The Black Radical Tragic

America and the Long 19th Century

GENERAL EDITORS
David Kazanjian, Elizabeth McHenry, and Priscilla Wald

Black Frankenstein: The Making of an American Metaphor
Elizabeth Young

Neither Fugitive nor Free: Atlantic Slavery, Freedom Suits, and the Legal Culture of Travel
Edlie L. Wong

Shadowing the White Man's Burden: U.S. Imperialism and the Problem of the Color Line
Gretchen Murphy

Bodies of Reform: The Rhetoric of Character in Gilded-Age America
James B. Salazar

Empire's Proxy: American Literature and U.S. Imperialism in the Philippines
Meg Wesling

Sites Unseen: Architecture, Race, and American Literature
William A. Gleason

Racial Innocence: Performing American Childhood from Slavery to Civil Rights
Robin Bernstein

American Arabesque: Arabs and Islam in the Nineteenth Century Imaginary
Jacob Rama Berman

Racial Indigestion: Eating Bodies in the Nineteenth Century
Kyla Wazana Tompkins

Idle Threats: Men and the Limits of Productivity in Nineteenth-Century America
Andrew Lyndon Knighton

The Black Radical Tragic

Performance, Aesthetics, and the Unfinished Haitian Revolution

Jeremy Matthew Glick

NEW YORK UNIVERSITY PRESS

New York and London

NEW YORK UNIVERSITY PRESS
New York and London
www.nyupress.org

LIBRARY OF CONGRESS CATALOGING-IN-PUBLICATION DATA

Glick, Jeremy Matthew.
 The Black radical tragic : performance, aesthetics, and the unfinished
Haitian Revolution / Jeremy Matthew Glick.
     pages cm.   (America and the long 19th century)
 Includes bibliographical references and index.
 ISBN 978-1-4798-4442-5 (cl : alk. paper)
 ISBN 978-1-4798-1319-3 (pb : alk. paper)
 1. Haiti—In literature. 2. Haiti—History—Revolution, 1791–1804—
Drama. 3. Haiti—History—Revolution, 1791–1804—Literature and the
revolution. 4. Blacks in literature. 5. Radicalism in literature. 6. Tragic,
The, in literature. I. Title.
 PN56.3.H35G55 2015
 809'.933587294—dc23
                                                    2015021342

References to Internet websites (URLs) were accurate at the time of
writing.

Neither the author nor New York University Press is responsible for
URLs that may have expired or changed since the manuscript was
prepared.

New York University Press books are printed on acid-free paper, and
their binding materials are chosen for strength and durability. We
strive to use environmentally responsible suppliers and materials to the
greatest extent possible in publishing our books.

Manufactured in the United States of America

10 9 8 7 6 5 4 3 2 1

Also available as an ebook

A book in the American Literatures Initiative (ALI), a collaborative
publishing project of NYU Press, Fordham University Press, Rutgers
University Press, Temple University Press, and the University of Virginia
Press. The Initiative is supported by The Andrew W. Mellon Foundation.
For more information, please visit www.americanliteratures.org.

THE
AMERICAN
LITERATURES
INITIATIVE

In loving memory of Barry H. Glick, Ivan Van Sertima, and Amiri Baraka

Contents

Acknowledgments

This book would have been impossible without the mentorship and encouragement of Brent Hayes Edwards, who saw me through the early stages of this project. Brent is a paragon of radical generosity. I am immeasurably grateful for seventeen years of his mentorship and consistent friendship. Time spent with Brent and Nora is the best thing about living in New York City.

Fred Moten's kindness and thoughtfulness is a model of radical commitment. I am so thankful for his friendship.

Bruce Robbins's and Michael McKeon's concern and guidance (in both scholarly and personal matters) continue to sustain me after twenty years. I have so much love for these guys. When I am at my best, I hope I'm achieving a fraction of their contributions.

Sampada Aranke read every word of this book in manuscript form. The only thing that surpasses Sam's dedication to Black radical thought and praxis is the warmth of her smile.

Richard Dienst kindly suggested key formulations to this book's prefatory sections. In a profound sense, we will need to build another world to adequately appreciate the brilliance and urgency of his scholarship. What Brecht said about Benjamin's "On the Concept of History" easily applies to the entirety of Richard's thought: One thinks "with horror about how few people there are ready even at least to misunderstand something like this."

Thanks to my students and colleagues at Hunter College for helping to clarify my priorities and understanding. Thanks to Thom Taylor of the Hunter English Department—for everything, really.

This book was written mainly in Brooklyn, New York, but also benefited from the generosity of two friends' willingness to share both their families and homes: Peter Bratsis (Kasos, Greece) and Marlene Hennessy (St. Andrews, Scotland).

Selma James makes the world less dangerous. I am grateful for her fellowship.

Mike Ladd's artwork from his album *The Infesticons: Bedford Park* (photographed by Nathalie Mourout) graces the cover of this book. Mike's friendship and our thirteen years as part-time roommates span two boroughs and two continents. It sustains me creatively and in many respects made this book possible.

Thank you to the anonymous readers at NYU Press for their sage criticisms and commentary. To Alicia Nadkarni at NYU Press—an absolute pleasure to work with. Salute to my dear friend David Kazanjian and to Elizabeth McHenry and Priscilla Wald for their belief in this project. Heartfelt thanks to Jennifer Backer for the stellar copyediting. Thank you to Marilyn Bliss for the stellar index. And Dhoruba Bin Wahad for letting me use epigraphs.

I am profoundly grateful to the following professors, friends, and comrades: Donald B. Gibson, Carter Mathes, and his family for always making me feel welcome, Shannon Mathes, the Mathes youth, Samantha Anderson, Elin Diamond, Wesley Brown, Ibrahim Noor Shariff, Cheryl Wall, Matthew Buckley, Chuck D, Mohamed Haroun, Maha Haroun, Carolynn Williams, Ed Cohen, Mutulu M1, Stic, Divine, and Tahir, María Josefina *Saldaña*-Portillo, Brian Rourke, Billy Galperin, Daphne Lamothe, Aldon Lynn Neilsen, William J. Harris, Leonard Bethel, Edward Ramsamy, Karla Jackson-Brewer, Elaine Chang, John McClure, Miguel Algarin, Cheryl Robinson, Phil Rosenfelt, Belinda Edmondson, Clement Price, Barbara Foley, Tzarina Prater, Anantha Sudhakar, Hortense Spillers, David Scott, Rachel Kranson, Brett Singer, Michael Daniel Rubenstein for his friendship, unconditional support, razor-sharp humor, and insight, Kelly Baker Josephs, Susie Nakley, Gary Zeitlin, Nikolas Sparks, Nick Mitchell, Yumi Pak, Anna Abramyan-Bagramyan, Eric Berger, Sommer Dowd, Anna Posner, Aryn Schwartz, Edwin Whitewolf, Matt Behrens, Nora Barrows Friedman, John P. Clark, Bill DiFazio, Kazembe Balagun, Sumayya Kassamali, Sonali Perera, Sara Salman, and Tanya Agathocleous; my chairs Cristina Alfar and Sarah Chinn for seeing me to and through the tenure process; Nijah Cunningham, Rupal Oza, Jennifer Gaboury, Harriet Luria, Kaiama L. Glover Dylan E. Rodriguez, Joi Gilliam, and Trauma Black; my man Cecil Brown; Barbara Webb, Tony Alessandrini, Daniel Vukovitch, Heidi Bramson and Ryan Joseph, Bill Germano, Sohnya Sayres, Manthia Diawara, Christopher Winks, Soyica Diggs Colbert, Ryan Howard, Rick Vitucci, Herman Bennett, Robert Reid-Pharr, Amiel Alcalay, Ashna Ali, Hillary Chute, Candice Jenkins, my friend Michael Pelias, and Stanley Aronowitz; *the Situations Study Group*; Alison Dell, Evie Shockley,

Tony Bogues, Ronald A. T. Judy, Meg Havran, Paul Bové, Nick Nesbitt, Margo Natali Crawford, Andy Hsiao, Jacob Stevens, Kristin Wartman, Brian Norman, Robert A. Hill, Christian Høgsbjerg, Rachel Douglas, Raj Chetty, Kamel Bell, Russell Shoatz III, Ankh Marketing, my dear friend Alan Vardy and the entire Vardy La Familia, my brothers Mario Ramirez-Hardy Africa and Siidiq "Creech" Booker; Rob "Sonic" Smith, Jun, Fred Ones, Thomas DeGloma, Sarah Jane Cervenak, Janet Neary, Robert Schnare, Minkah Makalani, Edgar Rivera Colon and Lillian, Samuel Sanchez and Nancy Nevarez, Yuri Kochiyama, Elombe Brath, Bernard White, Darryl Scipio, Tinaya Wos, Dax Devlon-Ross, Ahi Baraka and Chumma, Mike Crockford, Maura Carey, Shaffy Moeel, Lennox Hinds, Martin Garbus, Tekitha Washington, Pam and Ramona Africa, the MOVE Organization, my dear friend Boots Riley; Walter Riley, Barbara Rhine, Selena Rhine, Nathaniel Mackey, Amina Baraka and the entire Baraka family, Louise S. Ammentorp, and Keith Joseph—the brightest and most committed of us all.

Thanks to the library staff at the British Library, the University of Hull, the University of St. Andrews, and the Marx Memorial Library (London) for their expertise.

Love and heartfelt gratitude to the Mechanic, Glick, Neufeld, and Onorato families: grandparents, uncles, aunts, cousins, and allies.

To Andrea, Rick, and Avery Ramsey, one of the coolest kids ever. Avery: Your rendition of "Tomorrow" made a very bleak time brighter. It is the most thoughtful present I have ever received.

To my grandfather Fred Mechanic—a fortress of decency and self-sacrifice.

To my family: Bethany, Ben, Scott, and sister Jeannie.

To my mother, Judy Glick—the strongest person I know.

An earlier iteration of parts of Chapter 2 of this book appeared as short articles in "Parsing Aftershocks and History," *Small Axe Salon* 9 (28 May 2012) and "Paul Robeson as 'Sporting Hero,'" *Small Axe Salon* 16 (9 July 2014).

The Black Radical Tragic

Introduction

The Haitian Revolution as Refusal and Reuse

The cost of Americanization, of equality, is to forget. In black
culture a narrative of antagonism is inscribed in its memory.

Hortense Spillers

To make a transition successfully, you need to be armed.

Samuel R. Delany

The Haitian Revolution is a grand refusal to forget. In defiance of our current conjuncture's predilection for amnesia, Haiti as the
first slave rebellion turned successful revolution (success defined here as
the creation of a sovereign state) continues to be an inspired site of investigation for a remarkable range of artists and activist-intellectuals in the
African Diaspora. Qualifying the Haitian Revolution as such assumes a
particular set of understandings about *firsts* (the question of beginnings)
and *successes* (the question of ends). Such assumptions merit interrogation,
in other words, they are sites of and sites for critical thought. The plays
and related objects of study examined in this book constitute staged repetitions of the Haitian Revolution. In our current political climate where
revolutionary antecedents are, at best, shortchanged for their theoretical
richness and, at worst, forgotten, Haiti brazenly insists on reminding.
Radical historiography on the Haitian Revolution, chronicling its combat-
ive trials and tribulations, constitutes one of the most fecund, conceptu-
ally rich subfields in African diasporic studies.[1] Its heroes, its plotlines,
and its military-strategic components continue to warrant novelistic,
operatic, cinematic, and painterly attention. The following is an examination of twentieth-century theatrical production's relationship to the political and methodological insights of the long nineteenth century's Haitian

Revolution from a tragic vantage point (tragedy as form and philosophical posture). It builds upon previous scholarship on C.L.R. James and Haiti to argue that we must pay greater attention to the aesthetic properties and speculative potential of such writings.

Haitian revolutionary strivings chart a path where everything seems to have happened first, if not earlier: (1) a sequence of antislavery armed resistance and *marronage* cohering as state sovereignty; (2) the military defeat of all the major European colonial powers constituting a palimpsest war of decolonization; (3) the hesitancy of the United States to recognize the new nation as preface to multiple U.S.-led military interventions and occupations; (4) ruthless almost immediate postwar reincorporation into a global matrix of insidious economic debt; and (5) Haitian dilemmas around organizing production (the collectivization of agriculture—Toussaint's policy of "military agrarianism") that precede twentieth-century challenges in Russia and China but are often prefixed with proper names from these sites, for example, referring to certain nineteenth-century Haitian agrarian production designs as "Stalinist." Haitian revolutionary precedents generate so much *use* in comparative, analogical, geopolitical, and, ultimately, theoretical valences.

This book is a call to take questions of radical leadership seriously. Dramatic staging, in its vocation of arranging bodies onstage, is well equipped to think both problems of leadership, as well as what Michael McKeon concisely identifies as a key tenet of dialectical method: "All 'wholes' may be, on the one hand, divided into their constituent parts, and on the other, collected into more inclusive wholes of which they themselves constitute one part."[2] The Haitian revolutionary dramas presented in this study constitute exercises in thinking sets in motion. Such sets refuse to relinquish the challenge of staging the dialectical dance of part/whole, division/recombination, assertion of presence/absence—the active working toward one's own redundancy—all of which is implied when utilizing the expedient shorthand: the interdependence of leadership and mass base.

I offer readings of dramatic performances by C.L.R. James, Edouard Glissant, Lorraine Hansberry, Paul Robeson, Eugene O'Neill, Sergei Eisenstein, and Orson Welles as sites of political knowledge. I conclude with a discussion of Malcolm X's 1964 Oxford Union Presentation Debate's interpretation of Shakespeare's *Hamlet's* "taking up arms against a sea of troubles" (III.i.57–60) and *The Autobiography of Malcolm X's* brief mention of philosopher Baruch Spinoza's excommunication, which I relate to a dream detailed in Spinoza's *Letter 17.* This book's central claim is both urgent and modest: quite simply it argues that the aesthetic properties bound to this cluster of dramatic works offers up political insight and constitutes a field ripe for speculative thinking on the interrelationship between Black radical pasts, presents, and futures, as well as the continued relevance of leaders and masses in Black revolutionary struggle. Radical reading has to reclaim the freedom to trace many kinds of mediation, from the inconspicuous to the world-historical, from dream-work to the *actuality* of revolution, from the anecdotal and gestural to the conceptual and *geistige*.[3] Evoking Jean-Luc Godard's designs for cinema, these plays constitute a theater of ideas. I advance prior attempts to talk about aesthetic organization's relationship to revolutionary organization. C.L.R. James's notion of tragedy developed in his theatrical and historical writings on Haiti foregrounds questions of revolutionary subject formation and representation central to those working from a Black radical vantage point. Theatrical and aesthetic endeavors act as springboard for thinking about the problem of leaders and masses in processes of revolutionary overhaul—the intersection of stagecraft with statecraft. Tragic form facilitates balancing the imperative to theorize individual political leadership's interdependence on collective mobilization and collective knowledge. Tragedy as the literary form par excellence for staging the dialectic of freedom and necessity is configured theoretically from a Black radical position as the interplay between democracy, self-determination,[4] and revolution. The problem of the gulf separating leader and mass staged by this cluster of plays should be thought of as symptomatic of the project of Black Revolution's labor to think the constitutive (tragic) gap and dialectical relationship between: (1) democracy: radical inclusion within existing political coordinates; (2) self-determination:[5] the right to choose within existing political coordinates; and (3) revolutionary overhaul: transformation of existent political coordinates into something radically new. From the orientation of a global Black Liberation Movement each of these three at any given moment constitutes a revolutionary threat to the hegemonic ordering of things. Rarely are they inseparable. This resonates with Greek finance minister Yanis Varoufakis's shrewd warning against "revolutionary maximalism": "The trick is to avoid the revolutionary maximalism that, in the end, helps the neoliberals bypass all opposition to their self-defeating policies."[6] The urge to dismiss an intervention as stunted reformism is usually a mistake—a mistake only as grave as asserting such reformism as endgame. The plays examined here stage that theoretical problem, that tripartite dialectical interplay, and constitute a laboratory for exploring its lineaments. Taken as a whole, this book ultimately argues that a Black revolutionary horizon is still an unsurpassable political project and imperative of radical political desire.[7] It is the condition of possibility to think and actualize a different system to surpass our current neoliberal coordinates. It represents the greatest theoretical reserve to fashion socialism for the Americas, the imperative that C.L.R. James insisted on when he demanded that "every principle and practice of Bolshevism needs to be translated into American terms."[8]

Haitian Revolutionary Drama as "Imitations I Can Use":
On the Application of Brecht's Messingkauf Dialogues

"Imitations I Can Use" comes from Bertolt Brecht's *Messingkauf Dialogues* (1939–1942), a theatrical dialogue in which the German Marxist poet-playwright attempts to write theoretical essays through other means—experimenting with genre, in this case, the closet drama or Socratic dialogue. Brecht claims a radical democratic tradition of Modern German letters, starting with Goethe's "Prelude in the Theatre" from Book One of *Faust*. In *The Messingkauf Dialogues*, The PHILOSOPHER, Brecht's stand-in character, tells an actor and dramaturge: "I'm looking for a way of getting incidents between people imitated for certain purposes; I've heard that you supply such imitations; and now I hope to find out if they are the kind of imitations I can use."[9] This offends some of the other characters that view the function of theater as edifying aesthetic experience that should principally resist utilitarian functions. In the cast of characters, it is "The ACTRESS" who is the most politically engaged. With complimentary brevity, Brecht lists her as "The ACTRESS [who] wishes the theatre to inculcate social lessons. She is interested in politics." *Der Messingkauf* means literally "the purchaser of brass." Brecht as The PHILOSOPHER is interested in the theater as "an apparatus" to convey certain representations "between men" in the service of negating and overcoming capitalist political economy. Yet with characteristic dialectical flair, his title-example is submerged in the logics of utilitarian capitalist exchange: "I can only compare myself with a man, say, who deals in scrap metal and goes up to a brass band to buy, not a trumpet, let's say, but simply brass. The brass dealer 'ransack[s] your theatre for events between people.'"[10] He reduces the instrument to its elemental components. "Just brass" strips the instrument (the apparatus) of its sentimental claims trumpeting the edifying impact of theater all the while preserving its fetish character as precious metal. A callous exchange-value as tool chips away at the aura of the theatrical performance. This is in the service of his political project to transform capitalism, a socioeconomic system that in its very essence prioritizes exchange over use yet works via an interplay of exchange-value and use-value that cannot be uncoupled. Indeed this is a *useful* optic to think of the plays examined in this study. Brecht (and James for that matter) was certainly interested in aesthetic value and entertainment. But the political function of dramatic works remains paramount. The discussion of plays that follow will be approached as "useful imitations"—springboards for artist-intellectuals to think through organizational problems related to the Haitian Revolution.

The analytical preoccupations of C.L.R. James and Brecht constitute one of the main theoretical frames informing my readings of twentieth-century Black radical theatrical production and historiography revisiting the Haitian Revolution. The other is an encounter between James and Raymond Williams. I'm interested in the cluster of ideas that coalesce around the proper names of C.L.R. James, Bertolt Brecht, and Raymond Williams and utilize these ideas to engage committed representations of the Haitian Revolution. Haiti is the generative site *par excellence* for creative work by African diasporic artist-intellectuals attempting to break free from impasses in their respective political conjunctures. Revisiting Haiti acts as a solvent against political ossification.

This analysis takes some of its philosophical cues from the ongoing work of Alain Badiou (and Sylvain Lazarus) on the relationship between proper names and singular (radical) political events:

> The point from which a politics can be thought—which permits, even after the event, the seizure of truth—is that of its actors, and not its spectators. It is through Saint-Just and Robespierre that you enter into the singular truth unleashed by the French Revolution, and on the basis of which you form a knowledge, and not through [Immanuel] Kant or François Furet.[11]

Consider three points. (1) Badiou's formulation privileges the revolutionary actors themselves as sites of knowledge and access (Saint-Just and Robespierre) over theoreticians of the event (Kant and Furet). It insists upon simultaneously undermining such an opposition, since certainly Saint-Just and Robespierre were also theoreticians. (2) Fittingly, Badiou casts his cautionary note on historical methodology in the language of the theater—both actors and spectators. (3) The category of theoretical spectatorship for Badiou is wide enough to encompass multiple centuries: both Kant and Furet fit the bill. Implied here is not just that the actors themselves constitute sites of philosophical knowledge but that the profundity of revolutionary events is in one sense coterminous with their very proper names. In another sense, such revolutionary pasts are re-accessed every time such proper names are evoked. Dramatic form in its enactment and repetition of revolution invigorates the organizational political forms of Black radical struggle while also enacting new vitality and conceptual density in order to transform a world. In this regard, the plays examined here constitute new purchase of life for the proper names related to this history. Twentieth-century plays dip back to an eighteenth- and nineteenth-century revolution and establish a fecund site to engage both Brecht's and Badiou's thinking. Hence the rationale for the generous periodization that is the long nineteenth century: twentieth-century artistic representations of a revolution that commences in the eighteenth century, completes its initial push in the early nineteenth century, animates Black radical culture work in the twentieth century, and continues to reverberate. The literary form I call the Black Radical Tragic builds on this scholarship and offers an aesthetic and critical lens to understand how genre choice, strategies of staging, and questions of mediation are keys for both theatrical and historical imaginings of the Haitian past and its relationship to a transformative future. I offer readings of a series of plays that pose the question: What insights are gained when we link problems of aesthetic organization with problems of revolutionary organization?

Chapter Overview

Chapter 1 looks at three North American and European avant-garde uses of the Haitian Revolution in performance and cinema theory: Eugene O'Neill's Haiti play, *The Emperor Jones* (1920), Orson Welles's radio-play on the Haitian Revolution, *Hello Americans*, Episode 3, "Haiti" (1942), and the Soviet film director Sergei Eisenstein's discussion of the Haitian Revolution and Alexander Dumas's *The Count of Monte Cristo* essay "A Course in Film Treatment" (1932), as well as an account of how a Russian novel about the French and Haitian revolutions structured one of Eisenstein's lessons in his professional role as distinguished professor of film craft at the VGIK (State Cinema Institute in Moscow, 1932–1935). It demonstrates how dramatic works and preparatory stages in crafting dramatic works (in the case of Eisenstein) function as a laboratory for political thinking. These three culture workers chart Haitian revolutionary lines of flight, retreat, and attack.

Chapter 2 reads the 1967 revisions of C.L.R. James's play *Toussaint Louverture* (1936)—retitled *The Black Jacobins*—and Edouard Glissant's *Monsieur Toussaint: A Play* (1961) as two case studies to further explore the tragic as a way of talking about the relationship between leader and masses in the Black Radical Tradition. C.L.R James prefigures the writing of his historical study on Haiti by composing and staging a play about Toussaint L'Ouverture in London shortly prior. I am interested in the differences, both strategic and structural, between James's play and the history. There are interesting implications of this unusual situation, where a play seems to have some formative relationship to a historical work on the same topic. I trace this via a revised version of the play written decades after James's historical study. James's revision tempers the individual bravado of Paul Robeson's performance as Toussaint L'Ouverture. Robeson haunts James's revision process, informing how his subsequent drafts figure the revolutionary leader's interdependence on the masses. The play anticipates the theatrical language employed in James's historical text. The theatrical reviews of James's play form a counterarchive, a way to capture the fleeting nature of a performance whose various iterations C.L.R. James scholars have gone to great lengths to sort and track. Through an analysis of Glissant's theoretical work on theater in Martinique, I enact a comparative Anglophone and Francophone analysis of Caribbean theatrical production. Glissant experiments further with James's formal use of stage directions and headings in his own Haiti drama to theorize theater's role in combating alienation and cultivating a sense of national identity in Martinique, with special attention paid to thinking about the interrelationship between the living and the dead.

Chapter 3 examines "tragedy as a force of dialectical mediation" in C.L.R. James's history, *The Black Jacobins*. It begins with a theoretical-aesthetic excursus that examines how James's London journalism prefigures his Haiti work, specifically his intimate engagement with questions of bodily compression and expansion in a certain Rodin sculpture witnessed upon his arrival to London. By way of Hazel Carby's stellar work on bodily compression, I put a series of Robeson photographs in dialogue with the insights of Rainer Maria Rilke (Rodin's secretary) on the work of his employer. I juxtapose Carby's formulation on the problem of thinking Paul Robeson as a political comrade and one of Brecht's final short poems as a way to think problems of mediation. Building on Robert Hill's scholarship, I discuss Hill's assertion of Robeson as representative for James of a heroic example of Black masculinity that shatters the colonial framework inherited by the British colonial legacy in Trinidad. James provides a useful example of narrative and theoretical triangulation—in his case, questions of form and the study of the Haitian Revolution (alongside the French and Russian revolutions) and the political challenges of his 1938 London milieu organizing against Italy's aggression against Abyssinia (now Ethiopia). Here I engage the accounting of James's use of tragedy in David Scott's brilliant study, *Conscripts of Modernity*. James's modification of both Aristotle's *Poetics* and Marx's critique of "The Great Man Theory" in *The Eighteenth Brumaire of Louis Bonaparte* offers an opportunity to analyze how James reads both texts and employs a strategy of what I call direct substitution, often in contrast with his steadfast dedication to a method that insists on thinking dialectically the relationship of severance and continuity.

Chapter 4 engages the Pan-Africanist dramas of Lorraine Hansberry as a way for her to think about questions of scale, leadership, and internationalism apropos of the civil rights movement. Her posthumous play *Les Blancs* represents a key flashpoint in the history of Black theater that explicitly connects the struggle of Black masses to the fate of nations on the African continent waging wars of decolonization. The scale of her dramatic field cognitively maps *the whole* of the capitalist world system. Her unfinished piece of musical theater, *Toussaint*, transforms her childhood infatuation with the Haitian struggle into a work of stagecraft. Through the use of musical tropes, creative manipulation of stage action, and deeply philosophical discourse presented in dialogue, Hansberry builds on O'Neill's and James's staging of Haiti's protracted liberation war. Hansberry's Pan-Africanist dramas resonate with the challenges of mapping the totality of a world. She privileges revolutionary use over a less generative revolutionary morality and employs the European classical music tradition to do certain work in her opera on Haiti. I revisit an earlier line of thought that suggests for James (and arguably for Mozart and Da Ponte), Don Giovanni constitutes a drive rather than an individual character. The opera works as a vengeance machine or vengeance ensemble. Hansberry's critique of Jean Genet's employment of dramatic abstraction is a way to criticize both American racism and French colonial policy in Algeria—a short interlude on George Jackson helps clarify the theoretical stakes of her stagecraft choices. My conclusion departs from Haiti only to return. I examine Malcolm X's reading of *Hamlet* during the 1964 Oxford Union

Presentation Debate and the discussions Malcolm engaged on Haitian revolutionary leadership with one of his companions, Caribbean writer Jan Carew, as well as Malcolm X's *Autobiography's* representational defiance of the excommunication of Baruch Spinoza for what it has to say about radical fidelity and a set of Haitian revolutionary reading protocols.

Dispersed throughout these pages are discussions of three keyword clusters: (1) self-determination; (2) firsts/repetition; and (3) mediation/immediacy. They serve as a clarifying role, a pedagogic aid that helps bring online the theoretical stakes and Hegelian resonances of this study, stakes that more often than not function by way of demonstration and juxtaposition rather than declaration—a dialectic of showing as opposed to telling. I begin with the most vexed: the compound formulation, self-determination.

Self-Determination

> The equality of nations and their right to self-determination is also a fundamental tenet of socialist doctrine. In its fully developed form, as elaborated in the work of V. I. Lenin, the right of nations to self-determination includes not just the right to cultural autonomy but also to full political independence. As in the case of the liberal theories already cited, however, for Lenin recognition of the right to nations to self-determination in principle does not, of course, imply an *a priori* endorsement of secessions and state divisions. This is because it is theoretically impossible to say in advance which solutions will allow for the optimal implementation of such rights in specific situations. Hence, Lenin argues, proletarian socialism "confines itself, so to speak, to the negative demand for recognition of the *right* to self-determination, without giving guarantees to any nation, and without undertaking to give *anything* at the *expense* of another nation."
>
> Joe Cleary

> I'm ceded—I've stopped being Theirs—
>
> Emily Dickinson

Amiri Baraka provides the following definition of self-determination in the 1993 updated version of the 1979 book-length essay *The Black Nation* (subtitled *The Afro American National Question*), a study commissioned by *The Afro American Commission of the Revolutionary Communist League (MLM)*, in which he served as chair:

> Self-determination is the right of nations to decide their own destiny. This is a democratic and political right; it includes also the right to political secession. Self-determination for oppressed nations is a major demand of the proletariat. Oppressed nations have the right, and through national liberation struggles and wars, achieve the power to decide their own destiny. Only by recognizing this right and concretely supporting the struggles of oppressed nations can the proletariat of the oppressor nation have principled unity with the proletariat of the oppressed nation in the common struggle against imperialism.[12]

Baraka immediately follows this gloss by referring readers to Lenin's writings on the "National and Colonial Questions."[13] I want to engage this formulation by lingering on *the question of questions*. A radical lexicon of questions might initially strike a contemporary student of Left movements as antiquated holdover from an early twentieth-century period rife with proletarian revolution, wars of decolonization, and screaming debates over correct political lines. A series of questions posed at some point by the Left—"The Women Question," "The Jewish Question," "The Negro Question," and "The Agrarian Question"—read as sidebars, something to be picked up and discarded, secondary priorities vis-à-vis the main task of proletarian revolution. Instead, why not take these formulations at face value, in other words, as actual questions—in the case of self-determination—a contingent, open-ended process and problematic that prioritizes mass participation and indeterminate outcome over easy resolution? A questioning political project that cannot fully define its content since such content is determined by way of revolutionary overhaul, crafting unknown future outcomes and thwarting present predictions—the theoretical unknown that Joe Cleary signals by way of Lenin. An etymological probing of *determine* of self-determination certainly warrants this. In Raymond Williams's analysis, *determine*, far from signaling a tidy, reductive fait accompli, charts a tension between *absolute* (determined) ends, contingent uncertainties, and prioritization of process over outcome:

> **Determine** came into English C14 from fw *determiner*, oF, *determinare*, L, rw *terminare*, L—to set bounds to. Several formulations with the Latin prefix *de* are complicated in meaning, but in this case the sense of "setting

bounds" is dominant in all early uses. The difficulty and the later ambiguity arouse when one of the applied senses, that of putting a limit and therefore an end to the process, acquired the significance of an absolute end. There are many processes with an ordinary limit or end, for which **determine** and its derivatives have been regularly used: a question or dispute is **determined** by some authority, and from this use, and the associated legal use in matters like leases, there is a more general sense which is equivalent to "decide": e.g.[,] "on a date to be **determined**." Associated with this is the sense which is equivalent to "settle"; fixing by observation, calculation or definition. What is distinct about all these uses is that **determining** is some fixed point or act at the end of a process, and that this sense carries with it no necessary implication, and usually no implication at all, that the specific character of the ultimate decision or settlement or conclusion is inherent in the nature of the process. **Determination** resolves or completes a process; it does not prospectively control or predict it.[14]

I want to encourage here a determination that "resolves or completes a process" but only to begin anew another process (the furthering of revolutionary goals) at another plane of struggle, accompanied by another set of problems, another set of contradictions, and, yes, another set of questions. To argue such a claim is teleological misses the point because it ignores indeterminacy of outcomes, which only appear as necessary after the fact and after contingency has its way. Different planes of struggle do not necessarily mean progressively higher planes. It most certainly "sets bounds"—in the case of Baraka's polemic, self-determination bounds his narrative both as a reading strategy for American history and as a fully developed Black radical *haltung* (a Brechtian idea signifying posture or stance). Self-determination as historical reading practice/*haltung* coheres Baraka's analysis. It organizes a narrative synthesis that includes examination of employment statistics, demographic/migration shifts, analysis of slavery and political economy, state-terroristic and extralegal repression of Black Reconstruction governments, the history of constitutional amendments, and an excoriating précis of socialist and communist formations' abdication of solidarities vis-à-vis global Black radical movements. In this regard, it is and it is not about solely a question of land, state sovereignty, and the right of nations. Here I encourage readers to consult the stellar scholarship of philosopher Omar Dahbour, particularly his formulation of "self-determination without nationalism (or liberalism)."[15] However, in the case of Haiti, sometimes the question of state sovereignty is in fact *the* radical question to ask, especially as it relates to the state's challenges to weather the ravages of global capital. This is surely the case in James Weldon Johnson's collection of essays, *Self-Determining Haiti*, which analyzes and forcefully condemns, among other things, the impounding of the revenue of Haiti by the National City Bank of New York in 1914 as well as the manipulation by the U.S. State Department as it relates to various U.S.-Haiti interstate conventions. Such is the prehistory of a series of military occupations and geopolitical U.S. interferences against Haitian sovereignty. Black self-determination is not solely a radical repurposing of a top-down Wilson-era conceptualization of international law. Yet it most certainly dialectically repurposes such conceptualization toward radical ends. Self-determination is a protocol for reading, one that demands keeping Black radical priorities front and center in theoretical-historical analysis and in evaluating "exacting solidarities."[16] In this regard, the essential and insightful work of scholars such as Brent Hayes Edwards and Cedric Robinson, in their respective concern for thinking through the "autonomy of Black Radicalism," might be read as what Baraka refers to as "vectors of self-determination."[17]

Before proceeding to C.L.R. James on "The National Question" and concluding with how this discussion relates to thinking philosophically about Hegel and Haiti, let us examine an earlier example from Baraka on Black self-determination, the conclusion of his 1968 commentary on the Impulse recording "New Wave in Jazz":

> These, and the others I mentioned before, names names, to conjure with, no one should forget. OK, speak of them as personalities if you want to. Sonny Murray is a ghost, listen to him thrash and moan with "Holy Ghost." Listen to Louis Worrell, Charles Tayler, Don Ayler, closely because they are newer and might be telling you something you never bargained for. Listen to Trane, Ornette, Sun-Ra, Milford Graves, Tchicai, Brown. Listen to everybody beautiful. You hear on this record poets of the Black Nation.
>
> New Black Music is this: Find the self, then kill it.

Here you get a demonstration of the tenuous relationship between a *self* (found then killed) and a liberated aggregate of selves. The self that is extinguished here can be thought as an aesthetic analogue to the revolutionary leadership as vanishing mediator—the only responsible vanguard model. Political work in order to qualify as radical work should strive toward its redundancy. Vanishing's abrupt immediacy is augmented by way of a protracted voluntarism. Properly pedagogic—the ends and means sync. Vanishing leaves a trace. Baraka's declaration of the jazz phonograph as archive of the "poets of the Black Nation" implies here the very notion of Black national liberation. I read this almost algebraic formulation ("New Black Music is this: Find the self, then kill it") as part taunt, part aspiration. Taunt because the structure of this sentence, mathematical in its force on both aisles of the colon, encourages a mediation that it forcefully denies. "New Black Music" is not like this—it *is* this. "Find the self, then kill it" as aspiration is not just a temporal projection into a liberated future because the poets of the Black Nation are not only here, their here-ness can be heard.

C.L.R. James is consistently hostile in regards to thinking Black self-determination bound up with a land base. I argue here for a viable form of Black self-determination to be found in James, despite such reservations. This viability is apparent when you examine chronologically a cluster of his interventions on the matter. So much of the identification of the Haitian Revolution as a pivotal *first*, autonomous radical statecraft won by an awesome series of armed struggles and strategic feats, is wrapped up philosophically and politically in matters of self-determination. In James's "Preliminary Notes on the Negro Question" (1939), a record of his conversations with Trotsky, we witness hostility to the self-determination thesis, written off by James as an idealist form of separatism. Yet there is also a consistent reckoning with the fact that American Blacks constitute the most militant segment of the population. On "black chauvinism" and the question of self-determination James writes, "In the concrete instance, black chauvinism is a progressive force, it is the expression of a desire for equality of an oppressed and deeply humiliated people. The persistent refusal to have 'self-determination' is evidence of the limitation of black chauvinism in America. Any excessive sensitiveness to black chauvinism by the white revolutionaries is the surest way to create hostilities and suspicion among the black people."[18] Both Baraka's and James's seemingly opposite conclusions dovetail in productive ways. James cedes to "black chauvinism" not just a "progressive force" but, implied here, a progressive materialist ("concrete")[19] force to effect radical transformation. For James "black chauvinism" is limited by the lack of what he views as the "refusal" of self-determination. However, such a radical refusal in another sense is an example of the very self-determination he shuns—choice that can be submitted to and is a product of thought.

In James's "The Revolutionary Answer to the Negro Problem in the United States" (1948), this tension gives way to a non-hesitant, active lauding of the "independent Negro Struggle." He employs a national terminology to advance his claims, all in the service of raising the problem of leadership within a Lenin-inspired framework:

> We say, number one, that the Negro struggle, the independent Negro struggle, has a vitality and validity of its own; that it has deep historic roots in the past of America and in present struggles; it has an organic political perspective, along which it is travelling; to one degree or another, and everything shows that at the present time it is traveling with great speed and vigor. . . .
>
> [Lenin] says that the dialectic of history is such that small independent nations, small nationalities, which are powerless—get the word, please— *powerless*, in the struggle against imperialism *nonetheless* can act as one of the ferments, one of the bacilli which can bring on to the scene the real power against imperialism—the socialist proletariat.
>
> Let me repeat it please. Small groups, nations, nationalities, themselves powerless against imperialism, nevertheless can act as one of the ferments, one of the bacilli which will bring on to the scene the real fundamental force against capitalism—the socialist proletariat.
>
> In other words, as so often happens from the Marxist point of view from the point of view of the dialectic, this question of the *leadership* is very complicated.[20]

Very complicated indeed. James presents a plea, a hedge against amnesia ("Let us not forget") in the form of a *reading-seeing* protocol. Note James's implication that cultural forms (and institutions) are sites for heavy analysis. James demands a "complex seeing" (a prerogative of John Berger's that I'll touch on later) of the actuality of Black radicalism in existent institutions. Like Baraka's listening session, such radicalism is both tomorrow and already here:

> Let us not forget that in the Negro people, there sleep and are now awakening passions of violence exceeding, perhaps, as far as these things can be compared, anything among the tremendous forces that capitalism has created. Anyone who knows them, who knows their history, is able to talk to them intimately, watches them at their own theaters, watches them at their dances, watches them at their churches, reads their press with a discerning eye, must recognize that although their social force may not be able to compare with the social force of a corresponding number of organized

workers, the hatred of bourgeois society and the readiness to destroy it when the opportunity should present itself, rests among them to a degree greater than in any section of the population in the United States.[21]

Consider one final example from C.L.R. James. At the start of his 1967 London talk entitled "Black Power," James recites what he will theorize in the form of a greeting: "Mr. Chairman, Ladies and Gentlemen, Black Power."[22] His stated purpose is to clarify Black Power, designated by him first as *slogan* and then as *banner*: "What I aim to do this evening is to make clear to all what this slogan Black Power means, what it does not mean, *cannot* mean." I want to signal how James thinks self-determination, charting "Black Power" by way of a return to the Haitian Revolution and Lenin's attack on those who would characterize the Irish rebellion of 1916 disparagingly as a putsch. James accomplishes this feat as a response to three Kantian questions: What do I know? What must I do? What may I hope? He tops off this inventory of questions with a philosophical rejoinder: *"every determination is negation."* Note the repetitive emphasis on study and the interrelationship between democracy and socialism as it relates to Black struggle:

> I had studied Lenin in order to write *The Black Jacobins*, the analysis of a revolution for self-determination in a colonial territory. I had studied Lenin to be able to write my book on *World Revolution*. I had studied Lenin to be able to take part with George Padmore in his organization that worked for the independence of all colonial territories, but particularly the territories of Africa. I therefore was in a position from the very beginning to state my position and to state it in a discussion that some of us had with Trotsky on the Negro question 1939.
>
> The position was this: the independent struggle of the Negro people for their democratic rights and equality with the rest of the American nation not only had to be defended and advocated by the Marxist movement. The Marxist movement had to understand that *such independent struggles were a contributory factor to the socialist revolution.* Let me restate that as crudely as possible: the American Negroes in fighting for their democratic rights were making an indispensable addition to the struggle for socialism in the US. [This is a key component of Baraka's line on self-determination, democracy, and socialist transformation.] I have to emphasize this because it was not only a clarification in the darkness of the Trotskyist movement on the Negro struggle in 1938–39. Today, 1967, I find in Britain here

a confusion as great as I found in the US in 1938, and nowhere more than among the Marxists.

Now I am going to quote for you one statement by Lenin in which he states the basis of his argument. His actual political programme you will find in the resolutions which he presented to the Second Congress of the Third International on the question of self-determination, and in that resolution specifically you will find that he mentions the Negroes in the US. But the basic argument which was the foundation of Lenin's policy is stated many times in the debates that he carried on before 1917 on the right of nations to self-determination, and I will quote particularly from his sharp observations on the Irish rebellion of 1916:

> To imagine that social revolution is conceivable without revolts by small nations in the colonies and in Europe, without the revolutionary outbursts of a section of the petty bourgeoisie *with all its prejudices*, without the movement of non-class-conscious proletarian and semi-proletarian masses against the oppression of the landlords, the church, the monarchy, the foreign nations, etc. . . . to imagine that in one place an army will line up and say, "we are for socialism," and in another place another army will say, "we are for imperialism," and that this will be the social revolution, only those who hold such a ridiculously pedantic opinion could vilify the Irish rebellion by calling it a "putsch."

Lenin is very angry and though often very sharp he is not often very angry. He explains how the Russian revolution of 1905 came:

> The Russian revolution of 1905 was a bourgeois-democratic revolution. It consisted of a series of battles in which all the discontented classes, groups, and elements of the population participated. Among these there were masses imbued with the crudest prejudices, with the vaguest and most fantastic aims of struggle; there were small groups which accepted Japanese money, there were speculators and adventurers, etc. *Objectively*, the mass movement broke the back of tsarism and paved the way for democracy. For that reason the class conscious workers led it.

Now it is necessary to continue straight on with Lenin, because he seems to me to have had some experience, some feeling, that people would not understand what socialist revolution was. And this is one of his sharpest passages. I give it to you in full so that you may see how strongly he feels on what is for him a vital constituent of the phrase, but the way in which he underlined what he considered absolutely necessary to the understanding of what a socialist revolution was:

> The socialist revolution in Europe *cannot be anything else* than an outburst of mass struggle on the part of all oppressed and discontented elements. Sections of the petty bourgeoisie and of the backward workers will inevitably participate in it—without such participation, *mass* struggle is impossible, without it no revolution is possible—and just as inevitably will they bring into the movement their prejudices, their reactionary fantasies, their weaknesses and errors. But *objectively* they will attack *capital*, and the class conscious vanguard of the revolution, the advanced proletariat, expressing this objective truth of a heterogeneous and discordant, motley and outwardly incohesive, mass struggle, will be able to unite and direct it, to capture power, to seize the banks, to expropriate the trusts (hated by all, though for different reasons) and introduce other dictatorial measures which in their totality will amount to the overthrow of the bourgeoisie and the victory of socialism, which however, will by no means immediately "purge" itself of petty-bourgeois slag.

Now the moment Trotsky agreed that the independent Negro struggle for its democratic rights was part of the way to the social revolution, the Trotskyist movement accepted it. They accepted it but I don't think they really understood it. At any rate, in 1951 my friends and I broke irrevocably and fundamentally with the premises of Trotskyism, and as independent Marxists, we advocated this policy, this Leninist policy, on the Negro question, and we believed that at any rate we understood this question thoroughly. We did not know what this policy contained in it. I began by telling you that early this year I listened to Stokely Carmichael and was immediately struck by the enormous revolutionary potential which was very clear to me. But I had no idea that before the end of the year I would hear from him the following:

> We speak with you, comrades, because we wish to make clear that we understand that our destinies are intertwined. Our world can only be the third world; our only struggle for the third world; our only vision, of the third world.

Stokely is speaking at the OLAS Conference, and the Negro movement in the US, being what it is, he makes very clear that this movement

sees itself as a part of the Third World. But before very long he says what
I knew was always inherent in his thoughts, if not always totally plain in
his words. I wish you to appreciate the gravity and the weight which a man
who speaks as Stokely has been speaking must give to the following words:

> But we do not seek to create communities where, in place of white
> rules, black rulers control the lives of black masses and where black
> money goes into a few black pockets: we want to see it go into the
> communal pocket. The society we seek to build among black peo-
> ple is not an oppressive capitalist society—for capitalism by its very
> nature cannot create structures free from exploitation. We are fight-
> ing for the redistribution of wealth and for the end of private prop-
> erty inside the United States.

In the opinion of myself and many of my friends no clearer or stronger
voice for socialism has ever been raised in the US. It is obvious that for him,
based as he is and fighting for a future of freedom for the Negro people of
the US, the socialist society is not a hope, *not what we may hope,* but a
compelling necessity. *What he or any other Negro leader may say tomorrow,
I do not know.* But I have followed fairly closely the career of this young
man, and I leave you with this very deeply based philosophical conception
of political personality. He is far away out, in a very difficult position, and I
am sure there are those in his own camp who are doubtful of the positions
he is taking, but I believe his future and the future of the policies which he
is now advocating does [*sic*] not depend upon him as an individual. [They
depend] upon the actions and reactions of those surrounding him and, to a
substantial degree, not only on what you who are listening to me may hope,
but also on what you do.[23]

A balance sheet and trajectory of these three C.L.R. James pronouncements on self-determination: (1) 1939: a simultaneous hostility to
territorial formulations of Black self-determination alongside an acknowledgment of the "concrete" revolutionary force of "black chauvinism." (2)
1948: the lauding of "the independent Negro struggle," one that has "a
vitality and validity of its own." (3) 1967: a praise song of "Black Power"
as vector of self-determination, arguably in which the precedent and theoretical antecedent is the Haitian Revolution. Black Power as "banner"
because although James wants to maintain its essence as anti-imperialist,
anticapitalist, militant demonstration of autonomy, it is tasked to accommodate the diversity of Black political tendencies and class formations,

comparable to what for Lenin makes the Irish Rebellion of 1916 and his own Russian Revolution effective models for study. In summation, Black self-determination, by way of Baraka and James, can be thought of as a generative example of *supplementary logic*: "an endless linked series, ineluctably multiplying the supplementary mediations that produce the sense of the very thing that they defer."[24] It is posture and standpoint, reading strategy and narrative cohesion tool. It has a relationship to a land base that it perpetually evades. It builds up leadership in combination and recombination as quickly as such leadership is surpassed. It determines and negates.

I conclude this discussion by thinking about the Hegelian philosophical pedigree of *the self* in self-determination. For Georg Wilhelm Friedrich Hegel self is a question of will. Here are two relevant passages from the second part (the "Morality" section) of Hegel's *Philosophy of Right*:

> As self-determination of will is at the same time a factor of the will's conception, subjectivity is not merely the outward reality of will, but its inner being.... This free and independent will, having now become the will of a subject, and assuming in the first instance the form of the conception, has itself a visible realization: otherwise it could not attain to the idea. The moral standpoint is in its realized form the right of the subjective will. In accordance with this right the will recognizes and is a thing, only in so far as the thing is the will's own, and the will in it is itself and subjective....

> In morality self-determination is to be construed as restless activity, which cannot be satisfied with anything that is. Only in the region of established ethical principles is the will identical with the conception of it, and has only this conception for its content. In morality the will is as yet related to what is potential. This is the standpoint of difference, and the process of this standpoint is the identification of the subjective will with the conception of will. The imperative or ought, which, therefore, still is in morality, is fulfilled only in the ethical sphere. This sphere, to which the subjective will is related, has a twofold nature. It is the substance of the conception, and also external reality. If the good were established in the subjective will, it would not yet be realized.[25]

Thinking the relationship between self and will in Hegel as it relates to the Saint-Domingue Revolution is essential to philosopher Frank Kirkland's rigorous and principled critique of Susan Buck-Morss's *Hegel, Haiti, and*

Universal History, a work that famously argues that revolution in Haiti inspired Hegel's "Lord and Bondsman" (sometimes referred to as "Master and Slave") section in his *Phenomenology of Spirit* (1807). One of Kirkland's main goals is to complicate our understanding of what Hegel means by his premise that "blacks do not have history in the 'true sense of the word.'"[26] I will not pretend to do this penetrating analysis justice here in terms of full coverage. That would be impossible without capitulating the whole arc of the argument precisely because what Kirkland enacts here is a slow, detailed "reconstruction" of how Hegel's philosophical categories engender or reject Buck-Morss's assertion of Hegel's Haitian revolutionary influence. Kirkland's essay resists summary by way of its model expository design.

Kirkland brings front and center philosophical primacy in engaging Hegel's categories and uses it to complicate Buck-Morss's anecdotal/philosophical synthesis. He spells out the inextricably linked relationship between Hegel's ideas of race and history (his racialism) and his theorization of his notion of "natural spirit." This is in service of his overall project to reexamine both Hegel's relationship to the Saint-Domingue Revolution[27] and Buck-Morss's argument about such, by insisting that one has to show how Hegel's philosophical concepts warrant or unwarrant claims about his views on Blacks and history, in general, and the Saint-Domingue Revolution in particular. Kirkland faults Buck-Morss's interpretation for relying "too heavily on what Hegel has said or not said rather than on what his philosophy is warranted to say or not."[28] Pursuing such a path leads to the conclusion that despite the fact that "Hegel never laid out this thesis with respect to Africans. . . . Nothing from his idealism would preclude it." Kirkland is by no means arguing that Hegel believed in the equality of races; he rather insists "we should not confuse Hegel's views on the comparative levels of development with the levels of development themselves. The development stage of any given race must be variable. A racial hierarchy may be rigid. By virtue of races' accomplishments, however, the stages of development cannot be and hence, the hierarchy cannot be constantly in stasis."[29] I want to signal two interrelated points: (1) Kirkland's theorization of *the right to revolution* and (2) how his meditation on Hegel's philosophical categories engenders his periodization of the Saint-Domingue Revolution. Kirkland's periodization charts "eight thresholds" of Haitian revolutionary activity. On "the right" to revolution:

Hegel's critique pertains to the idea that the *right* to act under the idea of freedom neither can be nor include the right to revolution. The capacity for or the act of revolution are not the right to it. On this point, Hegel agrees with Kant that there can never be a right to revolution, but with a major difference. Kant regards revolutions as matters of the "state of nature." They are catastrophes spurred "naturally" by a sovereign when s/he violates the rights of the people and by people's belief that they have a right to rebellion for themselves against the sovereign for such violation. However, for Kant, both the sovereign and the people are wrong. The sovereign as a despot vacates the civil state to re-enter, rather than to exit, the "state of nature." The people are oriented toward acting under the idea of freedom outside of their obligation to enter and remain in the civil state.

Hegel, on the other hand, does not regard revolutions as steps back into the "state of nature." They are rather action-repertoires of violent resistance, which fail necessarily to be effective rationally in a normative sense. To be rationally effective in a normative sense is for a free person to have a justifying reason for an action or action-repertoire whose authority would rest on political arrangements enabling such a reason to be institutionally recognized. It is impossible, Hegel maintains, for revolutionary activity to be rationally effective in a normative sense. Albeit free, it cannot sustain a reason whose authority rests on political institutions incorporating it as a norm to be acknowledged. The "negative freedom" as Hegel puts it, exhibited in revolutionary activity is "the destruction of the whole subsisting social arrangement, the elimination of individuals who are objects of suspicion to any social arrangement, and the annihilation of any organization which tries to rise anew from the ruins."[30]

In the periodization below, the following acronyms are employed: SDR (Saint-Domingue Revolution), SASC (Hegel's *"Self-Alienated Spirit-Culture"*), SD (Saint-Domingue), and PhS (*The Phenomenology of Spirit*):

For the sake of a "Black Atlantic" reconstruction of SASC, the SDR was the first "racial revolution." Hence it cannot avoid, even philosophically, the role racial chauvinism played in it. It involved enslaved blacks and creoles as well as free persons of color (post-1791) increasingly acquiring freedom and the right to act freely over 13 years of conflict crossing eight thresholds: (a) the previously mentioned slave insurrection (1791); (b) the collapse of SD's colonial system and the immediate abolition of slavery in SD (1793); (c) warfare against England and Spain on behalf of France (1793–1798); (d) the general acquisition of the right to act freely in SD for one and all from France (1794); (e) SD's attempted yet failed transformations from a plantation colony to a free society (1795–1800); (f) the constitutional main-tenance of the right to act freely, under French sovereignty, in SD for one and all (1801); (g) the violent campaign against France's attempt to turn SD back into a plantation colony and forfeit SD's constitutional maintenance of the right to act freely for all its people (1802–1804); and (h) the consti-tutional emergence of both Haitian sovereignty and self-determination of one and all as Haitian people to think, act, and live rightly under the idea of freedom (1804).

From enslaved bossales and creoles to black insurgents against enslave-ment to guardians of emancipation and the right to act freely for one and all, there is a development and transformation of an ethno-racial people now responsible for the development and transformation of SD from an institutionalized plantation slave colony to an emergent and promising free society. All of this can be rendered consistent with both Hegel's PhS, under SASC, and his later philosophical position.[31]

Adjudicating whether or not the sequence of events in Saint-Domingue coheres to Hegelian philosophical categories on the *right* of revolution does not abdicate the responsibility to *think* such revolution. Kirkland expertly inhabits what I'm calling Haitian Revolutionary Reading Pro-tocols in his insistence on disaggregating the different "thresholds" that cohere in what we call the Haitian Revolution. In a sense, the Haitian Revolution is an abstraction that assumes and subsumes its component parts, parts that become manifest by way of reading. Taking the time to concede to this history a site to think Hegelian philosophy proffers a sort of care that inspires a delineation of different stages and different actors in these events. This is why his essay insists on mostly naming this sequence the Saint-Domingue Revolution. Self-determination is one facet, one crossed-over threshold in a series. In the words of anthropologist Gary Wilder, self-determination in the Black radical context is not a "ready-made solution."[32] How one parses such a series has everything to do with what archive one examines to calibrate beginnings and ends. Hegel's *Phi-losophy of Right*'s coupling of self-determination with will is an opportu-nity for the German idealist philosopher to think subject-object relations, freedom, and how such internal struggles of will get materialized vis-à-vis variable and in motion "external reality."

The theoretical overture that follows resonates with the proper name (Toussaint) *L'Ouverture*—The Opening. It is a political primer for the entire work, an *opening* up of its theoretical stakes, sometimes by way of examples not directly referencing Haiti but speaking to it nonetheless. Staking the *how* of this associational claim by way of modeling, in other words, by way of its dialectical presentational structure, is its main task: "The principle of the organization of thinking is in actual fact the 'content' of the work."[33] The *how* is actualized continuously by way of mediation.

An interview with C.L.R. James in the November 1971 issue of *Black World* is subtitled "Pan-Africanism: A Directory."[34] The discussions in the next pages constitute further entries in an ever-expanding Pan-African directory. Consider Gordon K. Lewis's gloss of Caribbean intellectual use and theorization of the proper name Toussaint, itself a roster of political openings:

> The varying and, at times, glaringly contradictory interpretations of the figure of Toussaint L'Ouverture are as good an example of the matter as any. For De Vastey himself, Toussaint, like Henri Christophe, is one of the great father figures of the new nation. For Ardouin, he is a tool of the whites in the struggle, because of his hatred for mulattoes. This irreconcilable difference of opinion was followed by other writers—both Haitian and foreign, and extends into the twentieth century itself. For James Stephen, Toussaint becomes the incarnation of the Oroonoko legend of the westernized, white black man, whose virtues are set off against the vices of the Emperor Napoleon. For Schoelcher he is essentially a good man corrupted by too much power—a view that naturally suggested itself to a disciple of Tocqueville. For Aimé Césaire—coming to the twentieth century writers—he is the catalyst that turns a slave rebellion into a genuine social revolution. For the Haitians François Duvalier and Lorimer Denis, he is a noble spirit fighting against the greed of the whites and the prejudices of the mulattoes, almost as if Duvalier was presaging his own elevation to black power as the historical successor to Toussaint. For C.L.R. James, finally, Toussaint takes on the form of a great revolutionary leader who has lost contact with the masses and lacks an ideology, almost as if James were perceiving in Toussaint a historical anticipation of the failure of the Russian Revolution after 1917 in its Stalinist phase to create a genuinely classless society.[35]

The overture enacts a method (etches out, pries an "opening") within which to think about dramatic usages of the Haitian revolutionary long nineteenth century. It constructs a tradition within which I want to operate. Adding to Lewis's inventory, I rehearse an overall methodology that presents a relay-circuit from Brecht to Williams to Fanon to James to

Brecht. The impact of such a relay-circuit simultaneously stakes its own claims on dramatic representations of the Haitian Revolution and charts directions for further use.

"The sound of that name the preceding century had quaked."[36] Michael Löwy's astute analysis of Thesis XII of Walter Benjamin's "On the Concept of History" (1940) clarifies: "The German text speaks not just of the 'sound' of his name [that of Auguste Blanqui], but of its *Ezzklang*, its sounding out like brass, and this is doubtless a reference to the tocsin, the alarm bell this armed prophet figuratively sounded to warn the oppressed of imminent catastrophe."[37] In the pages that follow, tragedy is pried away from its generic and classical moorings. It sounds an alarm by way of its evocation of proper names. Tragedy is retooled as a way of approaching history as though we can buy brass there.

Overture

Haiti Against Forgetting
and the Thermidorian Present

The history of scaffolding has been dismantled.
Lisa Robertson

An effective historical method can only be practiced through a mode
of inquiry that not only can begin the process of defining one's goals
but also pursue and complicate those goals at every stage of study.
Michael McKeon

The Provocation and Invitation of an Unmarked Coffin: Port-au-Prince, 1859

One of the *mise-en-scènes* framing Laurent Dubois's *Haiti: The Aftershocks
of History* begins "Sacrifice," an examination of the failure of the United
States and the Vatican to diplomatically recognize Haiti:

> In December 1859, an elaborate official funeral was held in the cathedral of
> Port-au-Prince. The Haitian president, Fabre Geffrard, oversaw the proceed-
> ings, while the head Catholic priest of Port-au-Prince officiated a high mass.
> In the nave of the church was the coffin, draped in black, lit up by candles, and
> decorated with an inscription naming the deceased as a "martyr for the cause
> of the blacks." After a rousing eulogy, it was carried to a cross at the edge of
> town by a large procession that brought together many of the town's prominent
> citizens. But the coffin was never placed in the ground, for it was empty.[1]

Dubois slowly identifies the figure in the empty coffin: North American
abolitionist and militant John Brown, executed days earlier in Virginia for

his role as architect of the raid on Harpers Ferry's Armory.[2] The tempo of Dubois's narrative disclosure doubles the coffin inscription's hesitation to name. Dubois's paced divulgence of John Brown's absent body—the way that the deceased is solely named by his political solidarities—"martyr for the cause of the blacks"—illustrates an analogous temporal dynamic in how the Haitian revolutionary plays examined in these pages engage a "poetry of the past":[3] aiming toward an undetermined radical futurity. Certainly there is a commonsense explanation for John Brown's empty coffin in Port-au-Prince (his dead body surfacing somewhere between the state of Virginia and his final resting place in North Elba, New York). The openness of such a declaration—the anonymity of words on a wooden coffin—refuses to specify a proper name. Anonymity signifies a future orientation and conjures radical possibilities, advancing by way of ruse, accident, reversal, and surprise. Haitian revolutionary citizenship and friendship are constituted as martyred solidarity that can be repeated. John Brown's absent body saves a space open in the queue—the roster of future allies. It carves out a space for the sequence of repetitions examined in this study.

"Ontological Equality" and the Proper Name

So much of how the Haitian Revolution of 1791–1804 circulates in the imagination of the African Diaspora is bound up in the proper names making up that history: Toussaint L'Ouverture, Jean-Jacques Dessalines, Henri Christophe, and the like. African diasporic thinkers revisit by proper name the protagonists of a sequence in Haitian revolutionary insurgency as analogical exercise to shed light on their own political conjectures. The revolution animates, qualifies, enriches, and frames their respective artistic-intellectual projects. I am using "analogical" in the conviction-laden sense established by Kaja Silverman in her recent work on painter Gerhard Richter: "Analogy is a relationship of greater or lesser similarity between two ontologically equal terms, not a relationship between one thing and something else that equals it."[4] Silverman's emphasis on ontology over an unspecified something else gently pushes up against the equivalent logics of capital. For Silverman, the commonality of death constructs a field of ontological oneness. For this study, the freedom dreams[5] and self-determination animus that propel Black radical struggles from Haiti's Toussaint L'Ouverture to Malcolm X (two of the proper names bookending this study) constitute a philosophical identity, that despite their differences in chronologies, locales, and national histories remain ontologically equal. Constant revision, rehearsal, and staging bind their equality. Constant struggle binds their equality. The formula *I identify my comrades by what they do*[6] is supplemented by the formula *I identify my comrades by what they make*. Not a racialist *a priori*—they are ontologically equal by virtue of what they gave their life to oppose. Yet a definition of ontological equality that defines itself solely in relation to death is never the whole story. Performance and repetition act as productive engine crafting identity within spaces of difference. They generate the field for this study, one in which performance actants do and make the Haitian Revolution.

Questions of Method and Presentation

Some preliminary words about the method of inquiry and presentation of this book are in order. This overture consists of three overlapping modes: first, *associative flow*, where the links between texts are loosely motivated; second, *miniaturized counterpoint*, where evidently small details acquire larger significance by being connected to comparably small details of other texts; third, *blocs of affinity*, where longer sequences or bigger structures are approached as if they share common concerns, even when they don't share a tradition or political orientation.[7] This study's political orientation is informed by Orthodox Marxism—in the singular sense advanced by George Lukács in the beginning of his *History and Class Consciousness*: "It is not the 'belief' in this or that thesis, nor the exegesis of a 'sacred' book. On the contrary, orthodoxy refers exclusively to *method*."[8] I understand this as a Fanon-inspired prerogative, which is not an attempt to annex Fanon to something called Marxism, stripping his theoretical work of its particularity. Rather I understand this as resonance—Edward W. Said argues a case for Fanon reading Lukács while composing *The Wretched of the Earth*.[9] This is a Black radical protocol. From *The Wretched of the Earth*: "Comrades, let us flee this stagnation where dialectics has gradually turned into a logic of the status quo."[10] As Immanuel Wallerstein in his exemplary corrective "Fanon and the Revolutionary Class" succinctly quips: "If Marx was not a Marxist, then Fanon surely was not a Fanonist."[11] I come to these two interrelated prerogatives (to place method front and center and to reinvigorate dialectics' Black radical edge) by way of Black radical study. Simply put, my intellectual and political training is such that I learned Marxism by way of Black radicalism, through the tutelage of Black radical thought.

It is not my intention to neuter the activist impulse of either Marxism or Black radicalism, which are both clearly not just methods but rather transformative politics. Rather, I just want to allow for a space of difference in which a study in aesthetics does another kind of work than a method for making revolution. Conflating both does a disservice to each. By claiming methodological primacy to Marxism, I am not privileging one revolutionary actor over another (for example, proletarians over insurgent anticolonialists or oppressed nationalities resisting the afterlives of racial slavery). Indeed it is that very parenthetical opposition, a kind of "check one please" mystification, the idea you could separate the two as discrete fields of allegiance, the work under review here challenges. Theorizing the nature of class formations in a specific conjuncture and *longue durée* as well as the corresponding need to gauge revolutionary capacities needs to muster the specificity of C.L.R. James vis-à-vis Haiti in *The Black Jacobins*, a specificity that opens up a dialogic exchange that expands, critiques, refutes, and corroborates James's findings and instantiates Haitian Revolutionary Studies as an unfinished field of inquiry.

This overture advances by a series of dialectical couplings. It brings together C.L.R. James and Raymond Williams (by way of James's 1961 review of Williams's *Culture and Society* and *The Long Revolution*) to further elaborate how the tragic functions in James. I rehearse an encounter between James and the writings of the working-class Welsh scholar-teacher-activist. Williams's *Modern Tragedy* alongside dramatic representations of Haiti has a great deal to offer our own political impasse in which antisystemic forces are often thought as unnameable, horizontally organized multitudes, yet there is never a shortage of proper-named, all-powerful, individuated bad men. This project mines the tension between the "unnameable" mass and the proper-named revolutionary subject.

The pairings following my discussion of Williams and James constitute the first two movements in a heuristic—the so-called tripartite Hegelian dialectic. "Three times, in a gesture of negation, the divine head moved from right to left."[12] Each introduces the three major questions that this book seeks to address: (1) Frantz Fanon and Paul Robeson's linking of the long nineteenth-century revolutionary Haiti with twentieth-century revolutionary Vietnam addresses questions of comparison. (2) Biographer David Macey on the conditions of production of Fanon's *Black Skin, White*

Masks and C.L.R. James's dissatisfaction with the archival sources of *The Black Jacobins* addresses questions of historical archive and the problem of immediacy. (3) And finally, the tension between Bertolt Brecht as *dramatis personae* (*The Messingkauf Dialogue's* Philosopher) versus Brecht as private journal writer is an opportunity to think about the complications applying Brechtian theory to African diasporic sources.

A further clarification on Hegelian method and expository organization is in order. Consider this qualification on *triads* (what Marx lambasted as "wooden trichotomies")[13] that argues the impossibility of formalizing resolution or synthesis in the Hegelian dialectic:

> The dialectic is often characterized as a tripartite process of thesis, antithesis, synthesis—though scholars are correct to point out that Hegel himself never used these terms, and that the third (synthesis) is misleading. Nonetheless, the dialectic typically involves the assertion of a category, which is then understood to lead to or to involve its opposite (or, at least, a conflicting category or claim). The two antagonistic categories are then "resolved" in a third, which often identifies the underlying unity between the two. (How these antagonisms are resolved varies considerably in Hegel, and is one of the reasons why "dialectical logic" is impossible to formalize.)[14]

In the presentational logic of this study, Haitian revolutionary plays function as open-ended, improvisational moments of synthesis. Put another way, the revolutionary dialectic is ongoing. My triadic organization is not an argument about how these works develop as a whole (except in their open-endedness as performances). Rather, it is just my signaling how this study is formally organized. Of course as Eisenstein reminds: formal organization is never just that. Fredric Jameson cautions:

> We need to ponder a methodological issue and to forestall one of the most notorious and inveterate stereotypes of Hegel discussion, namely the thesis-antithesis-synthesis formula. It is certain that there are plenty of triads in Hegel, beginning with the Trinity (or ending with it?). It is also certain that he himself is complicitous in the propagation of this formula, and at least partly responsible for its vulgarization. It is certainly a useful teaching device as well as a convenient expository framework.[15]

It is the prerogative of dramatic form to warrant constant rehearsals, revision, and reenactment. Indeed, rehearsals never cease as long as people stage the plays and the texts find their audience. Accessing the archive of twentieth-century African diasporic dramatic imitations of the long nine-teenth-century Haitian Revolution (long because it commences at the end of the eighteenth century yet its political challenges have yet to be sur-passed) provides clues for how to think this "impossible" formalization. Thinking through the staging of this impossibility names the task ahead.

Revisiting Raymond Williams's Modern Tragedy

> Even to name something, is to wait for it in the place you think it will pass.
>
> Amiri Baraka, *Home: Social Essays*

Take a quick detour from Haiti for the lecture halls of Cambridge Uni-versity, in which Raymond Williams[16] engaged a radical student body on the aesthetics and politics of dramatic tragedy and revolution. In *Mod-ern Tragedy* (1966), Williams tacitly critiques George Steiner's *The Death of Tragedy* (1961), which argues that secular modern society has no more room for tragedy since it has both killed its gods and extinguished the possibility for collectivist restructuring of its economic organizing of pro-duction.[17] Steiner's thesis privileges Greek Attic tragedy as the exemplary mode rendering all later tragic drama moot. Such an error is one of a nar-row Eurocentrism[18] (although not labeled as such by Williams). Steiner aspires toward the materialist weight of George Thomson's *Aeschylus and Athens: A Study in the Social Origins of Drama*,[19] yet fails to yield its seri-ous political insight. Kenneth Surin situates the intellectual atmosphere at the time of Williams's composition of his text as one in which "the terms of the exchange on the nature of tragedy were those of an intellectual poli-tics very specific to the teaching of English in Cambridge in the 1950s and 1960s."[20] Williams leaves a teaching post in adult worker education for a lecturing position at Cambridge, where he reconfigures his insights from an earlier study, *Drama from Ibsen to Eliot* (1952), to satiate the interests of Cambridge radicals more interested in talking about insurrection than the complexities of stage design. *Modern Tragedy* marks the tension between tragedy as literary genre and its colloquial meaning as terrible calamity:

> Tragedy has become, in our culture, a common name for this kind of experi-ence. Not only the examples I have given, but many other kinds of events—a

mining disaster, a burned-out family, a broken career, a smash on the road—
are called tragedies. Yet tragedy is also derived from a particular complicated
yet arguably continuous history. The survival of many great works which are
all tragedies, makes this presence especially powerful. This coexistence of
meanings seems to me quite natural, and there is no fundamental difficulty
in seeing their relations and distinguishing between them. Yet it is very common for men trained in what is now the academic tradition to be impatient
and even contemptuous of what they regard as loose and vulgar uses of "tragedy" in ordinary speech and in the newspapers.[21]

Williams uses this multiple signification of tragedy (the "coexistence of
meanings") to chart how its meanings are classed linguistic phenomena,
housing assumptions about continuity, tradition, and progress. He opens up
the term so it can both encompass literary theatrical production and signify
the life hurdles, defeats, and upsets of day-to-day working-class life. Williams glosses the progression of the tragic in European philosophy and cultural production and provides a counterreading that focuses on character
emphasis and politics. From Hegel's proposition that genuine tragic action
needs to include "the principle of individual freedom and independence, or
at least that of self-determination"[22] (recall that for Hegel self-determination involves the question of will), to Schopenhauer's secularization of fate
and positing of tragic suffering rooted in the human condition, Williams
sketches tragic development in philosophy. He ends the trajectory with
"the death of liberal tragedy" (Arthur Miller and Tennessee Williams) and
the radical rejection of tragedy (Bertolt Brecht). Williams's critical Marxian influences render him suspicious of a dramatic tragedy that restricts its
focus on the fate of the individual: "The identification of the 'world-historical individual' with the 'tragic hero' is in fact doubtfully Marxist. It shifts
attention from the objective conflict, which is present in the whole action, to
the single and heroic personality, whom it does not seem necessary to regard
as tragic if he in fact embodies 'the will of the world-spirit' or of history."[23]

The Haitian revolutionary plays examined in subsequent chapters push
against the above claim. This cross-section of Black radical theatrical production is not yet prepared to let go of its identification with the "world-
historical individual," even if such an individual is framed quite different
than it is in Hegel. Certainly not because of Williams's reasoning that such
a focus is "doubtfully Marxist." It is not useful to exorcise the productive
tension between individual and mass base, even with the admirable goal
of finally getting past such divisions.

Williams defines "Liberal tragedy" as "that of a man at the height of his powers and the limits of his strength, at once aspiring and being defeated, released and destroyed by his own energies. The structure is liberal in its emphasis on the surpassing individual, and tragic in its ultimate recognition of defeat or the limits of victory."[24] It is the fault of us moderns that we read backward, imposing upon Greek tragedy a focus on the individual. The thrust of Greek tragic drama is not individual psychology but rather human history as "man's inheritance and relationships, with a world that ultimately transcends him." For Williams, Christianity contributes an alteration of this Greek worldview with an added emphasis on the individual culminating in a Romanticist notion of tragedy in which Prometheus and Faust are heroic exemplars of humanist individual rebellion.[25] Williams sees Henrik Ibsen as representative of the "crux of liberal tragedy" in which "the heroic liberator [is] opposed and destroyed by a false society," that is, "the liberal martyr."[26]

The tragic form and aspiration of the hero take the form in Ibsen as an understanding of inheritance or debt: (1) the dissolving of the self in the form of a proto-Freudian inheritance and (2) the material inheritance of a bankrupt, false society. Ibsen alchemizes such inheritances in his intensified dramatic forms. By the time we get to a post-*Crucible* Arthur Miller, the Ibsenian tragic martyr fails to console. Individual self-sacrifice is no longer a viable option or exit strategy. There is no way out of the quagmire. "Proctor, in *The Crucible*, had died as an act of self-preservation: preservation of the truth of himself and of others, in opposition to the lives of the persecuting authority. . . . This sense of personal verification by death is the last stage of liberal tragedy."[27] *The Crucible's* heroic martyr cynically morphs into the disconnected individuals depicted by Arthur Miller in *Death of a Salesman* and *A View from the Bridge*: "In Willy Loman's death the disconnection confirmed a general fact about the society; in Eddie Carbone's death, Miller has moved further back, and the death of the victim illustrates a total condition."[28] This rings the death bell for liberal tragedy.

Compare this no-exit assessment with Gloria T. Hull's pronouncements on Black Theater: "Because of their historical and present experiences, black writers could never accept these conditions as being 'in the nature of things' and thus succumb to the defeatist, nihilistic attitude that characterizes modernism. Joseph Walker, the popular playwright and actor (*The River Niger*), once affirmed that he and other young black writers still believe in human possibilities and thus have not abandoned the concept of 'the hero.'"[29] Miller's heroes and Hull's heroes unevenly occupy the same world system and this unevenness is both rationale and catalyst for radical solutions. The gaps in need of mediation between the claims of bourgeois democracy and the actuality of racism, that is, premature Black death, and national oppression offer analytical provocations. Such unevenness warrants different heuristics for judging the efficacy and representational currency of the individual hero, collectivist action, and the interdependence of both.

In a key passage from *Modern Tragedy*, Williams unpacks the relationship between tragedy and revolution:

> What seems to matter, against every difficulty, is that *the received ideas no longer describe our experience* [emphasis added]. The most common idea of revolution excludes too much of our social experience. But it is more than this. The idea of tragedy, in its ordinary form, excludes especially that tragic experience that is social, and the idea of revolution, again in its ordinary form, excludes that social experience that is tragic. And if this is so, the contradiction is significant. It is not merely formal opposition, of two ways of reading experience, which we can choose. In our own time, especially, it is the connections between revolution and tragedy—connections lived and known but not acknowledged as ideas—which seem most clear and significant.[30]

With troubling complementariness, both bourgeois and revolutionary histories risk insufficiently accounting for the full range of experience subsumed within "received ideas." This is a product of both their form and content.[31] Both C.L.R. James and Raymond Williams work with great care to provide correctives to the exclusion of "too much . . . experience" in revolutionary narratives. James's chorus in his Haitian dramatic and historiographic writings marks a prior realization of Williams's challenge. His chorus signifies a mass base of Haitian social actors containing the freedom drive, aptitude, and structural position needed to make a revolution, rendering mediation by individual leadership sometimes central, harmful, and in some instances superfluous. Both men recoiled from the Soviet Union because of its degeneration under Stalin's leadership. James's Haiti writings stretch experience to accommodate both the voices and actions that evade more narrowly conceived narratives of revolutionary triumph.

C.L.R. James's Filling in the "Angry Silences" of Raymond Williams

Stuart Hall[32] in a tribute for his friend Raymond Williams rejects the twin poles of celebration and condemnation:

> I recently did this memorial lecture on Raymond Williams, called "Culture, community and nation." In the first half, I talked about the importance of Williams's work on culture, on structures of feeling, and on "lived communities," and so on. But in the end I offered a critique of that conception of culture, because of its closed nature, because of its reconstituting itself as a narrow, exclusive nationalism. The lecture explored hybridity and difference, rather than "whole ways of life," etc., which can have a very ethnocentric focus. A lot of Raymond Williams's work is open to the critique of ethnocentrism, just as he is open to the critique of being oddly placed in relation to feminism. These absences don't mean that one has to repudiate the work. I've always opposed the absolutist way of approaching such questions, where you either advocate everything a writer says, in the manner of a covert or disciple, or you have to repudiate everything. Williams has his strengths, his important insights; he is a major figure, etc. But from the position of how British cultural studies is being practiced now, one sees Williams's work differently. One begins to engage with it critically, rather than celebrate or venerate it.[33]

Two benchmarks of Williams's work that interest C.L.R. James are the studies *Culture and Society* and *The Long Revolution*.[34] The former is a lexicon meant to develop critical faculties in the study of literature and culture for his working-class adult-education students. The latter theorizes the need to bring about socialism as gradual, deep comprehensive change not just in the organization and relations of production but also in the so-called superstructure—all the facets of culture and society impacting working life. For C.L.R. James in his critical review entitled "Marxism and the Intellectuals" (1961), the absent agent in both *The Long Revolution* and *Culture and Society* is the revolutionary proletariat itself.

James commences his review by crediting Williams, whom he refers to as "the most remarkable writer that the socialist movement in England has produced for ten years or perhaps twenty" for exposing "lying propaganda" and delivering a "knock out blow" to the capitulation to the middle class by the British Labor Party.[35] James cites Williams:

Before World War II the condition of the working class in England was a world-wide scandal. Poverty, unemployment, social degradation in many "depressed areas" seemed permanent. Undoubtedly, the Labour victory in 1945 improved working-class conditions of life. What is called "prosperity" is that the worst of the shocking conditions have been eliminated. The Conservatives accepted the change and promised, if they got back to power, not to go back to the old days. They have got back to power since 1951. They spend a vast amount of their resources and energy seeking to convince ordinary people that, owing to this new prosperity, labour must now desert the very idea of labour politics.[36]

After showing how Williams demystifies the notion of progress masking the betrayal of the working class by the Labour Party, James catalogues the writer's various accomplishments. Williams argues for a concept of culture that is broad enough to frame its meaning as a "total way of life of the whole people." For James, Williams is a socialist thinker of the highest order who exposes "the pretenses of capitalist society and its tricks."[37] What is the exact nature of James's qualms? What is James getting at by stating: "Mr. Williams [is] not a Marxist"?

Williams "does not seem to be aware of what Marxism is" because he neglects the centrality of "the labour process" and "the role of production" and "ignores the idea of revolution completely."[38] James offers up a corrective and a sketch of the development of the British working class, filling in the silences. He emphasizes the centrality of production that anticipates Stuart Hall's internationalist framing by linking the British worker's fate with the rest of the world's toilers. Williams fails to maintain any "conception of the spontaneous creativity of the working class."[39] The belief in the inevitability of socialism (a belief that for James is key to Marx's method) would disturb Williams as some sort of retrograde "Marxist jargon."[40] The intellectual is hobbled by the wish to do something in response to the deepening capitalist crisis. James lauds Lenin's decision both in 1905 and 1917 at the height of revolutionary upheaval to take time to study both Hegel and Marx. His applause for Lenin's ethos of study is wrapped up in a simultaneous faith in workers to make the correct stance in the service of revolution without the mediation of an intellectual class. It is this double bind—coupling intellectual study with a simultaneous disdain for intellectual mediation—that warrants paying close attention to this review. This double bind animates James's Haitian revolutionary production in its entirety.

For James (unfairly I think), Williams projects his own analytical shortcomings in terms of the failure to grasp that revolution is about seizure of power from below, onto and by the workers themselves.[41] James's faith in the analytical capabilities and political judgment of everyday people rightfully gets scripted in both the dramatic form and historiographic work of his Haitian period. He, like his interlocutor, hungers for a more expansive definition of tragedy yet refuses to sell short the potential for progressive movement on behalf of workers acting alone themselves. The push and pull of mediated mass action is central to James's writings on Haiti and tragedy. They are problems for aesthetics as well as problems of politics. Their challenges are, among other things, challenges of reading.

The Haitian Revolution as Disavowal and Proliferation: Two Việt Minh Juxtapositions, Frantz Fanon and Paul Robeson

> The body calls.
> Yeah, the body, it calls out.
> It whispers at first.
> But it ends with a shout.
>
>   Devendra Banhart

> I honestly think, however, it's time some things were said. Things
> I'm going to say, not shout. I've long given up shouting.
>
>   Frantz Fanon

Let us continue constructing theoretical scaffolding by coupling a disavowal with a comparative proliferation: two interventions by Black liberationist thinkers, in which the authors triangulate their contemporary political conjunctures, the long nineteenth-century Haitian Revolution, and the mid-twentieth-century struggle of the North Vietnamese against French occupation.[42] Consider the conclusion to Martinican psychiatrist and Algerian revolution combatant Frantz Fanon's *Peau noire, masques blancs* (1952) and African American intellectual artist-activist Paul Robeson's column in the periodical *Freedom* entitled "Ho Chi Minh Is the Toussaint L'Ouverture of Indo-China" (March 1954).

When twenty-five-year-old Frantz Fanon submitted his medical thesis *Peau noire, masques blancs* for his degree (composed in Lyon between 1951 and 1952, originally entitled *Essai sur la désaliénation du Noir*) his committee was less than thrilled. It was swiftly rejected for its unorthodox form and political content. Fanon submitted an entirely different document[43]—a study of *Friedreich's ataxia*, a hereditary syndrome that negatively impacts the spinal cord (and possibly the cerebellum)—to receive his accreditation. History would absolve Fanon's concept of *sociogeny* established in *Black Skin, White Masks*. Yet in the moment, for a young Martinican attempting to gain his credentials as a medical doctor, it was *ontogeny* by way of dissertation committee decree that ruled the day.[44] Fanon's *Peau noire* calls for a process of dis-alienation that de-links Blacks from colonial symbolic logics. Both its content and its form as a doctoral thesis defy academic convention. The composite nature of Fanon's education propelled by his revolutionary commitment to convey the depths of alienation felt by African diasporic subjects in the French medical establishment and French society *tout court* animate this text—it is a synthesis of psychoanalytic theory, literary criticism, anticolonial *cri de guerre,* and dialectical thought. Toward realizing these transformative goals, Fanon supplemented his medical studies at Lyon by enrolling in the Philosophy Department at the School of Liberal Arts. Because Fanon was a pioneer of interdisciplinarity, the range of material informing his text makes classifying the book a challenge.

> He attended courses taught by Merleau-Ponty and by André Leroi-Gourhan. His interests ran to ethnology, phenomenology, and Marxism, but existentialism and psychoanalysis took top billing. Fanon was an avid reader with wide-ranging reading habits: Lévi-Strauss, Mauss, Heidegger, Hegel, as well as Lenin and the young Marx. Among the books he had borrowed from the Rue Blondel, he discovered the works of Leon Trotsky, but put off reading *Capital* and never got around to reading it in the end. In Paris he formed relationships with people who had deep political commitments and who helped pique his interest in Marxist methodology, but he never developed a need for clear cut political affiliations with the Communist Party least of all. He was especially drawn to psychoanalytical works and to Sartre's philosophy of the subject. He read Freud as well as the handful of works by Jacques Lacan that were available at the time.[45]

Fanon's study regimen raises the question of what kind of book is *Black Skin, White Masks*. Heuristically for the purpose of understanding its conclusion's reference to Haiti, I want to think of it as a lamentation. In *The Messingkauf Dialogues*, Brecht writes:

Crying doesn't express sorrow so much as relief. But lamenting by means of sounds, or better still words is a vast liberation, because it means that the sufferer is beginning to produce something. He's already mixing his sorrow with an account of the blows he has received; he's already making something out of the utterly devastating. *Observation* has set in.[46]

The keyword here, *observation*, clinically resonates. Soon-to-be credentialed Doctor Frantz Fanon's observations in *Peau noire, masques blancs* refuse to shout; yet true to Brecht's maxim, they register suffering and generate "something out of the utterly devastating." Fanon's work does not take leave of the body per se (quite the contrary); yet the backstory about obstacles in his medical accreditation might indicate that some forces in the French medical establishment wanted him to stay there. I begin here because there is something imperative in thinking about the conditions of how *Peau noire* was produced (Fanon dictated it to his wife, Josie). This speaks to the register of performances, the listening of speech, utterance, and gesture that accrues in the rest of this study. There is insight wrapped up in the limits and possibilities of Fanon's pacing body, the curvature of his spine, the breath strokes of his speaking voice giving dictation. In other words, thinking of *Black Skin, White Masks* understood as lamentation reveals something to us about the challenges of historical archive and the project of recapturing moments past. This something has a great deal to offer analysis of Black radical dramatic performance with regard to the problem of historical archives. For now, I want to examine a curious disavowal of the Haitian Revolution in the conclusion of *Black Skin, White Masks*.

Disavowal is a bit harsh here. It is more the case that Fanon refuses to be limited by comparison to accomplishments of Black radical pasts: "Je suis un homme, et c'est tout le passé du monde que j'ai à reprendre. Je ne suis pas seulement responsable de la révolte de Saint-Domingue."[47] *Reprendre* as both rework and recapture marks the challenge here for English translators. Here are Charles Lam Markmann's and Richard Philcox's translations, respectively:

I am a man, and what I have to recapture is the whole past of the world. I am not responsible solely for the revolt in Santo Domingo.[48]

I am a man, and I have to rework the world's past from the very beginning. I am not just responsible for the slave revolt in Saint Domingue.[49]

The variant translations of *reprendre*—rework and recapture—function as fruitful shorthand for examining the work of the plays examined in this study. Such dramatic texts function, within a dialectical intermediate space, poised between rework and recapture. Recapture relates to the etymological root—*ceptio* (concept) in reconceptualization. A theater of ideas worth its revolutionary credentials is always also a theatrical archive of concepts. Philcox's "I am not just responsible" implies a proliferation of responsibilities, whereas Markmann's "I am not responsible solely" implies a related refusal of restricting influence. Fanon's meditation on Vietnam represents a Black radical reading of what Marx in the nineteenth century theorized as the problematic tendencies of revolutionary movements to receive their inspiration from "the poetry of the past." An examination of the internal logic of *Black Skin, White Masks* complicates an understanding that for Fanon this signifies an easy endorsement of Marx's cautioning revolutionary movements on the dangers of temporal dips backward. Markmann's recapture resonates with Black radical thought's ongoing dialogue with notions of fugitivity as well as Walter Benjamin's germane rejoinder to Marx's *Eighteenth Brumaire* in which Benjamin insists that the oppressed garner tools of resistance from "image[s] of enslaved ancestors rather than that of liberated grandchildren."[50] Twentieth-century representations of the Haitian Revolution take their inspirational cues from both sources. Rework in the Philcox translation can be read as an insistence on forward motion. Rework implies refashioning "from the very beginning" all of yesterday's theoretical and praxis-based templates for face-forward revolutionary action.[51] In both translations, the assertion about not being limited to Haitian revolutionary pasts echoes W.E.B. DuBois's insistence on not tethering influences on Black radical pedagogy.[52]

Consider Fanon's corrective about causality, Indochina, revolt, and the question of temporality:

> It is not because the Indo-Chinese discovered a culture of their own that they revolted. Quite simply this was because it became impossible for them to breathe, in more than one sense of the word.
>
> When we recall how the old colonial hands in 1938 described Indochina as the land of piastres and rickshaws, of houseboys and cheap women, we understand only too well the fury of the Vietminh's struggle.
>
> A friend of mine, who had fought alongside me during the last war, recently came back from Indochina. He enlightened me on many

things—for example, on the serenity with which the sixteen- or seventeen-year old Vietnamese fell in front of the firing squad. Once, he told me, we had to kneel down to fire: the soldiers, confronted with such young "fanatics," were shaking. To sum up, he added: "The war we fought together was child's play compared with what is going on out there."

Seen from Europe, such things are incomprehensible. Some people claim there is a so-called Asian attitude toward death. But nobody is convinced by these third-rate philosophers. It wasn't so long ago that Asian serenity could be seen in the "vandals" of Vercors and the "terrorism" of the Resistance.

The Vietnamese who die in front of a firing squad don't expect their sacrifice to revive a forgotten past. They accept death for the sake of the present and the future.[53]

In order to understand Fanon's present/future radical insistence here it is helpful to look again toward Walter Benjamin—this time, in the form of his contention that true criticism is anti-comparison. For Benjamin, the function of criticism is not "to instruct by means of historical descriptions or to educate through comparisons, but to cognize by immersing itself in the object."[54] What kind of critical insights are gained via immersion in *Black Skin, White Masks* in terms of trying to classify it as a genre? Thinking of the text as a lamentation (along the lines of Brecht's definition) might account for the strange juxtaposition of Haitian revolutionary irrelevance and Indo-Chinese revolutionary urgency. Perhaps *Black Skin, White Masks* can be thought as a Caribbean lamentation, the production of *One Continual Cry* like David Walker's *Appeal to the Colored Citizens of the World (1829–1830).*[55]

Fanon frames the conclusion of *Black Skin, White Masks* with a passage from Marx's *Eighteenth Brumaire of Louis Bonaparte*:

> The social revolution cannot draw its poetry from the past, but only from the future. It cannot begin with itself before it has stripped itself of all its superstitions concerning the past. Earlier revolutions relied on memories out of world history in order to drug themselves against their own content. In order to find their own content, the revolutions of the nineteenth century have to let the dead bury the dead. Before, the expression exceeded the content; now the content exceeds the expression.[56]

In *Black Skin, White Masks*, stripping the past of "all its superstitions" implies engagement with such revolutionary pasts. Stripping is a gesture of active revisiting and rehearsal. History in this quote plays the role of form—in this case the Vietnamese peasant, whose radical political action exceeds all past expressions precisely because her actions are authentically generating what has yet to be determined. Philcox's/Fanon's use of expression reminds readers that the form that captures such action is in itself an ideological act with sometimes dire consequence.

Fanon's text begins with a statement that links questions of temporality to questions of insurrection. Fanon warns the reader to not expect an "explosion" today since its arrival is either "too early" or "too late" and he ends with a "final prayer": "O my body, always make me a man who questions!" Thinking together the first and last lines of Fanon's study anticipates questions of immediacy addressed in my next pairing. Fanon quells his audience's expectations for an explosion, a curious initial move. His matter-of-factness conceals more than it clarifies and is generative in such concealment. Asserting that the explosion is either "too early" or "too late" only guides the reader in not expecting it to happen today. It is precisely not setting coordinates for an arrival (or in the spirit of prior revolutionary manifestos, conjuring an explosion into being through, riffing off Martin Puchner, anticolonialist speech acts).[57] Rather, it is either the assertion of a temporal deferral or a declaration of tardiness. The reader is just left with a warning against the temptations of immediacy. Paradoxically, the text concludes by situating the author's infinite desire ("always make me a man who questions!") within the frame of his finite ("O my") speaking body. The arc of Fanon's argument is not hostile to African pasts, Haitian or otherwise. Early on in his first chapter, "The Black Man and Language," Fanon indicates enthusiasm pertaining to the research of Cheikh Anta Diop, the Senegalese scholar of African antiquity. It is rather that the act of lamentation, the aggregate of observations of both revolutionary pasts and the endured sufferings such pasts were poised to oppose in the prior chapters, functions as a sort of exorcism (a spoken purgation) that strains the relevancy of slave revolts in Saint-Domingue compared to the present militant action of the Vietnamese combatant.

It is helpful to contrast the scale of *Black Skin, White Masks* as full-length study as lamentation with Paul Robeson's "Ho Chi Minh Is the Toussaint L'Ouverture of Indo-China," a short piece of journalism, unanxious in comparing Vietnamese presents with Haitian pasts. Robeson begins this periodical article by synchronically juxtaposing two populations by way of a collective recollection of the Haitian Revolution:

As I write these lines, the eyes of the world are on a country inhabited by 23 million brown-skin people—a population one and a half times the number of Negroes in the U.S. In size that country is equal to the combined area of Mississippi, South Carolina and Alabama. It's a fertile land, rich in minerals; but all the wealth is taken away by the foreign rulers, and the people are poor.

I'm talking about Vietnam, and it seems to me that we Negroes have a special reason for understanding what's going on over there. Only recently, during Negro History Week, we recalled the heroic exploits of Toussaint L'Ouverture who led the people of Haiti in a victorious rebellion against the French Empire.

Well, at the same time that the French were fighting to keep their hold on the black slaves of Haiti, they were sending an army around to the other side of the world to impose colonial slavery on the people of Indo-China. And ever since then the Indo-Chinese have been struggling to be free from French domination.

"My children, France comes to make us slaves. God gave us liberty; Burn the cities, destroy the harvest, tear up the roads with cannon, poison the wells, show the white man the hell he comes to make!"

These fiery words, addressed to his people by Toussaint L'Ouverture when Napoleon sent Leclerc with an army of 30,000 men to re-enslave Haiti, are echoed today by Ho Chi Minh, but like the blacks of Haiti, the plantation workers of Indo-China have proved unconquerable.

In 1946 France was forced to recognize the Republic of Vietnam, headed by Ho Chi Minh; but like the double-crossing Napoleon in the time of Toussaint, the French colonial masters have come to hate this struggle, they call it "the dirty war"; and their rulers have not dared to draft Frenchmen for military service there.[58]

Robeson proposes a question and provocation that links the political destinies of African Americans and Indo-Chinese: "Shall Negro sharecroppers from Mississippi be sent to shoot down brown-skinned peasants in Vietnam—to serve the interests of those who oppose Negro liberation at home and colonial freedom abroad?" In ballistic short-burst prose of newspaper column, Robeson performs constant recourse to the language of simultaneity—"As I write these lines," "At the same time." The temporal logic of his piece collapses in its narrative strategies the geographical divide separating "Negroes in the U.S." with the militarily engaged Vietnamese as a formal strategy to emphasize how that very same geographical divide obfuscates political interconnectedness. "Negro History Week" is an exercise in collective recollection—a communitarian mining of the poetry of the past that works to prescribe both present and future decisions.

As Fanon biographer David Macey writes, "Under the colonial system that developed from the seventeenth century onwards, the role of the West Indian colonies of Martinique, Guadeloupe, and Saint Domingue (now divided into Haiti and the Dominican Republic) was defined with brutal clarity. Their sole *raison d'être* was to supply the metropolis with tropical produce."[59] Surely Fanon in neighboring Martinique was privy to the historic centrality of Haiti for producing agricultural wealth for Europe from the blood of coerced Black labor. France's defeat by General Giap's Việt Minh forces at Dien Bien Phu was central in his mind and more temporally present than a long nineteenth-century slave uprising and revolution in neighboring Haiti.[60] His disavowal of Haitian revolutionary pasts only makes sense when you think of *Black Skin, White Masks* as a totality in which the catalogue of observations—the "making something out of the utterly devastating"—is necessary to go through in order to get beyond.

The plays examined in this book continue this Herculean effort and respond to Ernesto Che Guevara's 1967 call to the Organization of Solidarity with the People of Asia, Africa and Latin America (OSPAAAL, also referred to as the Tricontinental) to "Create two, three, many Vietnams"[61] by staging two, three, many Haitian revolutions.

"The Pure Pleasure of Writing at Last Language As One Hears It": *Questions of Immediacy and the Historical Archive*

Let us turn to a page from the 1978 "Author's Note" of *Monsieur Toussaint: A Play* by Edouard Glissant, Fanon's childhood friend:

> At the time of publishing this acting version, the conditions of theatrical production prevailing in the Antilles are such that the result cannot be considered as "up-to-date," but rather as a complementary substitute by which the accurate portrayal of our situation becomes known more and more. Hence the question of the speech of Haitians in the drama must be considered. It may for example seem strange that a character like Mackandal, a black maroon of the preceding century, who appears to Toussaint as a sort of primeval conscience, would speak to the latter in French, instead of Creole. I have tried however to resist resorting to the procedure of "creolizing,"

the artificiality of which would have been obvious. The linguistic environment of the play can be determined at the time of its production. The Creole tongue is sufficiently adaptable in its written form so that producer and actors can work together to complete by improvisation what the author has intended. It goes without saying that the sprinkling of Creole lines appearing in this version (incantations and chants syntactically incoherent, mixtures of Guadeloupean, Haitian, and Martinician sonorities) indicates above all the pure pleasure of writing at last a language *as one hears it.*[62]

Fanon's proposition in the seventh chapter of *Black Skin, White Masks*—"the black man is comparison"[63]—presents a sort of technical challenge, a problem of writing "at last a language *as one hears it.*" Comparison in its written form in both French and English resonates with Fanon's discussion of Adlerian behavior disorder. Yet the homonym comparison in its Antillean variant does slightly different work. In Creole, comparison as adjective means "contemptuous" or "contemptible."[64] Contemporary readers of Fanon's work cannot access the spoken emphasis placed on *comparison* that his wife, Josie, heard. Its trace indeed marks the text, but the definitional inflection of the performed utterance is lost upon its speaking. Where does it go? This is the challenge signaling a generative limit in writing (related to audience) as well as a cautionary warning about the theoretical challenges of archival exploration: How to capture Martinican sonority in French translation that does a kind of theoretical work? Glissant privileges a presentist (and collectivist) concern—the producers' and actors' ability to improvise—over fidelity to representing Haiti linguistically *how it really was.* Process trumps an idealist commitment to so-called accuracy, and forward march trumps atavistic return. Interpretive communal processing is the privileged future mode for engaging various pasts. Continuing with *Peau noire, masques blanc,* I return to *reprendre,* in this case its tertiary definition, *reprendre* as to catch (as in catch one's breath) and correct (as in to correct oneself speaking), as a way of thinking about problems of immediacy and the historical archive.

Frantz Fanon's 1952 *Black Skin, White Masks* in some sense can be heuristically thought of as a collaboration between Fanon and his wife, Marie Josephe Duble (Josie). Recall that Fanon dictated and Josie recorded. This assertion of collaboration cannot be stretched too far. Dictation and transcription push toward collaboration yet never quite constitute it. Still, the transcriber performs small acts of interpretation, bringing voice to page. Fanon biographer David Macey misses an opportunity to theorize this fact and instead restricts the following commentary to the level of imme-diacy. His theorization of the composition of *Black Skin, White Masks* is locked in sense perception:

> Fanon never learned to use a typewriter and dictated his text to Josie as he strode up and down the room like an actor declaiming his lines. Traces of the oral origins of the text are visible in the sudden breaks and changes of direction, as Fanon suddenly recalls or thinks of something. If there is an element of free association here, it is Fanon and not his informants who is free associating. When he writes, or rather says, "When my ubiquitary (*ubiquitaire*) hands caress these white breasts, I am making white civiliza-tion and dignity mine," he is speaking to the young woman he will marry.[65]

Compare this commentary to C.L.R. James's self-criticism pertaining to the archival sources of *The Black Jacobins*. From his July 1971 lecture enti-tled "How I Would Rewrite *The Black Jacobins*" given at the Atlanta-based *Institute of the Black World*:

> Now, in rewriting *The Black Jacobins*, I could, under different circum-stances, tell you about certain principles and then try to fit what I have to say into those principles. I will not do it, it would constitute too great a strain.
>
> The kind of thing that I want to talk about can be seen on page 10. A Swiss traveler, Girod-Chantrans is his name, has left a famous description of a gang of slaves at work:
>
>> There were about a hundred men and women of different ages, all occupied in digging ditches in a cane-field, the majority of them naked or covered with rags. The sun shone down with full force on their heads. Sweat rolled from all parts of their bodies. Their limbs, weighed down by the heat, fatigued with the weight of the their picks . . . strained themselves to overcome every obstacle.
>
> It's a very famous description, and I used it. *Today I would not do that.* I would write descriptions in which the black slaves themselves, or people very close to them, describe what they were doing and how they felt about the work that they were forced to carry on. I don't blame myself for doing this in 1938; it is a famous inscription. It is accurate enough, but I wouldn't do that today. I don't want today to be writing and say that's what *they* said about how *we* were being treated. Not any longer, no. I would want to say

what we had to say about how we were treated, and I know that the information exists in all the material. But it was easy enough in those days to go ahead.[66]

The pronominal labor of the italicized *they* and *we* is imperative. James reminds the historians in the audience about the importance of perspective in framing historical truths, the importance of partisan sourcing in generating a universal claim. Certainly there are accounts of the enslaved Africans themselves; yet still there is an almost utopian persistence in James's insistence here. James's labors to dip backward in the archive, his striving to access the most unmediated voices of "the black slaves themselves," reveals a utopian desire to gain access to a past without thorny mediation.

Contrast this with Macey's archival project to capture a moment of production lost to history in the genesis of Fanon's *Black Skin, White Masks*. Macey's commentary represents a surrendering to immediacy. The consequence of this move is that for a brief moment, he only sees Fanon (a Black man) locked in sensual immediacy speaking to Josie (a white woman). J. Fanon had her own take on the subject of so-called interracial relationships. In a 1978 interview at Howard University's *African-American Center*, she argued that posing their marriage as a political problem antagonistically conflicts with Fanon's work and political vision-praxis where the revolution itself changes signs, technologies, and power relations (three prime examples will suffice: Fanon's writings on the veil, the radio, and Western medicine).[67] In J. Fanon's analysis stasis is never triumphant and process trumps immediacy:

> It is my opinion, and I believe that it was also his—otherwise he would not have contracted nor remained in this interracial marriage—that there was no contradiction. In his works, he states clearly that it is through a revolutionary process that we can understand and resolve racial problems. Otherwise, we find ourselves in dead-end situations that are impossible to resolve—the sort that we can never put to rest. For example, critics can reproach a black American for marrying an Arab woman because her skin is lighter than his and so on, and so on.
>
> In a certain phase of the struggle, such a position can have for a time a positive and beneficially unifying effect. However, it remains a limitation. We are not going to limit each other to race! Otherwise, where is the revolution?[68]

The utopian desire of James to access an unmediated archive trumps Macey's surrender to the immediacy of a more recent revolutionary past. I am setting the question of "dictation" in Fanon against the question of "citation" in James: two distinct modes of composition rendered problematic by the circumstances of these writers, the way the necessity of their respective conjunctures bind.

Productive Contradictions of Brechtian Use

> Wir leiten unsere Ästhetik . . . von den Bedürfnissen unseres Kampfes ab.
>
> We derive our aesthetics . . . from the needs of our struggle.
>
> Bertolt Brecht

The question of use is key for Brecht[69] in crafting his revolutionary aesthetics and remains a central preoccupation for scholars and practitioners working within a Brechtian framework. Brecht's entire corpus of plays, poems, narrative fiction, song-cycles, and essays can be understood as an extended meditation on how to effectively use art in furthering a project of socialist revolution. A few examples suffice. The prefatory materials in two of Brecht's most significant poetry volumes, *Devotions for the Home* and the *Svendborg Poems,* contain meditations on use: "Both collections open with an address to the reader, advising on the attitudes to adopt while reading the poems. Whereas in the earlier collection the 'instructions for use' could still afford to be playfully blasphemous and tongue-in-cheek, the introit of the *Svendborg Poems* is constrained to warn readers, solemnly, and apologetically, that they would be unwise to place too much reliance on writings based on partial, imperfect and outdated sources of information."[70] This speaks to Brecht's worry that the distance exile creates a gulf separating his Nazi-ridden German homeland and his Svendborg escape taints the use-value of the poetic offerings in the *Svendborg Poems.* A May 1935 letter by Walter Benjamin refutes Theodor Adorno's concerns that Brecht's Bolshevik sympathies are detrimental to the development of Benjamin's ongoing encyclopedic *Arcades Project.* The letter extols Brecht's usefulness. According to Benjamin, Brecht's "decisive" influence infuses Benjamin's work with productive "aporias" instead of "directives":

> Then followed the decisive encounter with Brecht, and with it the culmination of every aporia connected with this work, which even then I still

refused to relinquish. The significant experience which I was able to gain from my work from this recent period—and it was by no means insubstantial—could not properly take shape before the limits of the significance had become indubitably clear to me, and all "directives" from that quarter as well had thereby become quite superfluous.[71]

In his critique of Kafka, captured in the infamous 1934 Svendborg "Conversations" between Brecht and Benjamin, Brecht outlines the "Parable of Use":

"I don't accept Kafka, you know." And he goes on to speak about a Chinese philosopher's parable of "the tribulations of usefulness." In a wood there are many kinds of tree-trunk. From the thickest they make ship's timbers; from those which are less thick but still quite sturdy, they make boxes and coffin-lids; the thinnest of all are made into whipping-rods; but of the stunted ones they make nothing at all: these escape the tribulations of usefulness. "You've got to look around in Kafka's writing as you might in such a wood. Then you'll find a whole lot of very useful things. The images are good, of course. But the rest is pure mystification. It's nonsense. You have to ignore it. Depth doesn't get you anywhere at all. Depth is a separate dimension, it's just depth—and there's nothing whatsoever to be seen in it."[72]

Note that far from being an easy dismissal, Brecht's hostility to Kafka's "mystification" poses the demand to read Kafka, to mine with great care Kafka for what is useful. The Chinese example here is germane. As Wolfgang Fritz Haug argues: "Fredric Jameson, in his beautiful book *Brecht and Method* . . . understands Brecht's *sinité* as a Lacanian 'tenant-lieu,' a place-keeper for the metaphysics that have become impossible."[73] Yet Brecht was also greatly influenced by Mao Tse Tung, who himself effected a dialectical negation of Chinese metaphysical thought in the form of engagement with Confucian thought. For the writers examined in this study, Haiti functions as similar place-keeper of impossible possibilities.

Offering up an interpretation of one of Brecht's poetic fragments, Benjamin writes:

"Carpenter . . . ": The carpenter we have to imagine here is an eccentric who is never satisfied with his "work," who cannot make up his mind to let it out of his hands. If writers are taking temporary leave of their *oeuvre* . . . then statesmen, too, are expected to show the same attitude. Brecht tells them:

You are amateur craftsmen, you want to make the State your *oeuvre* instead
of realizing that the State is not supposed to be a work of art, not an eternal
value, but an object of practical use.[74]

Brecht's joining together the artist with the politician, the way that political practice is paired with craftsmanship (even in Benjamin's negative
comparative valence), speaks to a great deal of James's concerns. James's
encounters with the workmanship of England's laboring class directly
inform the political sensibilities that produce the writings of his Haiti
period. Both men share a labor-centric political worldview as well as an
Epicurean sensitivity to artisan beauty that is deeply political. Benjamin's
commentary recalls one of Brecht's 1934 journal entries where he questions the usefulness of his endeavors as a playwright, compared to his
unfulfilled vocational dream of becoming an artisan cabinetmaker:

i am a playwright.
     I would actually like to have been a cabinetmaker, but of course you
don't earn enough doing that. I would have enjoyed working with wood.
you don't get really fine stained and polished wood much any more, the
beautiful panelling and balustrades of the old days, those pale, Maplewood
tabletops as thick as the span of your hand that we found in our grand-
parent's rooms, worn smooth by the hands of whole generations. and the
wardrobes i've seen! the way the edges were bevelled, the doors inlaid, the
internal compartments offset, and such beautiful proportions. seeing a
piece of furniture like that made you think better thoughts. the things they
could do with a wooden fork-handle, these craftsmen have all gone now.
Even in these times of ours there are good things to be seen. in bond street
in london in a shop window i saw a big cigar-box, six plain maple boards
and an iron catch, but it looked marvellous. the cigars were a guinea apiece.
at a casual glance the unadorned box would have made one thing, "this
tobacco is so costly that they can't even lay out a shilling for the packag-
ing, a guinea is the bottom price they can take, and at that the planters are
starving." but on further inspection one could see that the firm had seen
fit to provide a case too that would satisfy the expectations of their fine
tobacco. . . .
     when I weigh up where abandoning myself to my enthusiasms has got
me, and what benefit repeated scrutiny has been, I recommend the latter. if
I had adopted the former approach, I would still be living in my fatherland,
but by not adopting the latter, I would no longer be an honest person.[75]

There is much to say about this extraordinary meditation. The journal entry (a private genre, not meant for public consumption) offers up a challenge to what counts as archival source material in a project that mines the pasts for insight. Here Brecht collapses exchange-value and use-value. The interpenetration of both use and exchange as constitutive of a Marxian understanding of value is a point that Gayatri Spivak's work has consistently emphasized with great precision.[76] Neither the beauty of the object nor the planters' wages escape Brecht's analytical purview. His expressions of remorse for choosing the vocation of playwright over that of cabinetmaker concedes the fact that he laments both the actors and the products of a bygone era of production: "these craftsmen have all gone now" and "you don't get really fine stained and polished wood much any more." Yet his observation still grants an almost anachronistic quality of craftsmanship to the most quotidian of objects—the cigar box. There is dialectical nuance here that complicates Brecht's own maxim: "Don't start from the good old things but the bad new ones."[77]

I couple James and Brecht throughout this work, in part to account for C.L.R. James's strange failure to mention Brecht in his capacious oeuvre on theatrical aesthetics and politics. Perhaps Brecht's official, unwavering support for the Bolshevik regime (a critical dialectic toward official Soviet policy is clearly visible by way of a deep examination of Brecht's thoughts) clashed with James's critical engagement with Trotsky. This will be explored further in my discussion of Paul Robeson and C.L.R. James. A similar ideological divide on the Russian question informs a productive tension but fails to break the friendship bond between James and Robeson. Nor did it break the friendship between C.L.R. James and Amiri Baraka.[78] Part of this book's labor is to explain why this is so. The lack of conversation between Brecht and James in hindsight is unfortunate since presumably they both would have had a great deal to talk about.

Before concluding, I want to signal a productive challenge in utilizing Brecht to think about Black radical aesthetic production. Again, from Brecht's *Journals*, this time, a Los Angeles entry from 17 May 1942 conveying an observation by one of his associates. Brecht relates a story told by his friend the Austrian actor and theater director Fritz Kortner: "kortner recounts how a negro polishing his shoes while he was having a haircut said, 'I don't like camminism, I like the russian system.'"[79] This recollection is cast in an absurdist mold in almost every facet—an inescapable fact whether or not it reflects the actuality of what happened. Black speech, the so-called "vernacular," is typographically registered along with phonetic spellings. We are presented with a representation of labor that is vertically spatially uneven—"a negro polishing his shoes." The journal entry mirrors the way the Hollywood apparatus might convey the uneven spatiality of a Black laborer to a white patron, yet Brecht implies by way of constituting it as part of his archive that the scene is worthy of thought. What can this possibly say to traditions of Black radical thought?

So much scholarship on Black radicalism is invested with situating Black revolutionary struggle on its own terms, in other words in its "autonomy."[80] Scholarship calibrates how such struggle is incorporated or dis-incorporated into a broader world system—a system inhabited by places, proper names, and events. The best of African diasporic inquiry mines art fashioned in struggle for a different vocabulary, a different optic to frame revolutionary desires. Form and content are always interpenetrating and the balance between the two constantly weighed. Santiago Colás's essay "Silence and Dialectics: Speculations on C.L.R. James and Latin America" expertly theorizes this interrelationship as: "James never just wrote *about* things—cricket, Cuba, *Moby Dick*, Lenin, and so on—he also wrote about *how* to write about them."[81] The articulated preference of "the russian system" over "camminism" foregrounds that concepts, the place-markers signaling events in the Black radical imaginary, often demand a different logic of naming. This necessity for a different protocol of naming, a different set of metrics for staging, is a materialist necessity. The "russian system" read here speculatively foregrounds the nation as proper name, whereas "system" marks its supplements: all that it entails, satellites, oppressed nations, stateless peoples, diasporic subjects linked in the orbit of such a proper-named system, one structured from within by uneven development. Perhaps "camminism" is the less desirable end of the formula because it purports a commonality that only initially self-determination can begin to initiate, a commonality whose condition of possibility is indeed self-determination in its myriad contingent possibilities. Self-determination as an act of interpretation and interpretation as an act of labor.

Consider the interpretive challenge to think the poetic relationship between shining shoes and polishing boots:

> nous n'acceptons plus
> ça vous étonne
> de dire: oui missié
> en cirant vos bottes

we won't take anymore
that surprises you
to say: *yessuh*
while polishing your boots[82]

Miguel Mellino's essay "The *Langue* of the Damned: Fanon and the Remnants of Europe" cites Macey's argument pertaining to the title of Fanon's *The Wretched of the Earth* as the linchpin his inquiry: "The obvious allusion to the '*Internationale*' ('*Debout, les damnés de la terre*' / 'Arise, ye wretched of the earth') is mediated through an allusion to something less obvious. Written in either 1938 or 1939 by Jacques Roumain, who was the founder of the Communist Party of Haiti, '*Sales nègres*' is first cited by Fanon in 1958." Mellino's goal is to "explore what has been missed in the gap between *Les damnés* and the final English translation of *The Wretched*. The signifier *wretched* does not convey the same—apocalyptic, messianic, redemptive—meaning as *damnés*. What is missing is precisely that *mediation* of the wretched through *les damnés* of Roumain's poem recalled by Macey. What is lost in translation here is nothing less than Fanon's *modernist* political imagination."[83] This fascinating textual backstory serves Mellino's "aim here to interrogate the existential grammar of the damned."[84] Mellino's provocation houses a peculiar gap—he does not engage the Roumain poem in question. A cursory investigation of its structuring moves (particularly its employment of the line break) resonates with how I am speculatively reading Brecht. The way the line—"that surprises you"—is constituted in its suspended singularity necessitates that the reader question whether or not the source of such surprise is (1) "we won't take it anymore," (2) the affirmative "yessuh" (which never really means just that), or (3) the meaning of the scene of labor—"polishing your boots." It is an invitation to contestation. It turns the problem of the ambiguity of a single-line affirmation, the addressee of such an affirmation, into the reader's problem or, returning to Brecht's journal, the patron's—if he indeed takes the time to listen.

A well-known consequence of the Haitian Revolution: the United States acquires the state of Louisiana from the French. The Classical Theatre of Harlem's 2006 staging of Samuel Beckett's *Waiting for Godot* on a roof in New Orleans during Hurricane Katrina is among other things a materialist equivalent of an allegorical and existential condition of dread. The predicament, what Bertolt Brecht would theorize as the social *gest* of two men, alone on a roof waiting on state drowning warrants an autonomous radical tradition. It demands the sustaining of such a radical tradition as materialist necessity. A byproduct of speculative engagement with Brecht's absurdist recollection is the reminder that although a great deal of Black radical thought demands autonomy in constituting its own categories, such autonomy is never removed from a world stage of references, geographies, and proper names. Black radicalism is always already radical internationalism. "I don't like camminism, I like the russian system" indeed. Haiti poses all of these methodological questions centuries earlier than the Russian Revolution of Brecht's journalistic musings. The best partisan minds of the Russian Revolution happily admit as much. The pages that follow chart one particular narrative trajectory of such returns.

1

Haitian Revolutionary Encounters

Eugene O'Neill, Sergei Eisenstein,
and Orson Welles

Ah, Haitians,—that is quite another thing! Haitians are the
écarté of French stock-jobbing. We may like bouillotte, delight in
whist, be enraptured with boston, and yet grow tired of them all;
but we always come back to écarté—it is not only a game, it is a
hors-d'oeuvre!

"A Flurry of Stocks," Alexander Dumas's
The Count of Monte Cristo

This chapter examines three Haitian revolutionary inspired
"lines of flight":

Lines of flight, for their part, never consist in running away from the
world but rather in causing runoffs, as when you drill a hole in a pipe;
there is no social system that does not leak from all directions, even
if it makes its segments increasingly rigid in order to seal the lines of
flight. There is nothing imaginary, nothing symbolic about lines of
flight. There is nothing more active than a line of flight, among ani-
mals or humans. Even History is forced to take that route rather than
proceeding by "signifying breaks." What is escaping in a society at a
given moment? It is on lines of flight that new weapons are invented, to
be turned against the heavy arms of the State. "I may be running, but
I'm looking for a gun as I go" (George Jackson).[1]

These three uses of the Haitian Revolution act as a kind of rehearsal
for our discussion of African diasporic dramatic performances of
Haiti in revolt. As Deleuzian "lines of flight" they do not propose

concrete solutions, nor do they aspire to dialectical synthesis. They do not proceed via "signifying breaks." The Haitian revolutionary example is one of repetition and persistence. As dramatic performances they "worry the line"[2] of demarcation separating imaginary, symbolic, and prioritized action. As works of drama inflected with past history or as preparatory exercises they do not simply constitute the Real. They relate but do not directly correlate to their historical referent: the Haitian Revolution. They resonate with Fredric Jameson's insight that "history is *not* a text, nor a narrative, master or otherwise, but that, as an absent cause, it is inaccessible to us except in textual form, and that our approach to it and to the Real itself necessarily passes through its prior textualization, its narrativization in the political unconscious."[3] A continuum of performance, they repeat therefore endure. New weapons get crafted by way of confrontation with the old.

Here are the three:

1. The late-night forest run of Eugene O'Neill's Emperor Brutus Jones.
2. A lesson given by Sergei Eisenstein to his students at the VGIK (the State Cinema Institute in Moscow), where he lectured from 1932 to 1935. A semester-long class in staging Haitian revolutionary combatant Dessalines fleeing a French infantry ambush via a line of flight out a window. As well as Eisenstein's essay "A Course in Treatment," consisting of his discussion of *The Count of Monte Cristo* and cinematic treatment for a Hollywood adaptation of Theodore Dreiser's *An American Tragedy.*
3. Orson Welles's radio play on the Haitian Revolution, in which the *queer* narrative arc flees from its long nineteenth-century Caribbean context, employing its theoretical knowledge to champion the United Front against twentieth-century fascism.

These three sites use the Haitian Revolution as source material to present radical innovations in aesthetics that speak to urgent political questions of domination and resistance. As a cluster, they function as an appropriate preamble to African diasporic theatrical uses of Haiti examined in this study.

The Theatrical Cauldron of the Black Radical Tragic: The "Yet" and "And" of The Emperor Jones

> To write ghost stories implies that ghosts are real, that is to say, that they produce material effects.
>
> Avery F. Gordon

> Yeah we got ghost writers, they just actually ghosts.
>
> Malik Yusef

Eugene O'Neill's *The Emperor Jones* (1920)[4] was composed in a climate of U.S. imperialist intervention in the Caribbean. Five years prior, President Woodrow Wilson sent three hundred marines to Port-au-Prince, Haiti. A constitution written in 1918 was imposed on that nation by then assistant secretary of the United States Navy, Franklin D. Roosevelt, undermining the Haitian combatant-statesman Jean-Jacques Dessalines's 1804 principle forbidding foreigners from owning Haitian land.[5] O'Neill's play stages both the fall of his protagonist Brutus Jones and an African American intervention in Afro-Caribbean sovereignty. The relationship of O'Neill's text to an understanding of Black radicalism generally, and Haiti specifically, is one of marked ambivalence. If "Western society," as Cedric Robinson writes, is the "social cauldron [for] Black radicalism,"[6] O'Neill's *The Emperor Jones*[7] presents a model theatrical cauldron. O'Neill's work provided unprecedented opportunities to Black actors and breathed new experimental life into the American theater. The play's movement is both progressive and regressive. It cannot resolve its structuring tension between its radical aesthetic and its foreclosure of its own radical political conclusions. I will focus on the political implications of O'Neill's use of abstraction and what he calls "super-naturalism."[8]

Shannon Steen recounts an objection to one of the play's stage directions voiced by actor James Earl Jones, lead role in the 1970 Caedmon Production's audio recording of the play. Jones took issue with O'Neill's description of the protagonist as "typically negroid, yet there is something distinctive about his face." He "questioned O'Neill's use of the conjunction 'yet' in this description, asking how our conceptions of this character would be different if O'Neill had instead used the conjunction 'and'; 'as if ordinarily there is not dignity in the negroid face . . . as if there is something keen and *un*negroid about him.'"[9] The "yet" of the play implies a discourse on Black essence that undermines the specific representation of Brutus Jones as individual in favor of a politics of expressionist abstraction overdetermined by a racialist calculus. The "and" signifies the latent possibility that undermines and escapes such retrograde formulation. Abstraction and particularity are in constant flux in the play. Each of its movements inherits the political consequences of how wide or how narrow it scopes its target. Even the Emperor's namesake houses this contradictory doubling. Carme Manuel references Norman Sanders's introduction to an edition of Shakespeare's *Julius Caesar* to illustrate the contrary, double-signification of O'Neill's character's first name: "At one extreme, we have the medieval Brutus condemned to suffer at the center of Dante's *Inferno*, as a man guilty of criminal assassination and personal betrayal; and on the other, 'the noblest Roman of them all,' Plutarch's 'angel,' the one just man, gentle and altruistic, among the wicked and envious conspirators."[10] *The Emperor Jones* exhibits a progressive and regressive movement, a tension between its radical aesthetic and underdeveloped radical politics. The critical tension between the "and" and the "yet" underscores the main problematic of the play. It marks an American model of Expressionism that stages an unresolved tension between racist primitivism and a radical attempt to foreground U.S. indebtedness to stolen Black labor and stolen Black life. In its formal construction and thematic content, *The Emperor Jones* balances a commitment to both acute specificity and a simultaneous radical and retrograde politics of abstraction.

The super-naturalism of O'Neill's aesthetic on one hand worries the line separating reality and fantasy in terms of what his character sees during his forest line of flight. The concept of haunting illuminates such work. For Tzvetan Todorov, the supernatural "often appears because we take a figurative sense literally."[11] To represent key moments of North American oppression of African people as figurative, haunting delusion performs a complex task in *The Emperor Jones*. It is a similar problem posed by the film version of Toni Morrison's *Beloved* (1998): abstract literary figuration accepts the challenge of representation, subtracting from it the burdensome hubris of conflating such representation with its traumatic real correlative. This feat is an acute challenge for film. Morrison's novel declares in a warning itself defies: "It was not a story to pass on."[12] One cannot represent the afterlives of American racial slavery, the genocide of New World Africans in a realist grammar, without betraying the horror of those experiences. Yet representation remains and, as such, performs critical work. To figuratively represent such signposts renders them as capable of overhaul. Latent in such representation is the possibility that these structures can and should be resisted and toppled. O'Neill does not draw out the latent potential in his work but offers it to the world for further development. The play exists as a multilayering of self-reflexive theatrical tricks: a psychodrama/hallucination, a play within the play. It maintains fidelity to its Modernist milieu by foregrounding its status as aesthetic object. The super-naturalist employment of haunting memories of an African American past bound up in militant resistance to enslavement has a great deal to say to Avery F. Gordon's notion of *haunting*. The ghost, Gordon argues:

> makes itself known to us through us through haunting and pulls us affectively into the structure of feeling of a reality we come to experience as a recognition. Haunting recognition is a special way of knowing what has happened or is happening.
>
> . . . The ghost is primarily a symptom of what is missing. It gives notice not only to itself but also to what it represents. What it represents is usually a loss, sometimes of life, sometimes of a path not taken. From a certain vantage point the ghost also simultaneously represents a future possibility, a hope. Finally, I have suggested that the ghost is alive, so to speak. We are in relation to it and it has designs on us such that we must reckon with it graciously, attempting to offer it a hospitable memory *out of a concern for justice*. Out of a concern for justice would be the only reason one would bother.[13]

I explore the specific contours of Brutus Jones's "haunting recognition" and demonstrate how such recognition proceeds by way of O'Neill's aesthetic innovation. I engage the aporias of representation bound up in O'Neill's Haitian drama in order to delve deeply into Houston A. Baker's prescient insight: "If only O'Neill had bracketed the psycho-surreal final trappings of the Emperor's world and given us the stunning account of colonialism that remains implicit in his quip at the close of his dramatis personae: 'The action of the play takes place on an island in the West Indies, as yet un-self-determined by white marines.'"[14] The "yet" of the "as yet un-self-determined" (in its veiled political critique) pushes up against the "yet" of James Earl Jones's critique. It is that constituted tension that makes the play such a site for heated contestation.

How does one reconcile the critique of O'Neill as symptomatic of certain white writers' racialist paternalism yet salvage some sort of radical *gestic* moment in the work that would engender revolutionary use? Edward Said's insights into Joseph Conrad help expose the latent liberatory kernel in O'Neill's flirtation with colonialist representation. Said on the problem of the *porter*:

> The horribly attenuated and oppressed black porters that Conrad portrays that [Chinua] Achebe finds so objectionable not only contain within them the frozen essence that condemns them to the servitude and punishment Conrad sees as their present fate, but also point prophetically towards a whole series of implied developments that their later history discloses despite, over and above, and also paradoxically because of, the radical severity and awful solitude of Conrad's essentializing vision. The fact that later writers keep returning to Conrad means that his work, by virtue of its uncompromising Eurocentric vision, is precisely what gives it its antinomian force, the intensity and power wrapped into its sentences, which demand an equal and opposite response to meet them head on in a confirmation, a refutation, or an elaboration of what they represent. In the grip of Conrad's Africa, you are driven by its sheer stifling horror to work through it, to push beyond it as history itself transforms even the most unyielding stasis into process and a search for greater clarity, relief, resolution or denial. And of course in Conrad, as will all such extraordinary minds, the felt tension between what is intolerable there and a symmetrical compulsion to escape from it is what is most profoundly at stake—what the reading and interpretation of a work like *Heart of Darkness* is all about. Texts that are inertly of their time stay there: those which brush up unstintingly against historical constraints are the ones we keep with us, generation after generation.[15]

What is the "antinomian force" underlying O'Neill's caricature of Brutus Jones? Is there a comparable Conradian horror in O'Neill's play? Conrad's representation of a "stifling horror" forces in its reception the need to push beyond it to an indeterminate cluster of possibilities. These include "clarity, relief, resolution, or denial." The staying power of O'Neill's work is in its very ability to brush up against such historical constraints and gesture toward future challenges facing anti-systemic and decolonizing forces. Surely this is what attracted the radical intellectual Paul Robeson to the production. There is a prophetic calculus implied in Houston Baker's remarks. It is a foregrounding of historical memory (poetry of the past) as it relates to the traffic in Black bodies as the building blocks of American Empire and the foundational material for American thought. I read *The Emperor Jones* as a meditation on colonialism that functions via coercive force and an overdetermined symbolic code generated from U.S. imperial encounters in the Caribbean. By presenting the audience with a series of sites and signifiers of racist tools of domination and American primitive accumulation (the slave block, the chain gang, the overseer guard), O'Neill makes space in the theatrical cauldron for further intervention by Black radical playwrights. He opens up a *discursive blood thing*—a space that refuses to sanitize its history as its condition of possibility. The use of abstraction renders visible the slave block, the grand spectacle of Western capital accumulation and its organizing social logic of white supremacy. O'Neill responds to an abstraction-based German expressionism with a historically grounded radical American model.

Eugene O'Neill's The Emperor Jones: *Haiti as Porter (Metaphor)*

The source material for *The Emperor Jones* comes from the armory of imagery generated by U.S. colonial encounters with Haiti as well as a biography of the Haitian leader, Christophe.[16] In a 1924 article for *New York World*, O'Neill proclaimed:

> The idea for *Emperor Jones* came from an old circus man I knew. I knew all the circus people. This man, who later was a sparring partner for Jess Willard, had been traveling with a tent show through the West Indies. He told me a story current in Hayti concerning the late President Sam. This was to the effect that Sam had said they'd never get him with a lead bullet; that he would get himself first with a silver one. My friend, by the way, gave me a coin with Sam's features on it, and I still keep it as a pocket piece. The notion about the silver bullet struck me, and I made a note of the story. About six months later I got the idea of the words, but I couldn't see how it could be done on the stage, and I passed it up again. A year elapsed. One day I was reading of the religious feats in the Congo and the uses to which the drum is put there; how it starts at a normal pulse-beat and is slowly intensified until the heart-beat of every one present corresponds to the frenzied beat of the drum. There was an idea and an experiment. How could this sort of thing work on an audience in a theatre?
>
> The effect of the tropical forest on the human imagination was honestly come by. IT was the result of my own experience while prospecting for gold in Spanish Honduras. In the first presentation of *The Emperor* with Gilpin in the role, the drum was not handled as skillfully as it might have

been, and I think the effect I hoped to get was lost. But in the revival with Paul Robeson playing the Emperor it really worked in accordance with my original scheme.

The circus represents a traveling performance that destabilizes the already shaky divide between high and low culture (the circus carnival as Bakhtinian carnivalesque) whereas "frenzy" points to the expressionist preoccupation with psychology. O'Neill's imaginative fabric connects Congo, Haiti, and Honduras. The silver bullet signifies a fanciful anecdote of recent Haitian history. In O'Neill's imaginary, the dismay inspired by U.S. colonial intervention in Haiti gets alchemized as the story of a Black porter's tenuous imperial reign on a Caribbean island.

The etymological *baggage* of porter speaks volumes. From John Berger's *And Our Faces, My Heart, Brief as Photos*: "The Greek word for 'porter' is metaphor"![17] The comparative work of metaphor in Berger's oeuvre is aptly theorized by Nikos Papastergiadis:

> The attention to the metaphoricity of all meaning also involves a shuttling moment in relation to place and time. Berger is quick to see that embedded within the etymology of metaphor is the "theory" which links the process of naming through differentiation and the dynamics of movement in creativity. "The Greek word for 'porter' is metaphor. And this is a reminder of how deeply the act of *transporting*, of dispatch and delivery, is intrinsic to the imagination." If the etymology of metaphor suggests the act of transporting, then we must also question the assumption in everyday and philosophical discourse that makes the link between metaphor and truth conditional on its transparency. When metaphor serves as the invisible "porter," that is, when metaphor doubles-up as the messenger and the message, then it is recognized not just as the image which serves as a proxy to reality, but as a linguistic fact that is constitutive of reality.... Metaphor is like a structure made *in* motion. Metaphor is not the moment of resolution, it does not declare, define, equate, or arrive once and for all, but rather the truth of metaphor is in its alliance with disparates, a sign which confirms a destination by suggesting a further direction. The truth of metaphor is not in what it contains but in the possibilities it suggests. It includes opposites not to rebound perpetually within them, but to scaffold up and beyond them.[18]

Haiti as comparison functions in this study simultaneously as messenger and message: a comparative gesture toward revolutionary pasts that garners insight into such pasts and constructs theoretical scaffolding to build revolutionary futures. All the authors in this study are always simultaneously talking about Haiti to talk about their present somewhere-else locale with the sole exception of O'Neill, who attempts to talk about Haiti by talking about some unnamed, unspecified, somewhere-else Caribbean island. Like Deleuze's "lines of flights" and Bergerian metaphoricity, the works examined here are provisional, gestural, and open-ended by way of their constant comparative temporal flux. As performances, they function in motion somewhat differently than metaphor in general. Haitian revolutionary dramas in their function as drama—their tendencies to be rehearsed, staged, revised—activate a past historical marker in the present moment of performance. They triangulate past experiential knowledge, present actualization, and future desire as its generic lot as performance.

How do we think the combination of high and low cultural references, colonial mythology of recent Haitian executives, and the author's own autobiographical streak (prospecting for gold in Honduras) as something other than just a quirky hodgepodge of artistic influence culled from the historical, experiential, textual, fanciful, and the personal realm? The etymological link between experience and experiment helps to clarify.

Etymological Resonances: Experience/Experiment

Raymond Williams thinks experience with experiment: "The old association between **experience** and *experiment* can be seen, in some for the most important modern uses, merely obsolete.... This can be summarized as (i) knowledge gained from past events, whether by conscious observation or by consideration or reflection; and (ii) a particular kind of consciousness, which can in some contexts be distinguished from 'reason' or 'knowledge.'"[19] To ground one's theatrical experimentation in the realm of the experiential—it is the hallmark of O'Neill's radicalism. His anti-mimetic experimentation establishes a productive framework to think about aesthetic representations of genocidal rupture that challenge realist modalities. Nathan Huggins captures the troubling propensity of O'Neill to slide in a racialist representational logic coupled with his more admirable goal of "breaking with the old habits of keyhole peeping realism":

Eugene O'Neill attempted something different. His early plays should not be considered part of the popular drama of the time. They were more special, *avant garde*. O'Neill's interest was something other than realism. August Strindberg's naturalism was the great influence on him, "super-naturalism" as the American chose to call it. His effort was to look beneath the surface realisms to the quick of human experience. "Yet it is only by means of some form of 'supernaturalism,'" O'Neill wrote, "that we may express in the theatre what we comprehend intuitively of that self-defeat-ing self-obsession which is the discount we moderns have to pay for the loan of life." Realism (or naturalism, as that term had come to be used in the theater) was inadequate. "It represents our fathers' daring inspiration toward self-recognition by holding the family Kodak up to ill-nature. But to us their old audacity is blague; we have taken too many snap-shots of each other in every graceless position; we have endured too much from the banality of surfaces." O'Neill proclaimed himself, and the new theater, to be breaking with the old habits of keyhole peeping realism, "squinting always at heavy, uninspired bodies—the fat facts—with nota nude spirit among them; we have been sick with appearances. . . . " Strindberg showed how to peep away the facile realities and to expose the quivering spirit-flesh which was living essence. In O'Neill's hands this "super-naturalism" some-times appeared to be primitivism.[20]

O'Neill's vision of tragedy neglects the subtle negotiation of people asserting freedom within necessity (captured by Marx in his *Eighteenth Brumaire* and echoed in James's *The Black Jacobins*) in favor of an exac-erbated individualistic focus. His is one of the atomized individual fight-ing up against systemic forces conceptualized so abstractly as to often render these individuals invisible. Yet that very same abstraction lends radical buoyancy to his plays. O'Neill's work is often treated as a general allegory of human ambition. It both encourages and undermines such a critical exorcism of its racialist overtones and historical particularity. O'Neill's super-naturalism gestures toward the flimsiness of structures and ideations whose base is American colonial power. In a 1924 conver-sation with Louis Kantor on his representation of African Americans in his play *All God's Chillun Got Wings*, O'Neill rallies against naturalism. When asked by Kantor why the naturalism of his play *Anna Christie* fails to inspire him anymore, O'Neill responded: "Because you can say practi-cally nothing at all of our lives since 1914 through that form. The natu-ralistic play is really less natural than a romantic or expressionistic play. That is, shoving a lot of human beings on stage and letting them say the identical things in a theatre they would say in a drawing room or a saloon does not necessarily make for naturalness."[21] Experience and Experiment are implicitly coupled again in this formulation—O'Neill's expressionist innovation is attempting to say something "of our lives." O'Neill takes great pains to abstract the significance of his plays, and outside of their particular racialist contexts. O'Neill's undermining of naturalism simultaneously underscores specific legacies of historical expression as much as it—in his own self-avowed presentation—is really about so-called humanity abstracted from a specific historical context. Despite such complications, O'Neill thinks American colonial power's undermining of the long Haitian Revolution by way of staging an eight-scene unfolding revolution.

The Latent Textual Prophetic in The Emperor Jones

By outlining the eight-scene breakdown of *The Emperor Jones* I pay special attention to the use of the drum as well as the proportion in the text between stage direction and dialogue and the increasing incursions of phantasms in the play. Much of the critical work of the play is performed by such structuring motifs. Stage directions dominate dialogue as the drama unfolds.

Scene one occurs "In the palaces of the Emperor Jones. Afternoon."[22] Dialogue outweighs stage direction in this initial offering. The natives of Brutus Jones's court have all run to the hills in anticipatory revolt. Jones's associate, Smithers, first interprets the drums before we hear them in the play: "Well, I bloody well wat's in the air—when they runs orf to the 'ills. The tom-tom'll be thumping out there bloomin' soon."[23] We learn the backstory of Brutus Jones's class ascendancy from "stowaway to Emperor"[24] and the origin of the charmed silver bullet. The tom-tom commences at a pulse of seventy-two beats per minute at a gradual, accelerating rate till the end of the play. In Scene two—"The Edge of the Great Forest. Dusk"—stage directions take precedence over dialogue. Brutus Jones is fleeing from what he assumes is the imminent revolt of his subjects and fends off hunger and fatigue during his first line of flight through the woods. He lifts up a series of white stones, none of which houses the food he had stored prior in anticipation of escape. This marks the first appearance of the "little formless fears" that taunt Jones—described as "black, shapeless, only their glittering little eyes can be seen. If they have any describable form at all it is that of a grubworm about the size of a creeping child."[25] By Scene three—"In the Forest. Night"—stage direction outnumbers dialogue. The scene notes a loud escalation of the tom-toms cut by an unidentifiable clicking noise. Panic sets in when Jones sees an apparition of Jeff, a man he stabbed to death during a craps game–related altercation. Scene three enacts the tension between the organizing logic of expressionist abstraction and historicist specificity. Scene four maintains the same setting and proportion as the prior. Jones becomes frantic at the continual sightings of "ha'nts." He perceives the phantom trace of a chain gang, in which he crushes with shovel the head of an abusive white guard who whips him. The interval and volume of the drums increase. Scene five's logic again has stage directions outweighing dialogue, in which a weathered tree stump resembles an auction block. The crowd of memory takes its toll—he laments killing his friend Jeff and a prison guard and views an apparition of a slave auction represented solely via stage direction—the auctioneer's expressionist "silent spiel."[26] Jones mounts the slave block, "all this in silence save for the ominous throb of the tom-tom." Scene six enacts a similar proportion. With his subjects in pursuit, Jones laments the fact that he has only one remaining bullet. He is incorporated into an apparition of a group of Black men performing a rowing motion that resembles the bottom of a slave ship. Escalation of volume and pace of the drums mark the conclusion of this scene. The seventh scene represents the most dramatic proportional tipping of the balance in favor of stage directions over dialogue: Jones finds himself part of an ensemble of chained, enslaved New World Africans. The "Congo Witch Doctor" performs a pantomime, a hypnotic dance to a rhythm of beating drums. Jones offers himself as ritual sacrifice 1 and wastes his final silver bullet shooting a crocodile-god apparition. In Scene eight dialogue is reintroduced, Brutus Jones is captured and killed, and the drumming has ceased.

The war between Expressionist abstractionism and historical specificity is written into the framework and structure of the eight scenes. Expressionist abstraction is tempered by the specificity of staging. Performance always entails improvisational possibilities, yet so much of the conceptual innovation of this play relies on stage directions, arguably the main force in a play tempering improvisational drive. Each scene and temporal progression of Jones's flight moves from concrete description to dream-mode, in which the tom-tom drums provide an Expressionist tonal/atonal continuity. In Scene two, Jones confronts his "formless fears," highlighting the fact that the primary battle takes place in the theater of Jones's psyche. The apparitions in Scenes two, three, and four are Jones's life memories. The white stones serve a metonymic function for the macrological organizational fabric of imperialism heralding the "formless fears." Scene five connects Jones to the historical experiences and phenomenology of objects constituting the transatlantic slave trade: especially the auction block, the slave ship. Dialogue and semirealist modes of representation are steadily replaced in the play with the language of marionettes and automatons. Mechanical descriptions—"something stiff, rigid, unreal, marionettish about their movements"[27]—work as multivalent signposts. They emphasize the cold, exchange-value logic of the trade in African people. They stage a foundational American opposition between the Black and the human. This is most apparent in the representation of the slave auction followed by the simulation of the slave ship:

(He sighs dejectedly and remains with bowed shoulders, staring down at the shoes in his hands as if reluctant to throw them away. While his attention is thus occupied, a crowd of figures silently enter the clearing from all sides. All are dressed in Southern costumes of the period of the fifties of the last century. They are middle-aged men who are evidently well-to-do planters. There is one spruce, authoritative individual—the auctioneer. There is a crowd of curious spectators, chiefly young belles and dandies who have come to the slave market for diversion. All exchange courtly greetings in a dumb show and chat silently together. There is something stiff, rigid, unreal, marionettish about their movements. They group themselves about the stump. Finally a batch of slaves is led in from the left by an attendant—three men of different ages, two women, one with a baby in her arms nursing. They are placed to the left of the stump, besides Jones.

(The white planters look them over appraisingly as if they were cattle, and exchange judgments on each. The dandies point with their fingers and make witty remarks. The belles twitter bewitchingly. All this in silence save for the ominous throb of the tom-tom. The auctioneer holds up his hand, taking his place on the stump. The group strains forward attentively. He touches Jones on the shoulder peremptorily, motioning, for him to stand on the stump—the auction block.

(Jones looks up, sees the figures on all sides, looks widely for some opening to escape, sees none, screams and leaps madly to the top of the stump to get as far away from them as possible. He stands there, cowering, paralyzed with horror. The auctioneer begins his silent spiel. He points to Jones, appeals to

the planters to see for themselves. Here is a good field hand, sound in wind and limb as they can see. Very strong still in spite of his being middle aged. Look at that back. Look at those shoulders. Look at the muscles in his arms and his sturdy legs. Capable of any amount of hard labor. Moreover, of a good disposition, intelligent and tractable. Will any gentleman start the bidding? The planters raise their fingers, making their bids. They are apparently all eager to possess Jones. The bidding is lively, the crowd interested. While this has been going on, Jones has been seized by the courage of desperation. He dares to look down and around him. Over his face abject terror gives way to mystification, to gradual realization.[28]

(He is well forward now where his figure can be dimly made out. His pants have been so torn away that what is left of them is not better than a breech cloth. He flings himself full length, face downward on the ground, panting with exhaustion. Gradually, it seems to grow lighter in the enclosed space and two rows of seated figures can be seen behind Jones. They are sitting in crumpled, despairing attitudes, hunched, facing one another with their back touching the forest walls as if they were shackled to them. All are Negroes, naked save for loin cloths. At first they are silent and motionless. Then they begin to sway slowly forward toward each other and back again in unison, as if they were laxly letting themselves follow the long roll of a ship at sea. At the same time, a low, melancholy murmur rises among them, increasingly gradually by rhythmic degrees which seem to be directed and controlled by the throb of the tom-tom in the distance, to a long, tremulous wail of despair that reaches a certain pitch, unbearably acute, then falls by slow gradations of tone into silence and is taken up again.[29]

Both scenes are framed as silent with the exception of the undercutting drum pulse. Drums not only signify a sort of psychological rhythm and mark the temporal regressive movement of the action; they also are the stand-in for the island revolution. The drums serve as communicative tools of revolt. O'Neill connects them with two central scenes of American cultural memory of forced coercion of African labor. This is the radical imperative in the text. Genocidal evaluative judgments about the financial worth of African people are scripted in the silent stage direction. The stage directions are the space of historicity, carnality, and materiality in O'Neill's drama. They are the structuring agent against forgetting. This foregrounding of a history constantly under erasure marks the prophetic strain in this drama. Brutus Jones is the only person given a speaking role at the auction. Drum structure, the "slow gradations of tone into silence," and returning again in the slave ship scene constitute a radical American rendition of the expressionist *le cri*. Munch's individualist scream is percussive and collective. Like Fanon, there is no need to shout the scream—observers are always already implicated in a structuring architecture of American racial slavery. The textual in O'Neill's play renders visible what is usually hidden. The agoraphobic psychological state is supplemented in O'Neill by bringing history back on the agenda. In the end, collaboration with colonial powers fails to deliver its promised contingency plan. The French gunboat supposed to transport Jones and his stolen loot to Martinique never arrives.

Filming Collaboration: A Leap into the Oceanic

In the 1933 film version of *The Emperor Jones*, Paul Robeson dives into the ocean water. The wide-angle shot captures the immensity of his shoulders and back span as he splits the sea, stumbling upon an unnamed Caribbean island. For a brief second, Robeson's dive of flight recalls and subverts binding legacies of oceanic transport of enslaved Africans. From this initial leap-dive-swim, Robeson the performer and Brutus Jones the dramatic persona (taking a cue from Brecht separating the two), casts off not just the prison barge but also the stifling apparatus of the Hollywood film. The ocean dive reclaims the best of O'Neill's text's super-natural logic. It is a delinking from the film's retrograde, realist undermining of the play's radicalism. A fleeting, in motion, cleansing that reclaims *The Emperor Jones* as staged drama from the carceral representation that is *The Emperor Jones* as cinema.

By opening up a discursive space that openly acknowledges and renders visible (however hazy) the material signposts of American trade in Black bodies, O'Neill's super-naturalist aesthetic brings history back online. O'Neill's expressionist aesthetic undermines a conservative realist grammar and renders visible an American legacy of coercion, enslavement, and failed reparation by precisely disavowing any claim to be able to achieve such a representation in a realist fashion. Brutus never seems to confront his constructed past head-on outside a feverish dream state. Rejecting a fraught "keyhole peeping realism," the work presents an example of radical individualism in the figure of Brutus Jones, cut off from a chorus. *The Emperor Jones* pushes up against the limits of its own racialist tropes as Modernist avant-garde American theater event in order to meet the challenge of foregrounding the brutality of American slavery, without the hubris of trying to tell it like it was. O'Neill's use of abstraction mutes the possibility of a representation of revolutionary agency yet highlights the frailty of oppressive ideology.

In speaking on the future of Black drama in Alain Locke's *The New Negro*, Eugene O'Neill affirms: "I believe as strongly as you do that the gifts the Negro can—and will—bring to our native drama are invaluable ones. The possibilities are limitless and to a dramatist open up new and intriguing opportunities."[30] In order to dwell on this vocabulary of possibility, I want to take a quick detour through Walter Benjamin's "Theses on the Philosophy of History" (completed in 1940 and first published in *Neue Rundschau* in 1950). By way of propositional logic and incantation prose style, Benjamin suggests how to employ the past in the service of achieving revolutionary amelioration in the present. The "Theses" reject both Stalin's myopic "productivist" ideology (producing rapid industrialization) and the liberalism of Social Democracy (producing piecemeal reform). *The Emperor Jones* is an interesting test case to think the temporal dynamics of Benjamin's "Theses":

> The true picture of the past flits by. The past can be seized only as an image which flashes up at the instant when it can be recognized and is never seen again . . . for every image of the past that is not recognized by the present as one of its own concerns threatens to disappear irretrievably. . . .
>
> To articulate the past historically does not mean to recognize it "the way it really was" (Ranke). It means to seize hold of a memory as it flashes up at a moment of danger.[31]

Jones's fragmentary, figurative world, in which visions of American slavery "[flit] by," provides a more productive model for representing the rupture of slavery and forced relocation, more so than a realist modality reliant upon the politics of identification. The collective chorus in O'Neill's work exists but it is not granted fullness in its representational complexity as a repository for critical thought. The individual in O'Neill's work is framed through the author's tendencies toward highly politicized hyperindividualism; yet that very hyperindividualism is undercut by both expressionist and racialist reliance on set tropes. Famously, Benjamin's "Theses" point to the fact that "the tradition of the oppressed teaches us that the 'state of emergency' in which we live is not the exception but the rule."[32] A decree pronounced by the sovereign to rationalize suspension of normative juridical checks and balances, indefinitely in a moment of so-called crisis. Benjamin's formulation has been rehashed in the critical literature to the point of exhaustion. I still want to suggest that perhaps Benjamin's insight helps explain why the critical reception of O'Neill's play is so vexed. The sovereign in this work (Brutus Jones) is both oppressor and oppressed. He declares the state of emergency yet is part of a tradition in which the exception is the rule. The play's continued appeal and staging relate to this conundrum as well as the text's willingness to simultaneously foreground and mystify its radical historicity. Surely O'Neill thinks about Haiti. The legacy of the long Haitian Revolution as he writes is being undermined in actuality by the U.S. Marines. The trajectory of the work as a whole consists of an African American fugitive line of flight followed by an African American encroachment on a sovereign Caribbean nation. O'Neill's dramatic text radically foregrounds the legacy of enslaved African labor as fundamental primitive accumulation and serves up a not-so-latent critique of American colonial ventures in Haiti; yet an aesthetic so apt in pointing out the flimsiness of colonial discourse—expressionist drama—cannot complete its revolutionary task. O'Neill's aesthetic is truly an unfinished revolution. Its progressive shaking up of the representational logic of American slavery and empire is undermined by its regressive reliance on racialist tropes. Perhaps completing such a task is too much to ask for dramatic performance. Regardless, O'Neill's *Emperor Jones* begins to pose all the right questions.

Dessalines Jumps out a Window: Eisenstein's Pedagogy of Mise-en-Scène and Mise-en-Shot

> For us Dessalines is a positive hero. Our sympathies are on his side. Therefore Dessalines determines the situation, the *mise-en-scène*, the break-up into shots. But if this episode has been produced, say, in America, produced by either conscious or unconscious—it makes no difference—servants of imperialism, the heroism we emphasize in Dessalines and for which we mobilize all expressive means would have been removed not only from the scenario treatment itself, but also from the *mise-en-scène* and shots.
>
> Sergei Eisenstein

> The question of montage is impossible without Eisenstein, whether they know it or not.
>
> Amiri Baraka

> Quiet as it's kept, Dessalines is the true Haitian hero of the Black liberation movement.
>
> Dhoruba Bin Wahad

Vladimir Nizhny's *Lessons with Eisenstein*, an account of Eisenstein's mid-1930s instructional seminars, asks the question: What is prospered by protracted attention to individual-leader/mass base dynamics in dramatic repetitions of the Haitian Revolution by way of the painstaking rehearsal of one actor's movement of flight?[33] Eisenstein's task is to assist would-be directors in the technical theoretical task of distinguishing *mise-en-scènes* (both in the theater and its culminating, so-called higher progression—cinema) from their component *mise-en-shots*.[34] In such a lesson part and whole get constantly unpacked and reassembled. This practical acumen is cultivated via a praxis-based problem-solving dialectic that constantly calibrates concerns of method with attention to the particularity of the filmed scenario. For Eisenstein, a free-floating, dogmatic, generalized method divorced from particularity is anathema. Here are the semester-long problems posed and solved collectively by the class:

1. A directorial treatment of the scene from Balzac's novel *Le Père Goriot* of Vautrin's arrest.

2. How to pre-stage then shoot a scene from John W. Vandercook's 1928 novel *Black Majesty, the Life of Christophe, King of Haiti,* in which Dessalines's invitation to dine with a French priest and some officers is a pretext to ambush him.

3. Parsing Dessalines's flight from danger (via a window) into multiple shots.

4. A minimalist challenge is to shoot the episode from Dostoyevsky's *Crime and Punishment* where Raskolnikov murders Alyona Ivanovna in a single shot.

Eisenstein shares with the group his rationale for thinking carefully about Dessalines's flight through a window: "S. M. explains that his choice of such an episode as 'Dessalines' has been dictated by the fact that its situation is so plain and straightforward, it is so much embodied in external action, that it will enable easy familiarization with those elements of production technique which have, in full measure, likewise to be applied in work on psychologically more profound and complex tasks."[35] "Easy familiarization" is a bit misleading here. The class spent the whole semester staging Dessalines's line of flight, staged on a small theater platform prior to filming. Every consideration recorded in *Lessons* measures choices of focus, angle, set arrangement, and tempo. Eisenstein assumes Dessalines's dignity against the naysayers and the smallest detail is mined for its theoretical consequences. Dessalines's focus of glance, the congregation of soldiers, the angle, in which sabers are cinematically captured all function as sites for a highly politicized reflection. This breaking down into parts, the centrality of preparation, signifies a cinematographic pedagogy that is analogous to the import of staged repetition central to my study.

Under Eisenstein's direction, the fact that Dessalines vowed to never look a French officer in the eye presents a technical and political problem that merits collective reckoning. He pushes his students to make their spoken contributions in class aspire to the Brechtian social *gestus,* what Elin Diamond defines as "the moment in performance when a play's implied social attitude becomes visible to the spectator."[36] When discussing the entry of a "serving-woman" who alerts Dessalines of imminent danger, he critiques the precision of a student's comment that "She upsets the whole plan." To that Eisenstein replies: "Wouldn't it be better to say that she arms Dessalines against his enemies?"[37] Every preparation, every rehearsal, every spoken utterance is grist for political reflection.

Eisenstein in the classroom, as master-director and film auteur, is *primus inter pares*—first among equals. This isn't just egalitarian pretense; rather, it is crucial to his philosophy of how film creation should proceed collectively toward revolutionary designs. This philosophy (a blueprint for work) often placed him at loggerheads with the Communist Party apparatchik's fetish for method: "The Talmudists of method—the academic high Marxists."[38] Eisenstein criticizes Plekhanov on this account for underestimating particularity, for neglecting attention to concrete objects in favor of "method in general": "We must build simultaneously a working process and a method. And we shall proceed not in the Plekhanov manner, for preconceived positions of 'method in general' to the concrete particular case, but through given concrete work on particular materials we expect to arrive at a method of cinematographic creation for the director."[39] Against "the methodists" with their "recipes" Eisenstein is interested in studying and conveying as many details as possible that make up phenomena. One should encounter the concreteness and specificity of the object of analysis then try it out. This is an aesthetic corollary to the Napoleonic military credo—"Engage Then Look"—which I will discuss later in terms of C.L.R. James.

From the start, Nizhny's account fashions Eisenstein's VGIK class collectively. Sergei Mikhailovich's plus the students in the class are characterized as a "twenty-headed director"[40] (Eisenstein's term). The students and professor constitute one thinking, working entity. Classroom organization mirrors the key philosophical animus that drives his understanding of film and its component parts. Like theatrical staging of revolution, the proportion of bodies is key: "As you see, when the content of the group's action is one, then the work of the group or mass is also one; but when the group is not united, but only generalized, all within the group will act in the various ways, though none the less preserving the outlines of a unity of action."[41] Nizhny's text is bookended by two pedagogical anecdotes:

At this first talk Sergei Mikhailovich said: "I can't teach you anything, but, look here, you can learn." It was a remark extraordinarily effective in making us sit up, and putting him on his mettle as a professor, too.

The point was this, that Sergei Mikhailovich was not so much directly, in the usual sense of the word, an instructor; what he did was to make himself available and open to those who studied with him, depending on their abilities, energies and tremendous efforts off their own bat, each could get from him whatever corresponded to his own ability.[42]

And:

> Late at night.
>
> I had come to see S. M. about matters connected with the course. We had agreed about everything, I am getting ready to go.
>
> "And how did you like 'Dessalines'?" S. M. suddenly asks me.
>
> "It didn't turn out too badly, after all . . . ?"
>
> I tell him my impressions and say that I marveled most of all at the ease with which he had improvised *mise-en-scène*, editing-units and shots.
>
> S. M. gives a ringing laugh, reaches down from a shelf a portfolio, hands it to me and asks me to say and have a glance at "some material that might interest you." He then leaves me alone and goes out, "so as not to disturb you," to visit his neighbor, Maxim Strauch.
>
> I open the portfolio.
>
> Before me are hundreds of sheets of paper and diagrams and drawings. On every sheet, notes. The majority, concerning Dessalines. On the top pages Dessalines escapes from encirclement by clinging to a huge mechanical fan that carries him right across the table as far as the window-ledge. A complete detailed plan of the fan is there, with its construction. But on almost the last page, in the margin is scrawled: "Too far fetched . . . !"
>
> Then follow fresh solutions.
>
> On the last pages are a *mise-en-scène* and shots that in many respects coincide with those arrived at in the lessons. Much evidence shows they are the fruits of long reflection.
>
> "Well, what about . . . ?" Asks S. M., coming back into the room.
>
> I only shrug my shoulders.
>
> He comes up to me and says:
>
> "What you took for improvisation cost me many sleepless nights. Do you think I would have let myself lecture the students without adequate preparation . . . ?"
>
> After a brief pause, he continues:
>
> "The aspect most important for me to put over is not the solution, but the method, the path, by which the director has to travel to reach his solution. Note that, reflect upon it, and talk to students about it, too in lesson time."[43]

In one fell swoop, Eisenstein's response deflates any pretense that his genius is automatic. He demystifies an understanding of improvisation as instantaneous runoff, a line of flight occurring somehow independent of strenuous preparation and reflection. "Many sleepless nights" is the con-dition of possibility for a well-executed improvisation. Moreover, it is the cost for such improvisational flex. This is imperative for students of Afri-can diasporic cultural production, in which improvisation as a conceptual framework occupies such great space (and rightfully so). Preparation and study serve as a template, a springboard that not only makes improvisa-tion possible, it is improvisation's steadfast requirement, its condition of possibility. The hundreds of annotated sheets of paper housed in the folio constitute credentials for leadership—an indispensable precondition for what Stokely Carmichael/Kwame Ture tirelessly emphasized as *Readi-ness*.[44] "I can't teach you anything, but, look here, you can learn" func-tions as declaration of leadership as vanishing mediator.[45] Vanishing, yet necessary.

Eisenstein's revolutionary pedagogy prioritizes rehearsal. Let us now turn to a discussion of Orson Welles's "The Islands." Welles, in the dra-matic progression/ordering of his radio drama, anticipates Aimé Césaire's *Discourse on Colonialism*, a work that implies that twentieth-century Nazism was a repetition of Western colonial enterprises.[46] The European super-exploitation of Africa, Asia, and the Caribbean was the rehearsal space for the twentieth-century Nazi project of genocide.

Orson Welles's "The Islands," Nazi Repetition, and the Subordination of National Liberation Struggles to United Front Politics

> They were good shows, I thought. All inter-American affairs. I did the A-B-Cs of the Caribbean. And they were very amusing. I didn't really do much of it—the writers were awfully good. And it was a good form. A-B-C: "A" is for "Antilles," "Antigua," and so on. We went through like that, and did little things and big things with music and stories each week. I'm queer for the Caribbean any-way—not as it exists, but as it was in my mind in the eighteenth and nineteenth centuries. The Caribbean is just great stuff. All of it. The whole idea of all these empires fighting over tiny little islands, and black independence and Spanish pride and the War of Jenkins's Ear and those great earthquakes.
>
> Orson Welles

On 29 November 1942, American radio broadcasted a bold, hybrid pro-gram produced and narrated by virtuoso Orson Welles. "The Islands"[47] in twenty-eight minutes chronicles the role of Toussaint L'Ouverture and Henri Christophe in the Haitian Revolution. The third installment in Welles's *Hello Americans* radio series, it is a montage of dramatic renditions, musical arrangement, interviews, and reportage of Welles's recent journeys in the Caribbean and South America. The genre-defiant programming is framed as the "A-B-Cs" of the Caribbean. Different countries were featured weekly, the first of which focused on Brazil and the origins of Samba. "The Islands" offers a rich aesthetic and philosophical synthesis combining the following:

1. *The Emperor Jones*'s colonial imaginary. Haiti is referred to as "the haunted island" or "Voodoo place" and houses witchdoctors and people willing to pop off Haitian Emperor-killing "silver bullets." Christophe laments that his time is up yet is consoled by the fact that his "ghost still walks" and his "secrets sleep with the bones."
2. Dramatic dialogue of testimonials from men and women who lost relatives and loved ones while building Christophe's massive architectural project, the Citadel.
3. The embedding of radical political critique (anti-fascist, anti-imperialist, anti-authoritarian, and internationalist) within a representation defaulting to stereotype.
4. Eisenstein's pedagogic compulsion that anticipates Fredric Jameson's suggestion to "Always Historicize."[48]

Welles's radio-play posits a singular field to think interrelating world-historical phenomena. Put another way, it refuses to regulate what happens in nineteenth-century Haiti to the restricted cosmos of Island haunts. Haiti's revolutionary historical knowledge speaks to Welles's crisis-laden historical present. It broadcasts the following warning against erecting historiographic Bantustans: "In all of the Americas the kings of Europe were the common enemy. . . . In France Napoleon rose with the revolution then betrayed it. Crowning himself emperor. In Haiti, Christophe rose with the revolution and Christophe crowned himself emperor." Taking its cues from *The Black Jacobins*, the radio program consistently triangulates the French Revolution and the Haitian Revolution alongside contemporary issues. It is a prime example of what Eisenstein theorized as *montage-as-conflict* versus *montage-as-linkage*. The framing of different mediums in the production, the quick cut-jumps from dramatic dialogue to music to political commentary, the span reaching from Revolutionary

Haiti to Revolutionary France all advance via conflict. Juxtapositions of phenomena propel the dramatic action forward and in such alter its constituent parts.

"The Islands" begins with Welles's signature greeting: "Hello Americans"—his addressee is hemispheric not nationalistic. His historical exposition initially freezes Haiti in a flurry of caricature, the *Africanisms* of the non-reflexive anthropologist's—Haunts, Voodoo, and the like—only to instantly undermine this logic in a single sentence. "This too, is Haiti" inaugurates a political discussion on the life-and-death struggle between Lords and Bondsmen; the participation of eight hundred Haitians during the American Revolution and America's historical amnesia as it relates to this record; France's selective application of Liberté in its policy on racial slavery; a discussion of Haitian assistance to Bolívar in his campaign to liberate South America; and a dramatization of Napoleon's betrayal of Toussaint.

In the last few minutes of the program something astonishing happens. This final move is anticipated eight minutes earlier when Welles as navigator announces a cut to the death place of Napoleon Bonaparte: "We take you now to the Island of St. Helena for a word or two from another dictator. You can't raise this particular spirit with tom-toms, steel drums, and kettledrums. Another ritual in Berlin." This contemporary reference to Nazism is tacked on with great stealth. Welles's voice is almost muted in its soberness. "The Islands" concludes with a story. Welles inserts himself in the narration and relates an episode in which his car breaks down in Haiti, long enough to witness a roadside burial service. The participants are trying to prevent the deceased from turning into a zombie. In reply to his question "How are Zombies made," Welles's Haitian interlocutor explains that they are created for the sole purpose of working tirelessly in the cane fields. Welles further questions whether or not zombies retain a sense of historical memory and why they do not return to their former homes. This is preamble for the sole interview segment in the program:

> I talked to many people in the West Indies about zombies. Wherever I went I heard these tall tales: In the Bahamas, Jamaica . . . Witchdoctors, duppies . . . Ghosts of dead men walk in the night and moan at the moon . . . Black magic, charms, witchcraft . . .
>
> Here are deep matters not to be dismissed by crying blasphemy.
>
> But the last word I got about the Zombie situation came from a West Indian. A young Negro doctor. I'd like you to hear what he has to say on these matters:

Mr. Welles. Mumbo Jumbo is dying out. . . . Anyway, it's dying out here in the Americas. All forms of mumbo-jumbo. Not just Voodoo. . . . When Citizen Bonaparte became Emperor Napoleon that was the mumbo-jumbo of old Europe. Fascism is mumbo-jumbo. He then goes on to posit that the people living under Hitler are zombies. They are the living dead. [This reverses Agamben's later formulation of The Camp: The living dead are the Nazis and their collaborators, not their victims.] The way we look at it that is what this war is all about: To Free the Zombies from their spell to get rid of the Witch Doctors. . . . I like what you had Toussaint L'Ouverture say tonight. This goes for all South Americans: "You will buy and sell us no longer. The slave trade is over. We have come to a new century."

—Cut to Welles's narration—

That is the best possible way to end this program. Thank you. Good-night Americans.

In contemporary African diasporic usages of the Haitian Revolution, Haiti functions in and for itself and simultaneously as a metonymic site of inquiry for Black radical struggle worldwide. The shift of focus from an African liberation struggle to marshaling support for the United Front against Hitler's fascism should give pause to students of twentieth-century Black radicalism. It recalls a great rift between Pan-Africanist partisans and revolutionaries loyal to the Soviet Union—chronicled with great expertise by historian Minkah Makalani.[49] In support of what was framed as the greater good (the fight against the greater evil), party policy dictated that combatants and intellectuals affiliated with national liberation struggles against French, British, and American imperialism cease fighting their occupiers (labeled by the Soviet Union as "democratic imperialists") and unite to fight German, Italian, and Japanese fascism. This was a scandal for anticolonial militants, the least of reasons being that Germany did not hold colonies. In a letter to Dr. Alain Locke, encouraging him to help with C.L.R. James's play, George Padmore concisely captures the ironies of such a shift in Soviet policy:

Shortly after your departure from Paris for the U.S.S.R. I arrived in France and remained there for several weeks doing a book "Africa in World Politics" which I have submitted to a publisher. I just received a copy of the German edition of my book on Africa. They made a splendid job of it, and strange it might sound, it is doing well in Germany. It is all the more ironical when it is recalled that the Nazis expelled me from there after Hitler came to power. The Germans are making a drive for colonies and no doubt feel that a book indicting their opponents—the British imperialists, by a Black would help to prove that they are not the only villains. It is all a game of Real politics.[50]

Here is how C.L.R. James puts in a recollection of the disillusionment of his Trinidad-boyhood mate, Communist turned Pan-Africanist Padmore, with this shift in Soviet tactics. Such disillusionment by no means equals a denunciation by Padmore of Marxism or its anticapitalist animus:

> I used to see him. In those days I was a Trotskyist, but we remained good friends and never quarrelled [*sic*] about our differences. He was reasonable man in many respects. One day in 1935, I remember it well, there was a knock at the door of my flat in London. I opened it and there was George. I said, "George, is something wrong?" He said, "I have left those people, you know." I was startled. He supported Moscow, I was against them, and he had left them. So I said, "Well, come in, sit down." I said, "What is it?" He said, "They are changing their policy." And George told me that they had now told him they were going to make friends with democratic imperialists, Britain, France and the United States; and that future pro-Negro propaganda should be directed against Germany, Japan and Italy, and played quite softly in regard to the "democracies." Padmore said, "But that is impossible." He said, "Germany and Japan have no colonies in Africa, so how can I say that the Negros in Africa must be emancipated, but they have friends in the democratic imperialists of France and England?" They say, "Well that is the line." He said, "Well, that may be your line, but that is a mess," and packed up and left.[51]

Directional shift in "The Islands" performs a different labor. It is not about subordinating the interests of anticolonial struggle to the struggle against Nazism. Yes, attention veers from a Pan-African concern for the American hemisphere to the fight against Hitler's fascism; yet that very same shift signals Haiti as pedagogically useful. The temporal progression and proportion of attention on late eighteenth-, early nineteenth-century Haiti compared to what was then contemporary Germany (twenty-five minutes to three) suggests something else. In Welles's hands, Haiti is an antecedent, a font of philosophical and strategic wisdom for carving out a strategy in the fight back against German fascism. As the epigraph framing this chapter section indicates, Welles is "queer for the Caribbean anyway—not as it exists, but as it was in my mind in the eighteenth and nineteenth centuries." Welles positions his own desire as crucial here. His emphasis on the Caribbean "in [his] mind" foregrounds questions of mediation. Linear historical chronology, place and time, natural and supernatural are all queered in Welles's radio play. Long nineteenth-century Caribbean landscapes bleed into and cast insight on twentieth-century fascisms. It is not a question of positing African interests as secondary; rather, it is a reminder that African diasporic historical memory has vital lessons to impart. It concedes to African diasporic historical memory its rightful understanding as reservoir of rich, abstract thought.

Such juxtapositions prod the mindful to consider the Nazi Holocaust as a doubling. Not a return of the repressed—that would imply temporary (if only symptomatic) cessation. Rather Nazism is the repetition that the Western democracies confuse as the anomaly. It is a repetition that forgot its precedent. It distorts correct understanding of such precedent by fiat of mystification. We conclude with Aimé Césaire serving notice:

And then one fine day the bourgeoisie is awakened by a terrific boomerang effect: the gestapos are busy, the prisons fill up, the torturers standing around the racks invent, refine, discuss.

People are surprised, they become indignant. They say: "How strange! But never mind—it's Nazism, it will pass!" And they wait, and they hope; and they hide the truth from themselves, that it is barbarism, the supreme barbarism, the crowning barbarism that sums up all the daily barbarisms; that it is Nazism, yes, but that before they were its victims, they were its accomplices; that they tolerated the Nazism before it was inflicted on them, that they absolved it, shut their eyes to it, legitimized it, because, until then, it had been applied only to non-European peoples; that they have cultivated that Nazism, that they are responsible for it, and that before engulfing the whole edifice of Western, Christian civilization in its reddened waters, it oozes, seeps, and trickles from every crack.

Yes, it would be worthwhile to study clinically, in detail, the steps taken by Hitler and Hitlerism and to reveal to the distinguished, very humanistic, very Christian bourgeois of the twentieth century that without his being aware of it, he has a Hitler inside him, that Hitler *inhabits* him, that Hitler is his *demon*, that if he rails against him, he is being inconsistent and that, at bottom, what he cannot forgive Hitler for is not *the crime* in itself, *the crime against man*, it is not *the humiliation of man as such*, it is the crime against the white man, the humiliation of the white man, and the fact that he applied to Europe colonialist procedures which until then had been reserved exclusively for the Arabs of Algeria, the "coolies" of India and the "niggers" of Africa. . . . At the end of capitalism, which is eager to outlive its day, there is Hitler. At the end of formal humanism and philosophic renunciation, there is Hitler.[52]

Summation: *The Enduring Edmond Dantès*

So much of the critical philosophical literature on dramatic tragedy wrestles with the twin poles of freedom and necessity. Dramatic texts function as templates, structuring frameworks, interpretive groundings for practitioners to think through contemporary political dilemmas and strategize future Black radical transformative paths. Like its tragic namesake it frames a hairsplitting freedom and necessity in motion, a dialectical interplay that recognizes the very dichotomy is a false choice. Dramatic plays, principally concerned with positioning, prioritizing, and orchestrating masses onstage, as well as calibrating a weighted interdependence between individual and group, function in a modality that I am calling the Black Radical Tragic. They are blueprints, theaters of battle that prepare its participants for that other Pan-African, proletarian battle—the battle to come. This provisionally binding quality of the dramatic genre, because of and in spite of such a quality, offers a springboard to test an endless proliferation of improvisation. If and when that binding becomes burdensome, hazard a Robeson dialectical oceanic leap. In summation, I want to consider the impact of a hero who refuses to remain dead—the vengeance machine known as Edmond Dantès—from Alexander Dumas's 1844 novel *The Count of Monte Cristo*.

Eisenstein writes of the novel: "It is the work of a Negro, but toiling as hard as he would have under the whip of an overseer. Dumas was actually of Negro descent, and he was born in Haiti, as was Toussaint L'Ouverture, the hero of a film I want to make, *The Black Consul*. The nickname of Dumas's grandfather—General Thomas Alexandre—was the 'Black Devil.' And Dumas himself was called 'fat back' by his envious contemporaries and rivals."[53] Eugene O'Neill's father was trapped for over three decades in the role of leading man in over four thousand theatrical productions of *The Count of Monte Cristo*. More than four thousand frameups, more than four thousand incarcerations, more than four thousand flights from the Château d'if, the prison housed on an island in the Frioul Archipelago in the Mediterranean Sea, more than four thousand tosses aboard plummeting "into a canvas ocean." Something is gained by in this extreme repetition.

The sea leap in *The Emperor Jones* vindicates Alexander Dumas and reclaims an oceanic line of flight co-opted via canvas repetition. Hampered in by his commercial success as lead, James O'Neill repeats the lines of flight, the acute decline and transcendence of framed fugitivity, the enactments of what Deleuze and Guattari might have called a "vengeance machine."

From a 1931 article in the *New York Times Magazine*:

> Forty-three years ago James O'Neill, the father of Eugene, was one of the idols of the American stage. As the innocent Edmond Dantès who eventually escapes from prison, becomes the Count of Monte Cristo and wreaks vengeance on his enemies, he was thrilling the theatergoing public. While Niblo's Garden was still a theatre on lower Broadway, while long-haired, fur-coated actors congregated about the Union Square Theatre, the elder O'Neill was nightly ripping the sack in which he been thrown into a canvas ocean. . . .
>
> "I Can still see my father," said the playwright, "dripping with salt and sawdust, climbing on a stool behind the swinging profile of dashing waves. It was then the calcium lights in the gallery played on his long beard and tattered clothes, as with arms out-stretched he declared that the world was his.
>
> "This was a signal for the house to burst into a deafening applause that overwhelmed the noise of the storm manufactured backstage. It was an artificial age, an age ashamed of its own feelings, and the theatre reflected its thoughts. Virtue always triumphed and vice always got its deserts. It accepted nothing half-way; a man was either a hero or a villain, and a woman was either virtuous or vile."[54]

What is the theoretical armature gleamed from market dictates forcing one to compulsively repeat a character's tragic ascent followed by his swift, fiery vindication? What could it mean to enact in performance a perpetual cycle of imprisonment and escape, suffocation and transcendence?

From the standpoint of the main questions my book asks, the Haitian novelist Alexander Dumas's serial melodrama comprises the true Spada family treasure.[55] The novel's generic conventions as a nineteenth-century French (Caribbean) serialized, melodramatic/adventure novel, replete with abrupt plot reversals, swift making and unmaking of all forms of alliance—romantic, filial, military, and political—has a great deal to say to revolutionary political projects. Its contradictions confound. A Marseille sailor, first citizen, then fugitive, then Count, keeps slaves (but specified only as set pieces in order to play off the role of rich beyond all account in order to enact his vengeance). One such slave's name resonates with Dumas's own homeland; yet she is figured as a rote Orientalist stock character—a "Greek-Turkish princess-slave-girl" named Haydee.

Eisenstein's mention of *The Count of Monte Cristo* in his "treatment" for a film adaptation of Dreiser's *An American Tragedy* models the political temperance, the lens I want to encourage (a properly Black tragic lens). Despite Eisenstein's grounded, anti-imperialist sympathies with the Haitian Revolution and his devotion to the historical backstory informing Dumas's worldview, the seasoned red veteran refuses to romanticize Dantès. Eisenstein maintains his admiration but simultaneously demystifies the function of the novel: "The gold fever of money-making and self-enrichment of the Louis-Phillipe epoch is no less a determining factor for the gilded legend of the fabulous wealth of the former sailor who becomes an omnipotent count, no less determining than Dumas's childhood memories of Scheherazade and the treasures of Ali Baba. And the very fact that a sailor could become a count, meant that 'anyone' might."[56] He pierces the core of the "social ideal" that is Edmond Dantès. Eisenstein thinks seriously about contextualizing the ideological work of literary forms (and characters) in the context of their time period:

> In the general chase after gold and aristocratic titles, the sailor, Dantès who became the mythically rich Comte de Monte Cristo, served as a splendid "social ideal" for the bourgeoisie who were feverishly enriching themselves. It is not without reason that to this image is ascribed the features of an idealized self-portrait. For Dumas himself, along with the others, bathed in the turbid sea of suspicious gold accumulated through the dubious speculations of the reign of *le roi bourgeois*.[57]

The Count of Monte Cristo offers up a normalization of political violence. Its *haltung* is one of materialist political resolve attempting to breathe amid melodramatic flourish. It does not fault Dantès for his recourse to vengeful political violence; it only laments that such recourse should occupy obsessively so much of his earthly vocation.

The novel parallels the sympathetic yet ambivalent relationship that the Dumas family had with Napoleon Bonaparte. Dumas's Haitian grandfather, Thomas Alexandre Dumas, joined the French army in 1786, served in an all-Black unit known as La Légion Américaine, and became a general in less than two years, fighting in the Revolt in the Vendé and in Bonaparte's Italian and Egyptian campaigns. He lost favor when he refused to participate in Napoleon's Syrian campaign and perished in 1806, a year after the ratification of the first Haitian Constitution.[58] The 1906 statue of General Dumas erected in Paris to commemorate the one-hundred-year anniversary of his death was removed by the Nazis prior to Hitler's visit to Paris. It has yet to be restored. Such literary generic, historical, and biographical factors converge as a sort of dialectical windfall making the ghost of Edmond Dantès the perfect patron-specter haunting work framed within a Black Radical Tragic vein. A tradition that is interested in vindication against white domination and colonial expropriation but not lacking in the tragic temperance necessary to see that task through with studied praxis.

"Haitians are the écarté of French stock-jobbing," Albert instructs Dantès. Écarté—the two-player French card game whose namesake means *discard*. The buying and selling of stocks in order to generate a profit changes quickly with the rapidity of romantic couplings becoming done and undone and the time it takes a promising working class sea captain to be stripped of all dignity and imprisoned in a serialized melodrama. This diminutive formulation—referring to coerced Haitian labor as a card game—falls short of acknowledging the deadly convergence of use- and exchange-value in the form of Haitian bodies and the labor extracted from such bodies for France's (if not all of Europe's) capital accumulation. The formulation does not do justice to the way such a rupture, in its foundational genocidal logic, overdetermines every aspect of where we live. The gaming metaphor signals the casino character of capital speculation and financial markets; yet the contributions Haitians made (and continue to make) are more tangible, entries in a ledger of sanguine sacrifice more acute. In this dialogue, Haitians are the *game* of choice for a craven European mercantilism. Yet Albert has to fess up to Haiti as the constant site of return for metropolitan moneyed interests. Such return marks a line of continuity linking Napoleon's imprisonment of Toussaint to Bush's abduction of President Aristide.[59] It is up to the African diasporic activist-artists examined in this study to chart another course of return to Haiti, to stake claim to another repeating regimen of use.

2

Bringing in the Chorus

The Haitian Revolution Plays of C.L.R. James and Edouard Glissant

Wife of mine, I must go into the hills for the freedom of all.

Monsieur Toussaint

Jacques Lacan suggests that there is open-endedness in Aristotle's *Poetics'* incompleteness—an example of the unfinished as generative: "I assume you know that what we have of the *Poetics* is only a part, roughly half, in fact. And in the half that we have there is only the passage referred to which discusses catharsis. We know that there was more because at the beginning of Book VIII in the numbering of Didot's classic edition of the *Politics*, Aristotle speaks of "that catharsis which I discussed elsewhere in the *Poetics*."[1] Lacan asserts that this has "over the centuries produced a flood—indeed a whole world—of commentaries."[2] A contestation over the meaning of classical terms—such as *hamartia*—animates C.L.R. James's Haiti writings. Building on one of his key influences—Aristotle—James encourages definitional contestation as a way to underscore the ongoing (unfinished) nature of his object of study: the Haitian Revolution.

Staging the Hamartia of Political Leadership

This chapter examines C.L.R. James's 1967 revision of his play *Toussaint Louverture* (1936), renamed *The Black Jacobins*, and Edouard Glissant's *Monsieur Toussaint: A Play* (1961) as two case studies to explore the use of the tragic to talk about the problem of revolutionary leadership. This is so despite their differences in language, performance locale, and conditions and time of production. The diasporic literary orbit this project implies does not purport to extinguish the temporal, linguistic, and national differences between the text and authors under investigation. Nor does it encourage ignoring their respective positioning in the world system. Rather, I enumerate the methodological insights garnered by engaging what I am calling the Black Radical Tragic.

Thinking about the problematic of revolutionary leadership in the midst of a collective project to encourage the stirrings of African independence and attempting to counter the 1935 Italian fascist invasion of Abyssinia, C.L.R. James in his historical study *The Black Jacobins: Toussaint L'Ouverture and the San Domingo Revolution* (1938) looks to the Haitian Revolution of 1791–1804 as a compass to direct his political activity. James and his milieu reach the conclusion that only a combination of ideological and armed struggle will decolonize the African continent. In the later edition of his study, James clarifies his application of tragedy as crisis in political leadership: "The *hamartia*, the tragic flaw, which we have constructed from Aristotle, was in Toussaint not a moral weakness. It was a specific error, a total miscalculation of constituent events."[3] Toussaint ceases communicating his strategic rationale to the masses of Haitian people, contributing to his capture, exile-imprisonment, and death. It is striking that James refers to Toussaint's error as "tragic," given that he had staged a play about the Haitian leader two years before the publication of *The Black Jacobins*.[4] I am interested in the differences, both strategic and structural, between the play and the history. Considering *The Black Jacobins'* status as one of the most important twentieth-century studies of Black radicalism, it is a welcome opportunity, the result of meticulous labor by both James and Robeson scholars, that we have at least three known versions of the play.[5] For James, prefiguring the composition of a historical narrative by staging a play accounts for the dramaturgical language of that history.[6] In light of the fact that James alters his play's title from *Toussaint Louverture* to *The Black Jacobins* in an effort to prioritize collective movement, I ask the questions: How does one write a narrative foregrounding mass participation, in motion and anchoring radical analysis, through the focus of an individual? How does the latter iteration of the play temper the initial version's individualist focus? James thinks through the first successful African revolution by examining the aesthetics of staging.[7] I consider some of the ways the narrative architecture of the play represents the subtle interdependence between individual and collective in revolt. Glissant explodes the gap between leader and base in his own Haitian Revolution play, whereas an engagement with his *theory of relation* suggests it wise not to rush to transcend it.

Tragedy is, among other things, a way to think and represent the dialectical mediation between leader and mass base. The classical tragic structure involves the protagonist mediating her relationship with the chorus. The chorus, in its classical sense, is often representative of the polis's mores and sensibilities. More often than not, the tragic gesture performs its political work as a dramatized transgression against something entrenched in the community's belief system: a religious or spiritual infraction, a political lapse, a general rift in the structures of feeling of a given body of people, or the competing loyalties to irreconcilable, antagonistic social codes. An obvious example is in Antigone's *Sophocles* (442 B.C.E.), wherein competing mandates of spiritual law and secular kinship obligation clash. Such competing mandates are actually constitutive of the social formation itself. *The Black Jacobins'* use of tragedy helps mediate a series of oppositions and disparate gaps. It conveys and bridges the relationship between (1) leader and mass; (2) aesthetic/art and history/science (Aristotle); and finally (3) temporalities—linking the study's period focus with the time period of its production. James's text thinks the Haitian Revolution of 1791–1804 alongside his 1938 interest in the burgeoning African independence movement. It highlights the difference between the real and the ideal. In other words, tragedy points out discrepancy or lack of fulfillment and infuses such discrepancy with political meaning. James's hope in the ability to bridge such a gap differs as his thought process develops. His additions to and revisions of *The Black Jacobins* are inspired by his frustration with how such liberation movements evolve, combined with the radical aspirations achieved by the Cuban Revolution. Similar to Edward Said's insight on how Jonathan Swift's prose in his *Modest Proposal* "mimics the cannibalism it propounds by showing how easily human bodies can be assimilated by an amiable prose appetite,"[8] James utilizes a tragic generic structure to formally highlight Toussaint's troubles. He views the problematic of individual leader versus mass base as integral to the task of writing history. Or as Fred Moten states in his discussion of the lyric qualities in a book collaboration between Congolese painter Tshibumba Kanda Matulu and ethnographer Johannes Fabian: "I intend to pay some brief attention to the mechanics of James's lyrical history in order to think what might appear only as a contradiction indicative of failure. It would have been a failure on the part of the author that replicates the military/political failure of Toussaint, a failure that operates perhaps in spite of, the author's mastery."[9] Both Said's commentary on Swift and Moten's commentary on James highlight how the writers' prose duplicates the problematic of their texts' thematic. Moten's "in spite of" points to a world outside the textual frame, perhaps radical history that as Fredric Jameson reminds is outside textual representation but can only be accessed by textual representation. The mechanics of James's writing reproduces through its formal composition Toussaint's flaw in political judgment. Moten theorizes the excessive lyricism and musicality of the Black Radical Tradition (as captured in James's prose and a series of paintings about the death of Patrice Lumumba). Such lyricism pushes a Marxian dialectic that dogmatically insists on a position in which the creation of a proletarian class is an integral precondition for socialist transformation (neither Lenin's nor Mao's position, by the way). It is James's dialectical that allows for different subjects—the peasantry, the ex-enslaved—to take center stage in the revolutionary drama.

I examine Edouard Glissant's essay "Theatre, Consciousness of the People" from his *Caribbean Discourse: Selected Essays* (1989) in relation to his dramatic take on the Haitian Revolution as a problem of leadership. Glissant dissolves the opposition between leader and mass through his concept of *depassé*. The Nation (in this case a self-determined Haiti) cannot exist without the dissolution of individual leadership into the whole. By radically affirming and expanding James's Marxian fidelity to totality, Glissant enacts a mechanism of *Du dépassement qu'on en réalise* and achieves revolutionary unity between leader and base through his philosophy of the *Tout*: "the dissolution of the individual in the Whole." The complexities of translating Glissant will be discussed further. Glissant radically updates James's concern with the tragic disarticulation between Toussaint and his base by severing the chasm between the two, wherein both are subsumed in the totality of the national polity: "Although the people become nation through Toussaint, the process is complete only with the sacrificial dissolution of their 'medium.' Glissant's Toussaint understands that his country 'needs his absence' and that he 'must go up into the woods for the sake of the general liberty.'"[10] The narrative architecture of James and Glissant's plays subverts the focus on the leader, tipping the scales more toward the subtle interdependence between leader and base.

Bringing Paul Robeson "Back into the Frame": 1936/1967

> I have heard of your name for a long time. I have seen your picture in my prison. At Peekskill the American fascists howled at you and the American workers defended you. After I left the prison I heard your voice at clandestine meetings of a peace committee in my country.
>
> I love you my brother because you are the voice of life and peace, the voice of the people. The voice of this great love unites the people of all nations and every race. The men of death are proud of their atomic bombs, we men of peace are proud of your voice. Do not forget, my brother, that you do not sing alone. The men of peace of every nation are by your side.
>
> Telegram from Nazim Hikmet to Paul Robeson

The Incorporated Stage Society's[11] London production of C.L.R. James's *Toussaint Louverture* (1936) opened at the Westminster Theatre to a majority critical review noting the play's overburdening dialogue.[12] James's 1970 essay on its lead actor, Paul Robeson, for the Atlanta-based journal *The Black World* cites two examples: Charles Darwin in *The Times* criticizes its dialogue for being "informative rather than suggestive" and lacking "suppleness." The saving grace of the performance is "Mr. Robeson's individuality," which "binds its episodes together." Robeson's appearance and voice "[bring] him out of the frame and [reduce] his associates the background." Ivor Brown notes in *The Observer*: "Probably poetry would better have honoured the great magnanimous figure of ebony which Mr. Paul Robeson presented like some tremendous tree defying hurricanes and finally overwhelmed by the small, mean blade of French dishonesty."[13] Both critics take great pains to point out Robeson's individualist performance as the play's grace-saving merit. I want to look at the structuring of the 1967 iteration to show how James wavers between focus on Toussaint, the revolutionary leader, and the Haitian masses. Reading this version against the first version's critics, I argue that the revision process works against what can only be imagined as Robeson's awesome virtuosity in stagecraft. Such virtuosity figuratively haunts James's 1967 revision of the play, informing its representational calculus coupling Toussaint's grandeur to the Haitian masses at every turn. The play's formal structure tempers both Robeson's individual magnitude and Toussaint's strategic brilliance, ensuring that both only make sense as part of a larger mass articulation. This will be traced by four means: (1) the interdependence of the Raynal episode with the Prologue, (2) the rapid-fire tempo of the play's dramatic action related to the status of Black labor prior to and following the revolution, (3) the function of music in the play, and (4) the portrayal of Toussaint's execution of his nephew Moïse.

Toussaint L'Ouverture's encounter with *Philosophical and Political History of the Establishments and Commerce of the Europeans in the East and West Indies* (1770), the multivolume treatise of abolitionist priest Abbé Raynal, is pivotal in molding Toussaint's consciousness and political desires. Raynal was an opponent of slavery in the colonies who preceded French abolitionist institutions such as the Societé des Amis des Noirs (represented pictorially in the first edition of *The Black Jacobins*). The act of closely reading the Raynal text ignites Toussaint's desire to lead. David Scott argues that Toussaint's reading of Raynal in *The Black Jacobins* history exists "as a source of considerable leverage for James's endeavor to hold the tension between the claims of agency and the claims of structure"[14] and "allows us to imagine a classic pedagogical scene of modernist self-fashioning drawn almost straight out of Rousseau's *Emile*."[15] The placement of the Raynal episode in the Prologue acts as a primer suggesting both a reading strategy and distillation of its meditation on the problem of political leadership.

The Raynal episode's relation to the short-burst action sequences in the Prologue works to complicate the individualistic fashioning of Toussaint's solitary moment of instruction. The intimate scene in which Toussaint shares his reading experience of Raynal with Madame L'Ouverture is coupled by a series of scenes of resistance and scenes of subjugation. Toussaint's engagement with Raynal's words is an act of repetition since Toussaint has read them a thousand times prior. Here James utilizes stage directions and headings to imply a supplement to the performance. The effect of their capitalization implies a certain allegorical quality that can only be read with text in hand.

The scenes are as follows: (1) THE SLAVES (in which five slaves chained together "mime digging with spades" sing a collective song of resistance), (2) THE BARBER (a scene in which a barber brutalizes an enslaved African for ruining the coiffure of a lady being tended to by four slaves), (3) THE SLAVES (the return of the five, who now "mime digging with pickaxes," raising the stakes on the arsenal of tools and incorporating the English translation of the song from a prior scene—"Eh! Eh! Bomba! Heu! Heu! White Man—vow to destroy / Take his riches away / Kill them /

Every one / Canga Li"), (4) THE THIEF (a slave is whipped and beaten for stealing a chicken), (5) THE SLAVE ("five silhouetted slaves pass heavy boulders slowly from one to the other" as an overseer cracks his whip), (6) THE ENTERTAINER (a scene in which a white man is boasting about torturously murdering an enslaved African—a scene of sadistic murder repeated in the 1938 study), (7) THE HOTEL (Henri Christophe, who goes on to be one of Toussaint's main generals and executive of a future Haiti, serves drinks to three white men complaining about French abolitionist actions and the minimal police presence in San Domingo), (8) THE FOR-EST (a speaker is shot dead after he articulates a vision of transatlantic antislavery resistance and Dessalines promises reprisals after his murder), and finally, (9) THE LEADER:

> *The lights come up on the area stage right. Toussaint L'Ouverture is sitting in a rustic armchair with a book open on his lap. His head is at rest and he stares into the night. His wife enters behind him.*
> Mme. *L'Ouverture*: Old man, why don't you come to bed. It is late.
> *Toussaint*: I can't sleep. There is something frightening in the air. And I have just opened my Raynal to read an even more frightening thing. The book just opened and I looked. The Abbé is saying: "A courageous chief only is wanted." I have read it a thousand times before, but it is as if I had seen it for the first time.
> Mme. *L'Ouverture*: Toussaint, you still feel this destiny for great things.
> *Toussaint*: Yes, I do. For a long time. Ever since the slave uprisings began. But *what* "great things"?
> Mme. *L'Ouverture*: Come to bed, Old Toussaint. You're tired.
> *Toussaint*: In a little while. (Madame L'Ouverture exits. Toussaint looks into the book again, then looks up as the lights fade to a solitary spot on him). "A courageous chief only is wanted." (*The lights fade to blackout.*)[16]

Recall the approximate but never constituted collaboration between Josie and Frantz Fanon. James's historical study *The Black Jacobins* cuts Mme. L'Ouverture out of the reading equation.[17] In the play, the ordering of the Prologue is instructive. To borrow James's terminology from the 1938 history, this episode stands alone yet is inseparable from the "sub-soil"[18] from which it arises. The subsoil is the prior bursts of mass action, which precede it. Toussaint acknowledges to his wife that he has read Raynal "a thousand times before" and that the slave uprisings have preceded this particular scene of instruction. James's Prologue dramatically illustrates how the revolution makes Toussaint. Raymond Williams notes that in classical tragedy the prologue constitutes "the scene preceding the entry of the chorus."[19] In James's departure the chorus is (always) already onstage. The start of the slave uprising infuses new meaning and new density into the Raynal text—it is the condition of possibility for Toussaint's crystallization of his duty. Early on in "THE LEADER" Toussaint theorizes the relationship between historical movement on the ground and the work of abolitionist political philosophy. The status of this scene in relation to the preceding episodes highlights Toussaint's separation from his constituents. The Raynal moment is not the solitary experience of instruction represented in James's historical work—in the play, Toussaint shares Raynal's written provocation with his wife. Its condition of possibility is dialogue. It is the apex of the motion that precedes it. By preceding Toussaint's engagement with Raynal's text with a collapsed rapid-fire staging of various scenes pertaining to bondage and liberty, James employs a synchronic temporal mechanism to underscore his main problem: the chasm and interdependence between Toussaint and the soon-to-be *Haitian* masses. It is this temporal movement that marks the rich accomplishment of the play. The 1967 version constitutes an acute distillation of the original version—a radical contraction of the 1934 text. There is in this quick succession of scenes a strategic calculus and situational tact in James's portrayal of Toussaint. This is nowhere more apparent than in the leaps and turns captured in just a single scene.

Act I, Scene II dramatizes the quick shifts in colonial allegiances to which Toussaint and his men are sworn by in pursuit of their singular goal of Liberté. James utilizes the sometimes truncated, sometimes fully elaborated French Revolutionary anthem—"La Marseillaise"—to structure the scene's thematic of strategic, contingent fidelity to different colonial European nations for the sole purpose of complete freedom for the Africans of San Domingo. As Toussaint tells Marquis, the Spanish general: "They will join anything, or leave anything, for Liberté."[20] The scene commences with Marat (aide to Dessalines) and Max (aide to Toussaint's nephew Moïse) lamenting about having to move a piano—labor he characterizes as "work for slaves."[21] The scene highlights the insecurity of the Black Jacobin toilers' juridical designation as "free men," its potentially fleeting status. This furniture-moving motif is repeated in *Act III, Scene I* in which soldiers are arranging furniture in Dessalines's "unofficial head-quarters."[22] The disillusioned Marat and Max problematize the distinction between free and enslaved labor:

> *Marat*: All this goddamn furniture to be moved. This is work for slaves.
> *Max*: They ain't got no more slaves.
> *Marat*: All right. No slaves, but fellas to do heavy work. I am a soldier.
> I am free. What is the use of being free and having to move a piano.
> When I was a slave I had to move the piano. Now I am free I have to move the piano.
> *Max*: You used to move the piano for M. Bullet. Now it is for General L'Ouverture.
> *Marat*: The piano is still a piano and heavy as hell.[23]

When Orleans, aide to Christophe, asks Max about the success of the revolution in France, Marat interjects:

> *Marat*: . . . Just like ours. The white slaves in France heard that the black slaves in San Domingo had killed their masters and taken over the houses and the property. They heard that we did it and they follow us. I am sure in France, the slaves do not move pianos anymore. They make the old Counts and Dukes move them.[24]

This dialogue works to foreshadow the tragic degeneration of the revolutionary process: Toussaint's failure to communicate to his base and to explain shifting allegiances. In these few lines, James the playwright with great economy gestures toward troubles ahead, the precarious footing of the ex-enslaved Africans. James condenses a sophisticated discussion on freedom in a scene about the quotidian labor of moving a piano. The characters reason in an effort to determine exactly how their lots have changed with their newfound freedom. Prior to this discussion Orleans declares himself a duke and later Toussaint chastises Dessalines for humming the anthem of the French Republic since he is contingently loyal to the king of Spain. Toussaint articulates his adherence to an Afrocentric version of monarchy to rationalize fidelity to Spain, the temporary, tactical stepping-stone for Haitian liberation:

> We are Africans, and Africans believe in a King. We were slaves and we believe in liberty and equality. But we are not republicans. Do not sing that

song again. La Marseillaise is the song of enemies. Our ruler is the king, the King of Spain.[25]

This exchange is immediately followed by a discussion between Marat, Max, Orleans, and Mars Plaisir, Toussaint's civilian aide, on the nature of freedom, how the French mantra of revolution translates across the Atlantic. Orleans states: "Everybody says Liberty-Equality-Fraternity. All right, Liberty is when you kill the master; Equality, he's dead and can't beat you again; and Fraternity. . . . What is that Fraternity?"[26] Fraternity is the contested term in this triad. Plaisir and Orleans infuse this triad of French Revolutionary idealism with reason, a radical actuality, and pertinence to their positionality. Mars Plaisir clarifies: "All right. Liberty, slavery abolished; Equality, no dukes. . . . No counts, no marquises, no princes, no lords, everybody equal. . . . And Fraternity, everybody gets together and be friends, nobody taking advantage of anybody, everybody helping everybody else."[27] James stages a dialectical movement from particular to universal back to particular. The concrete claims of the French Revolution do not extend to a colony in which the Black majority is denied liberty. James's characters demand definitional precision. Lieutenant Moïse enters with news from France that the former slaves of San Domingo are now welcomed as citizens and Toussaint immediately puts the Spanish general, Marquis, under arrest. Toussaint alone dictates key decisions about political alignment:

> *Toussaint*: . . . Look at these people, General. Some of them understand only one French word—Liberté. (*Moïse is now gesturing to the crowd of men, who are eagerly listening.*) They will join anything, or lead anything, for Liberté. That is why I can lead them. But the day that they feel I am not for Liberty, the day they feel I am not telling them everything, I am finished. They are all listening to us now. As soon as you and I have finished speaking, they will know what we have said, because Moïse, my nephew, is translating what we say into Creole. Many discussions have taken place in front of these men while Moïse translated. They know that the Spanish San Domingo Government declared slavery abolished here, that they repeatedly sent to us asking us to join the Republic. But they also understand, Marquis, that when the Government in France abolished slavery, I would be joining them; not before. Now that slavery has been abolished, we go at once. Our soldiers are strategically placed in relation to yours; they have always have been. Marquis, your sword please.[28]

Here is the tragic dispensation of a Black radical praxis casting its net of strategic allegiances wide, the cohesive glue holding together a constantly shifting strategy is Liberté. The play stages the qualitative and quantitative differences between bondage and freedom as a temporal problem grounded in labor. The speech works to foreshadow Toussaint's strategic stumble into irrelevancy and death: "the day they feel I am not telling them everything, I am finished." Moïse the translator articulates in Creole Toussaint's exposition to the men. He is the communicative bridge to the masses. Toussaint's speech to the Spanish general Marquis, after he is placed under arrest, is a moment of performance that focuses all attention on him. The music at the conclusion of the monologue grounds Toussaint's actions to the collective:

> (*Moïse takes the Spanish flag and the Spanish General off. Toussaint exits followed by Dessalines and Christophe. One slave returns the chair to its place behind the table. Another follows Christophe to the exit to ensure that the officers are gone. He returns to the crowd of slaves who are excitedly conferring among themselves. Other ex-slaves converge from all sides to hear the news. A shout goes up, out of which comes a joyous "La Marseillaise." Drummers enter to accompany the rocking anthem as the men begin to jump up ad lib. Offstage men start a chant that cuts through the repeat of "La Marseillaise." The chant eventually drowns out "La Marseillaise" completely as more sing the former and less the latter.*
>
> *When all the men are chanting "Enfin les Français ont donne liberté," a priestess enters with a voodoo container which has three compartments—to hold small jars—and a central lighted candle. She kneels facing the audience in front of the drummers who are seated on a bench. Then three women dancers enter with a new chant, "La Liberté," in counterpoint to the men's chant. Each woman brings in a jar with which they appear to sprinkle the floor. They converge on the priestess and deposit their jars in her container. The drums and chanting stop suddenly. A new rhythm starts immediately.*)[29]

The reference to musical compositions elaborates James's philosophy of revolutionary leadership as a precarious balancing act. The "new rhythm" cuts and augments the singing of "La Marseillaise." The kernel of "La Marseillaise"—"La Liberté"—is what matters. *Act I, Scene II* concludes with Toussaint's fiery oration coupled with a Dionysian scene of mass revelry. Through the process of revision, James incorporates the trace of Robeson's solitary oration and collectivizes it. The music and dance combination works to trump the contingent partially translated French musical anthem housing a limited ideation of liberation. "La Marseillaise" is cut and augmented to a more site-specific interpretation. It is the collapsing and coupling of scenes of individual performative bravado with mass-driven *carnivalesque* (yet less temporary than the reversals typically troped in the *carnivalesque*) celebration that defines the originality of James's play. The celebration affirms African rituals and structures such rituals as tools of resistance.

Mozart's Don Giovanni *as Vengeance Machine*

> That Leporello has to complain of meager diet and shortage of
> money casts doubt on the existence of Don Juan.
>
> Theodor Adorno

Along with "La Marseillaise," James's play mobilizes the European operatic tradition, particularly Wolfgang Amadeus Mozart's 1787 opera *Il dissoluto punito, ossia Il Don Giovanni—The Dissolute Man Punished, or Don Giovannii*,[30] specifically the first act aria: "Vendetta ti chieggio, la chiede il tuo cuore." Allusion to the opera helps underscore the revisionist bent of James's entire historical project. It brings into focus the forces and actors marginalized by victors' accounts of history while also subjecting vengeance to rigorous thought. A brief engagement with Liane Curtis's article "The Sexual Politics of Teaching Mozart's Don Giovanni"[31] helps clarify. The full title of Mozart's work foregrounds the oppressive violence, brutal objectification, thwarted sexual assault, and inevitable punishment central to Mozart's opera. These are the same elements that are neglected and wished away in some of the critical reception of the work. The "dissolute man punished" gets eclipsed and only Don Giovanni, the rugged individualist and master of his passions, survives. Part of what C.L.R. James's use of *Don Giovanni* wagers is the possibility that Giovanni might not be an individual at all but a motive force.

The opera stages sexual violence and retribution. Based on the *Don Juan* legend, it begins with a masked Don Giovanni fleeing from Donna Anna in pursuit, who has just fended off his attempted rape. In the finale ball scene Don Giovanni is dragged to hell, punishment enacted from beyond. The ghost of Donna Anna's father, Don Commendatore (murdered by Don Giovanni), summons Don Giovanni to his infernal descent. Edward

W. Said argues that "the terrifying Commendatore in *Don Giovanni* embodies the stern, judgmental aspect of Leopold's relationship with his son (discussed by Maynard Solomon illuminatingly as Mozart's obsession with Hegel's Lord/Bondsman dialectic)."[32] James's weaving Mozart into his drama not only works to parallel themes of lord and bondsman but also stages the relationship between revenge and justice. It serves as structuring agent, a signpost, for James to delineate different developments in the Haitian revolutionary process.

James introduces the aria in *Act I, Scene I* of his play via M. Bullet, owner of the slave plantation in which Toussaint L'Ouverture labors. The scene begins with her playing the vengeance aria on the piano alongside Marie-Jeanne, a "mulatto slave" who becomes central as the plot progresses. This auspicious beginning is in contrast with James's 1934 *Toussaint Louverture*'s commencement with a minuet from *Don Giovanni*. James's translation of the aria in the mouth of Mme. Bullet foregrounds through repetition the question of vengeance:

> I demand revenge of you, your heart demands it,
> Your heart demands it.
> Remember the wounds in that poor breast,
> Recall the ground, covered, covered with blood,
> Should the fury of a just anger, of a just anger
> Wane in you . . .
> I demand revenge of you, your heart demands it,
> Your heart demands it.[33]

Mme. Bullet (whom Toussaint will help flee from revolting ex-slaves, thwarting Dessalines's plan for execution) conveys to Marie-Jeanne the occasion for her viewing the opera. She sees Mozart's *Marriage of Figaro* with her husband in Prague. They go to Paris and get word that *Don Giovanni* will be performed in Vienna and set sail. Her piano recital is followed by M. Bullet's entrance into the room with whip in hand. This follows Dessalines's war cry: "Kill Master. Burn down plantation." From the onset of the action in the Prologue, James asserts the international character of this uprising:

> *Speaker*: My brothers, I have been running all night to tell you. The slaves of the French Islands of Guadaloupe and Martinique are fighting their masters. The white slaves in France are fighting their masters. You here in

Fort Dauphin, you have toiled in the fields and got no rewards except lashes
with the whip; the land belongs to you, your blood and sweat is mixed up in
the earth. You must join your brothers in revolt we must fight.[34]

Marie-Jeanne repeats humming "Vendetta ti chieggio" after she has a
consultation with Hédouville, general of the French army. James portrays
her as a valuable strategist and utilizes Mozart to make this point. She
pretends to cower to the charms of General Hédouville in order to learn
of a plot involving General Pétion and the mulattoes. She gains valuable
information for the revolution, defying Dessalines's expectations of her
treachery and hums the aria after deceiving Hédouville.

The Mozart aria is reintroduced in the play upon Marie-Jeanne's discovery of Dessalines's plot to set up Toussaint for capture. After the mid-
point of *Act III, Scene I* Toussaint disappears completely out of the action
in the play. When Marie-Jeanne declares to Dessalines her intention to
spend time with Madame L'Ouverture and her family, stage directions
read: *Dessalines turns to her with fury. The orchestra quietly but clearly
begins to play "Vendetta ti Chieggio la Chiedo il tuo cor."*[35] He harshly chastises Marie-Jeanne. This is the final use of Mozart as a structuring agent
in the play.

Sit down, woman, and listen to me. (*Marie-Jeanne continues to stare at him
but makes no move. Dessalines strikes her twice across the face and forces
her down into the chair. The orchestra plays the Mozart aria more strongly
than ever. However, as Dessalines speaks it gradually declines until by the
time he is finished it has died away.*) Sit down, I tell you: I have arranged
for Toussaint to be captured, not killed. He will not be killed. General
Leclerc has been wanting to put his hands on Toussaint since his surrender.
I always told him them that if they did without my consent an insurrection would break out at once, all over the island. Now the insurrection is
near. The man who stands in the way, Marie-Jeanne, is Toussaint. Don't
say a word, woman. It is Toussaint who stands in the way. He will never
give the signal the people are waiting for. He still believes in liberty and
equality and a whole lot of nonsense that he had learned from the French.
All I have learnt from the French is that without arms in my hand there is
no freedom. The people still believe that Toussaint is their leader; but I am
their leader and when he goes they will know that. From the time he had
to kill Moïse he has not been the same man. Moïse was right. But he had to
be shot then. Now the whole thing is changed. Moïse's ideas are flourishing

in new soil. You see Samedi Smith out there and his men. There are thousands more. When Toussaint is removed they will look to me. And I will lead them. We will drive every Frenchman into the sea. Now you can talk. These last months you were often puzzled at what I was doing. Now you know. (*Marie-Jeanne looks up at Dessalines as if she is seeing him for the first time.*) Toussaint has to go. And it is the French who have to take him.[36]

This final iteration of Mozart precedes the last example of music used as a structuring agent conveying James's thematic points. In the concluding scene in which the masses of people receive word of Toussaint's death, Dessalines declares himself emperor and demands the orchestra play a minuet. A minuet in this instance signifies a sterile, farcical repetition of the liberating force found in the retranslated, refracted Mozart aria. Its artificial plasticity contrasts starkly with the echoes of the aria, signifying a pessimistic conclusion to the revolutionary epoch revealed onstage. The minuet performs a kind of ironic bitterness that is disclosed in the play. According to James, Dessalines's order to execute the whites is prompted by Cathcart, the representative of British trading interests. It signifies a regression from the simultaneity of Mozart's music compositional pallet in the ball scene of the opera. The minuet is in effect a musical analogue to Fanon's Europe, "where they are never done talking of Man, yet murder men everywhere they find them."[37] The minuet conceals the violence that is its condition of possibility through the sterile ting of its melodies. This resonates with *Figaro*, in which according to Wye Jamison Allanbrook the title character masks "his insolence in the noble *politesse* of the minuet."[38] The Mozart aria recedes as the monologue progresses, signifying the distortion of Toussaint's vision of liberation as well as the necessary and contradictory truth in Dessalines's words.

James's use of Mozart revises and reframes the composer in the same radical context against critical revisionism that affronts Curtis. Yet Giovanni's libertine excess resonates with the revolutionary vocation of pushing an ideo-logic to its very end. As Mladen Dolar argues: "Don Giovanni takes an ethical stance that could be read in accordance with Lacan's slogan 'ne pas céder sur son désir' (not to give way at to one's desire . . .). The disturbing thing about him is not that he has vast quantities of women—all aristocrats are assumed to do that—but that he raises pursuing pleasure to the level of an ethical principle for which he would rather die than renounce. . . . Whereas *Figaro* ends in the spirit of liberté, égalité, fraternité, for *Don Giovanni* liberté is placed beyond and in opposition to égalité and fraternité, in a zone where pure liberty coincides with pure evil."[39] Maynard Solomon argues against reading *Don Giovanni* as ultimately offering up revenge as a viable strategy and analytical preference: "But Mozart despite his determination to get even when he himself has been mistreated, understands—at least, it is his rational/Masonic creed—that vengeance, because it indulges individual passion at the expense of objective reason, is an insufficient remedy for injustice."[40] Instead, Solomon offers up music as Mozart's preferred solvent, partially because music "is endlessly repeatable."[41] In his use of *Don Giovanni*, James extracts and amplifies the revenge kernel of the opera and endlessly repeats it, paralleling his play's Haitian combatants honing in on *liberté*, employing such *liberté* in the service of their own radical use. Indeed echoing Eisenstein, the radical form (and dramaturgical tactic) is content. It is not solely Giovanni that constitutes revolutionary resolve by way of an uncompromising fidelity. As Maynard Solomon points out, the rebuffed "noble Elvira retained her grand passion for him [Giovanni] and would follow him to the ends of earth despite his rejection of her redemptive love."[42] Music in *The Black Jacobins* parallels the push and the pull competing tactics for *taking* freedom. Such an act of seizure insists on actors seeing its logic through to the end—revolutionary commitment as pure follow-through—not pure in the sense of devoid of contradiction but pure in the sense of unwavering fidelity to the end. *The Black Jacobins* challenges the audience to both register and distinguish qualitative and quantitative difference between moments acted out in the revolutionary process onstage, moments that retroactively constitute a whole after the sequence reaches its conclusion. Like the triumvirate of principles announcing the French Revolution, music represents a global import of liberation culture as material force shaped and utilized by the Haitian masses. It represents that wide, calculating net of influences and contingencies that constitutes the Black Radical Tragic. It is a formal mechanism that James uses in crafting his play, a format to explore his meditation on the strategic blunders marking such a revolutionary process.

In the *Don Giovanni* ball scene, Mozart writes and performs three pieces of music simultaneously. The entire (class-stratified) community is invited to the party regardless of rank or social status, and Mozart scores accordingly. Three orchestras play three dances simultaneously and each dance is a classed musical form: the minuet, the allemande, and *contradanse*. "È aperto a tutti quanti" ("It is open to everyone"), asserts Don Giovanni. "Viva la libertà!" replies the ensemble.[43] Dolar modifies the call-and-response aspect of this exchange and renders the lines as solely Don Giovanni's: "This ballroom is open to all, you're at liberty to enter."[44] In the text, Don Giovanni's libertine invitation is both responded to and translated by the ensemble as political principle: "Long Live Liberty!" In Dolar's transcription, Don Giovanni asserts his power by welcoming all while consolidating his power by reminding the ensemble of their liberty. The mass character of the guest list, the fact that all are invited to the dance, and the simultaneously scored ball scene are byproducts of vengeance normalization in the work. The negation energy of the "Vengeance Aria," vengeance as a structuring agent in the opera, clears at least a fleeting space for *equal footing*—dancing, fleeting, equal footing. Yet all this discussion of call and response assumes ontological integrity—the existence of individual dramatic personas. Let us go further than this by way of the framing epigram from Adorno.

In James's 1934 *Toussaint Louverture*, he scripts General Hédouville distinguishing between freedom and "ordered" freedom: "Liberty, yes, but not license."[45] Liberty versus license: "That Leporello has to complain of meager diet and shortage of money casts doubt on the existence of Don Juan." Here Adorno employs necessity (Leporello's "meager diet and shortage of money") to question a reading of Don Juan's libertine freedom as anything but figurative. We only actually see Don Giovanni fail at seduction. His thousands of erotic conquests are *catalogued*, not performed. Leporello's license is the condition of possibility for Don Giovanni's excessive liberty. Yet this is not quite precise. Instead of condition of possibility, Leporello's needs cast doubt on Don Giovanni's ontological integrity. Adorno doubts whether Don Juan exists. Instead of existence as individualist characterization, Adorno understands Don Giovanni as desiring machine, less a character and more a composite of drives. Adorno opts for the archetypal Don Juan instead of the particular Don Giovanni. It is almost as if specific attention to Leporello's diet and salary encourages thinking Giovanni stripped of the particularity of his dramatic personae. Yet in congruence with the sort of tragic temperance this study is arguing for, asserting Giovanni's nonexistence runs the risk of minimizing the way in which his actions impact catastrophically other individuals (Donna Anna, for example), thus reinstating the tendency to put women's suffering under erasure. The tragic framework heralded by both C.L.R. James and Raymond Williams cannot abandon its obligation to refuse concealing the individual in a calculus of suffering. For C.L.R. James, the entire opera works as an ever-proliferating vengeance machine[46] folded into the dramatic fabric of *The Black Jacobins*. Ripped from its initial context, it serves as musical theatrical fodder within Haitian revolutionary theatrical settling of scores.

The Heresy of Fidelity: The Measures Taken, Mauser, and the Purging of Moïse

> To use Brecht without criticizing him is betrayal.
>
> Heiner Müller

Nothing captures Toussaint's leadership challenges more poignantly than the execution of his nephew Moïse, who stands for breaking up the large estates and an uncompromising fidelity to the Black masses of Haiti.[47] James scripts Moïse as Toussaint's interpreter, translating directives into Haitian for the majority of fighting men and women. In *The Black Jacobins* history, James couples the execution of Moïse with this degeneration in revolutionary communication—Toussaint "was now afraid of the contact between the revolutionary army and the people, an infallible sign of revolutionary degeneration."[48] In the historical study, the execution of Moïse poses the hypothesis that it is fidelity to the revolution rather than equivocation or opportunism that has to be purged. Slavoj Žižek theorizes an understanding of heresy as an excess adherence—his analysis of the affront that Gnostic (Cathars) narratives posed to a hegemonic Catholicism. For Žižek the Cathar "dualist belief in the Devil as the counter-agent to the good God; the condemnation of every procreation and fornication, i.e. the disgust at Life in its cycle of generation of generation and corruption"[49] was a reviled threat to Catholic orthodoxy because it dares to thinks Catholic ideology to its logical end. This is a definition of heresy not as violation by aberration but as violation by radical adherence to a doctrine that the hegemonic power has to disavow in order to perpetuate its comprised existence:

> In short, what the Cathars offered was the inherent transgression of the official Catholic dogma, its disavowed logical conclusion. And, perhaps, this allows us to propose a more general definition of what heresy is: in order for an ideological edifice to occupy the hegemonic place and legitimize the existing power relations, it HAS to compromise its founding radical message—and the ultimate "heretics" are simply those who reject this compromise, sticking to the original message.[50]

Lacan argues that the Cathars are "the pure" and "the word in its original sense doesn't mean illumination or discharge, but purification."[51] Toussaint's execution of Moïse as a purge of *heretical belief*—James's incorporation of this episode is not an endorsement of Toussaint's actions; it is a strategic employment of dramatic tragedy's classical protocols utilized to interrogate the enduring problem of "the purge" in revolutionary politics. The overall narrative logic of both James's play and history posits Toussaint in a heroic light. Here James insists in his Black Radical Tragic framework a ruthless criticism of Toussaint's purge of his nephew alongside facing and claiming that purge as part of the same radical tradition Toussaint's error betrays. Tensions between Moïse and Toussaint are introduced early on in the play. In *Act I, Scene II*, Moïse brings news of France's declaration of emancipation and full citizenship for enslaved Africans in Haiti. James's *gestic* stage directions read: "His enthusiasm is momentarily checked by Toussaint's glance."[52] James dramatizes the relationship between the masses' fidelity to Moïse and how such fidelity threatens Toussaint's authority: "They shout 'Long live Moïse!' What they mean is 'Down with Toussaint.'"[53] "They" refers to the masses of Haitians fed up with trying to decipher Toussaint's decisions. James dramatizes Moïse's and Toussaint's competing radical visions: the error trying to appease the whites at the expense of the Black masses, and the necessity of a radical program of land redistribution. James centers Mme. Bullet as another decisive force signaling Moïse's death. She alerts Toussaint of a rumor that if he names Moïse as his successor all the whites will flee the island. Toussaint delays signing Moïse's death warrant until the final hour. In response to the French invasion, Toussaint and Dessalines pursue a scorched-earth policy and Toussaint signs the order. Moïse's voice signals an unwavering commitment to the principles of the revolution. In its excessive adherence, he poses the greatest threat. As Dessalines asserts, "Moïse is a very dangerous man; he is dangerous because he believes everything he says."[54]

Moïse's sincerity for revolution—the fact that "he believes everything he says"—is in excess of the strategic balancing act that Toussaint falters in—his failed attempt to secure and prolong his legitimacy in the eyes of the Haitian masses. For Toussaint, compromise is not shorthand for class collaboration in general—it is collaboration in the actuality of the specific struggle James is engaging: "In allowing himself to be looked upon as taking the side of the whites against the blacks, Toussaint committed the unpardonable crime in the eyes of the community where the whites stood for so much evil. That they should get back their property was bad enough. That they should be privileged was intolerable. And to shoot Möise, the black, for the sake of the whites was more than an error, it was a crime. It was almost as if Lenin had had Trotsky shot for taking the side of the proletariat against the bourgeoisie."[55] By purging Möise, "Toussaint like Robespierre, destroyed his own Left-wing, and with it sealed his own doom."[56] Compromise is a strategic flexibility in service of achieving the goal of Liberté. For Möise, such compromise strikes at the heart of everything he believes and represents a capitulation to the same goal. In the presentational logic James stages, both men are correct, but Toussaint is unequivocally and tragically mistaken. Their mutually exclusive antagonism smacks of *Antigone*-esque lack of reconciliation and indeed constitutes the tragic as such.

David Scott's study on James and tragedy announces its preoccupation with temporality by way of Shakespeare's *Hamlet*: "The time is out of joint. O, cursed spite, / That ever I was born to set it right!"[57] The centrality of timing speaks to Dessalines's verdict evaluation of a Möise just and precise in his sentiment but despite that fact (strictly in the problematic that James stages) necessarily had to be shot. It is not in the least an endorsement of this execution; rather, it is an insistence that this execution be faced and claimed as part of the revolution's legacy. James offers up the execution as something to think about. It is not a question of determining whether or not it is sound or just to violently purge a cadre member from the safe distance of two centuries and the comfort of a scholar or theater attendee's chair. As Carolyn E. Fick argues:

> It was Möise, and not Toussaint, nor even Dessalines, who still bore scars of the whip and horrible measures of his own life as a slave, who embodied the aspirations and needs of the rural masses. More than that, he also believed in their economic and social legitimacy, and, if he did not ostensibly organize the insurrection, he nevertheless wholly supported it in opposition to Toussaint.[58]

James forces his audience to inhabit the problematic he stages. Antagonistic variations in leadership style signified by the proper-name binaries Toussaint/Dessalines, Toussaint/Möise, and so forth provide a thought template to think about questions of revolutionary leadership and strategy. If the goal is lauding the Black Jacobin with the most mass-base and uncompromising class-consciousness, and commitment to the imperative of breaking up the land for redistribution, Moïse wins every time. His uncompromising fidelity to justice is at odds with the strategic mandate to secure a hegemonic block of influence. Moïse's rigidity simply cannot be reconciled with a sense of "good timing." As the Darwin review states: "one feels that he has been mistaken in his calculations but not in his ultimate purpose" in conflict with Toussaint's "cautious eye for the political reality as he understands it." Moïse represents the true believer whose fidelity to the revolution, a fidelity that poses a challenge to the notion of timeliness as a strategic concern in waging a hegemonic struggle for support from various social bases, makes him a liability for the revolution—not in the actuality of the Haitian Revolution but in the actuality of the archive that James accesses and stages. His execution is a tragic loss because and not in spite of its very necessity within the heuristic James's play enacts.

Brecht Versus Brecht

A Brechtian digression on revolutionary violence (the purge) and the *Lehrstücke* is useful here. In this case, a repetition with a difference of Brecht's *The Measures Taken* (1930) in the form of Heiner Müller's play *Mauser* (1970)[59] helps to explain the work of execution in *The Black Jacobins*, despite the aversion Müller expressed toward "the misery of comparison."[60]

The Measures Taken presents the problem of violent purges to a revolutionary panel of two judges—both the "control-chorus" and the targeted worker-audience of Brecht's *Lehrstücke*, or learning play. Masked radical agitators undergoing illegal party working in China inevitably kill one of their comrades, whose fidelity to the revolution translates to eagerness, hastiness, and poor timing. First the "Young Comrade" places the ensemble in danger when he impulsively protests the mistreatment of barefooted rice barge workers, resulting in the group being driven from the work site, unable to continue agitation. Then he gets caught handing out illegal leaflets in a factory and fails to enact a united front of workers against scab labor. He reacts with hostility to the contempt a rich merchant has for "coolie" laborers, failing to secure the purchase of arms by the merchant to be used against the English. Finally, he insists on a hasty attack of the enemy barracks and refuses to work to win over the soldiers so that they can see their class interests as on the same side as that of the workers. The comrades chastise him: "Yours is an impetuous revolution that will last a day and be throttled tomorrow."[61] In protest he rips off his mask and destroys their supply of leaflets and risks exposing the agitators to enemies in pursuit. His strategic blunders continuously jeopardize their clandestine mission abroad. Their rationale for killing the comrade—necessary prerequisite to flee from pursuers and their eviscerating the trace of his body in a lime pit—is presented to the Brechtian chorus for judgment. The Young Comrade agrees to the necessity of his murder, making *The Measures Taken* an example of Brechtian *Einverständnis*, what Jonathan Kalb expertly defines as "informed agreement to loss of life or self or to other drastic action in the interest of the collective."[62]

Brecht underscores the audience's capacity for critical thinking, distinguishing his learning play from the "aristotelian play": the *Lehrstücke* replaces the audience as "collective individual" of the aristotelian play with a "collection of individuals" that are "capable of thinking and reasoning." Furthermore, "the aristotelian play is essentially static; its task is to show the World as it is. The learning play [*Lehrstücke*] is essentially dynamic; its task is to show the world as it changes (and also how it may be changed)."[63] *The Measures Taken* boldly suggests: "What vileness should you not suffer to annihilate vileness?"[64]

Note the unscrupulous merchant's "Song of Commodity":

> What is Man anyway?
> Do I know what Man is?
> How should I know who should know?
> I don't know what Man is.
> All I know is his price.[65]

This is the point of entry for Heiner Müller's Brechtian critique, radicalizing the *Lehrstücke* form both "with and beyond." Andreas Huyseen argues that *Mauser* "stands with and beyond Brecht's *The Measure's Taken*. . . . As such, it both accepts and critiques the conditions upon which it rests. And in refusing to close its contradictions, it offers the form of the *Lehrstücke* as a means of going through and overcoming them."[66] Pursuing Brecht's logic to the extreme, Müller's *Mauser* answers Brecht's *The Measures Taken's* question of "What is a man?" with another question: What is a human?

The title *Mauser* is a triple word-play: a noun that means both mouse-catcher and a bird's annual process of moulting, it is also the name of the pistol most commonly used in the Russian Revolution. The play tells the story of a man named simply "A" who is deranged by his task of executing "enemies of the revolution" at a critical point during the Russian civil way, launching into a fit of orgiastic killing. He too is asked to assent to his own death and, toward that end, is subjected to a repetitious, rhythmic litany of ideological statements by ambiguous entities such as "Chorus [A]" and "[A] Chorus" which blur his identity with the group's. These ambiguous headings and the recurrent issue of *Einverständnis* are both "copied" from Brecht's *Lehrstücke*.[67]

The CHORUS and Character A constantly interchange roles so as to make differentiating between the two impossible.

With its circular action and intentionally ambiguous dialogue indications, *Mauser* cannot be said to have such a singular protagonist. Part of what is so disturbing about the play is the absence of a fully human, and hence convincingly heroic, center on which audiences and players may fix their sympathies. In the Rotbuch edition of the work, Müller illustrated this point by appending an assemblage of photos by Ralph Gibson in which a cropped shock of hair and bare shoulder abut a cropped waist and hand wielding a cocked pistol, creating a composite beast made only of weapon and minimal head. The assemblage reinforces the impression of extreme absurdity left by the text, which presents a presumably dialectical debate concerning human identity and human rights within a space so emotionally charged it leaves little space to think.[68]

In 1986 Heiner Müller proclaimed: "To use Brecht without criticizing him is betrayal."[69] Criticism in the form of *Mauser* takes the form (like Moïse in relation to Toussaint) of excessive fidelity, excess that thinks Brecht's *Lehrstücke* to its logical extreme. "If Brecht's *Lehrstücke* grew out of an attempt to negate the bourgeois theater and drama, then Müller's *Mauser* can be regarded as the negation of the negation."[70] Critical heresy (as opposed to betrayal) works as a surplus of allegiance. Moïse believes in everything he says! Müller stages his dramatic intervention as a heretical Brecht. *Mauser* plumbs the depth of the concept of the human to explicate its lack of coherency in a time of revolution, a time where ideally all conceptual groundings (like philosophical and genre-based understandings of tragedy) are strained. *Mauser*'s chorus responds to the aggregate character A (CHORUS)'s rationale for excessive murder with the following logic:

Your task was never killing human beings
But enemies. The fact is we don't know
What a human being is. We only know
That killing is a job that must be done
But a human being's more than just his job.
For until the Revolution's won
In Vitebsk as in cities everywhere
Shall we know what a human being is.
The human is our work, for we expose
What's hid behind the masks or buried deep
In the filth of its own history, the face beneath
The leprous sores, the living core within
The fossil, for the Revolution tears
The masks from off the faces, obliterates
The body's leprous sores and washes off
With bayonet and gun, with tooth and knout
The filth encrusted over what is human
Which rising from the chain of generations
And tearing off its bloody navelcord
And recognizing in the lightning flash
Of true beginnings its own self and those
Like it, each one according to its kind
Tears the human from the human by the roots.
For death means nothing, what counts is the example.[71]

Reacting to the more salacious and provocative parts of this passage (the aesthetization of violence, the lauding of destruction as generative) misses the point. Müller in the role of *heretical Brecht* assumes the problematic of Brecht's *Lehrstücke*, deconstructing, criticizing, and sublating its critical insights. In the volume *Germania*, the chapter staging an encounter between Müller and Brecht is entitled "Brecht vs. Brecht." Critique, the minimum to avoid betrayal, involves subsuming the position of the one you are criticizing and pushing that position to its end. Its most forceful guise, as Alain Badiou reminds, musters the resolve of axiomatic choice in mathematical proofs. Badiou charts a course, a "historical sequence that goes from the great Jacobins of 1792 after the 9th Thermidor, to the last storms of the Cultural Revolution in China and the 'leftism' everywhere else in the world." This sequence summons the authority of math not in its veracity or objectivity but in its willingness to face the consequence of its moves to the very end:

In mathematics we have first of all a kind of primitive liberty, which is the liberty of the choice of axioms. But after that, we have a total determination, based on the rules of logic. We must therefore accept all the consequences of our first choice. And this acceptance does not amount to a form of liberty; it is a constraint, a necessity: finding the correct proof is a very hard intellectual labour. In the end, all this strictly forms a universal equality in precise sense: a proof is a proof for anyone whatsoever, without exception, who accepts the primitive choice and the logical rules. Thus, we obtain the notions of choice, consequences, equality, and universality.

What we have here is in fact the paradigm of classical revolutionary politics, whose goal is justice.[72]

Mauser implies that far from being too radical, Stalin was not radical enough. He fails to acknowledge that you cannot know what a "human" is until revolution stays its course and until categories in radical flux settle and cohere. This makes killing rationale a temporal problem of great magnitude. Whereas both Brecht's *The Measures Taken* and James's *The Black Jacobins* offer up a political execution, then explore the ambiguous aspects of such an execution's rationale (Moïse and the Young Comrade), *Mauser* goes further by way of a deep fidelity to Brecht's problematic of revolutionary political violence. The CHORUS makes clear that the definition of human being is unclear and that revolution reconfigures existing categories. In this ever-changing labor to define the human, James's play is more *The Measures Taken* and less *Mauser*. The balancing staged in *The Black Jacobins* as it relates to Toussaint's execution of his nephew never breaks its rationalizing (both positive and negative) frame to approach the kind of radical transfiguration exhibited by Dessalines, who, rather than "kill the whites" in the newly liberated Haiti (according to James prompted by British imperial interests hence unnecessary), establishes a criteria of nonracial citizenship, a new kind of human being whose only criteria constitute practice and radical choice, a practice constituted primarily by allegiance to the fledgling African nation of Haiti regardless of "color." Execution is prefaced by political choice, by a willingness or an unwillingness to claim the new abolitionist nation. The vengeance and justice machine that is the Haitian Revolution produces nothing less than a new definition of the human.

Edouard Glissant's Collectivity of the Living and the Dead

> Toussaint L'Ouverture, as a man, had his limitations. But he did his
> best, and in reality he did not fail. He was captured, imprisoned,
> killed; but his example and his spirit still guide us now. The last
> two years, from 2004 to 2006, the Haitian people have continued
> to stand up for their dignity and refused to capitulate. On 6 July
> 2005, Cité Soleil was attacked and bombarded, but this, and many
> similar attacks, didn't discourage people from insisting their voices
> be heard. They spoke against injustice. They voted for their presi-
> dent this past February; they won't accept the imposition of another
> president from abroad or above.
>
> This doesn't mean that success is inevitable or easy, that powerful
> vested interests won't try to do all they can to turn the clock back.
> Nevertheless, something irreversible has been achieved, something
> that works its way through the collective consciousness. This is the
> meaning of Toussaint's famous claim, after he had been captured by
> the French, that they had cut down the trunk of the tree of liberty
> but that its roots remained deep.
>
> As for Dessalines, the struggle that he led was armed, and neces-
> sarily so, since he had to break the bonds of slavery once and for all.
> But our struggle is different. It is Toussaint, rather than Dessalines,
> who can accompany the popular movement today.
>
> Jean-Bertrand Aristide

Glissant's Haitian Revolution play offers a gentle corrective to President
Aristide's spirited formulation.[73] Decoupling Toussaint from Dessalines as
popular accompaniment degrades the armature gleamed from the Haitian
past in service of radical futures. Whereas C.L.R. James labors to integrate
Toussaint within the collectivist scenes of his drama, Edouard Glissant's
Monsieur Toussaint: A Play offers a Toussaint who in his most isolated,
private moments is haunted by a constitutive collective. Glissant's *Toussaint* can never escape collectivity in order to etch out space to think his
interdependence on it. This speaks to Glissant's views on his native Martinique, his dissatisfaction with its juridical status as a "Department" of
France. As J. Michael Dash argues: "The total integration of Martinique
within a French sphere of influence meant a number of things: the loss of
control over internal affairs, the erosion of a local creole culture and the
relentless europeanisation of all areas of life. Even Césaire himself, under

whom these changes were ironically taking place, would soon recognize that departmentalization carried with it the risk of metropolitan tyranny and was relentlessly leading to what he called 'progressive underdevelopment.'"[74] The Haitian Revolution is used to think about Glissantian questions of opacity and interrogates revolutionary nationalist aspirations and what constitutes "the whole" in Glissant's thought.

In the monad of his mind and ensemble onstage, Toussaint is both simultaneously radically alone and frantically hosting. In other words, the dead visit and visit often. In Glissant we are offered a different type of chorus, differing from James's, yet realizing James's full implications. In a sense, Glissant's Toussaint is James's Toussaint actualized, brought to its logical conclusion. Like Shakespeare's *Coriolanus*, Glissant's Toussaint *completes* James's Toussaint. He sees the revolution through to its end (figuratively, since he is in his French cell and never enters the liberated homeland). The reward of such completion is an expanding ken of vision that easily traverses the worlds of the living and the dead. Toussaint emphatically learns: "There is a world elsewhere" (*Coriolanus* III.iii).[75] Glissant's poetics accesses this world as an optic to reexamine the tension between leader and base as integral to the labor of nation building.

Monsieur Toussaint: A Play (1961) was first staged at the Theatre International of the Cité Universitaire (Paris, 21 October 1977, Theatre Noir). It was again performed on the occasion of the 200th anniversary of the death of Toussaint (7–9 July 2003), in a courtyard at Fort de Joux, near Pontarlier in the French Juras, where an imprisoned Toussaint froze to death. Césaire's mise-en-scène is revisited and modified: "A lone man imprisoned in whiteness.... A lone man defying the white screams of white death."[76] "Lone man" Toussaint entertains many visitors and listens to their criticisms. Dash reads *Monsieur Toussaint* as staging two competing avenues of liberation: Toussaint's French Revolutionary internationalism and Mackandal's commitment to *marronage*, the opposition between "liberal leader with the radical maroon, the compromises of acquiescence with the negation of revolt."[77] A useful heuristic indeed, but perhaps acquiescence simplifies the matter. It risks morphing Toussaint's strategic blunder into a form of resignation, a brand of battle fatigue. Acquiescence houses a moralistic connotation that is arguably not helpful for thinking politics and a turncoat connotation not helpful for making sense of Toussaint. Glissant constitutes a dramatic field to examine ideas explored in his dense body of scholarship on poetic language, collective memory, depersonalization, and national recognition.[78] Wherein James prefigures and frames the way he thinks about leadership in his historical study *The Black Jacobins*, drawing upon the theme of Toussaint as individual protagonist mediated by the Haitian masses as chorus/bass, Glissant explodes such concerns by thinking and staging that binary to its logical dissolution, while also theoretically insisting not to "unify" such binaries. This is congruent with what Peter Hallward with great verve shows as Glissant's ever-developing theoretical grasping with the concept of Totalité.[79] Both James and Glissant stage the Haitian Revolution as a way to think about the relationship of *the whole* to revolutionary movement.

The acts of Glissant's play are framed by titles that work to constitute a vision of totality in which all binaries are evoked, exploded, and reconstituted: leader/base, past/present, secular/sacred, metropole/periphery, and, most important, dead/alive. Act I is entitled "The Gods," Act II "The Dead," Act III "The People," and Act IV "The Heroes." In lieu of a Jamesian Prologue that sets up the complicated opposition between Toussaint as leader-protagonist and the mass base chorus, Glissant's framing recalls the historical synchrony of Robeson's journalism linking Toussaint to Ho Chi Minh:

> *The play is set in Saint-Domingue and at the same time in a cell at the Fort de Joux where Toussaint is being held prisoner; he wears the uniform of a general of the Republic, a scarf knotted around his head, a plumed hat resting on his knees.*
>
> *Around him will appear: Maman Dio, in a long gray dress and scarf; Makandal, in sackcloth pants and a torn-up shirt, with one sleeve tied to the waist because he has lost an arm; Bayon-Libertat, in boots and a large straw hat; Moyse, dressed as a general, with a patch over one eye; and Delgrès, in a commander's uniform. These are the dead who haunt Toussaint alone; they are unseen by the other characters.*
>
> *Each time the action takes place in Saint-Domingue and requires Toussaint's presence, the latter moves into the space at the front of the cell, but it is understood that he never escapes from his ultimate prison, even as he relives his triumphant past. There is no clearly defined frontier between the world of the prison in France and the lands of the Caribbean island.*[80]

The realization of transatlantic linkages connecting metropole with colony, the inseparability of Toussaint's commencement of the revolution and Dessalines's completion of it (what Fred Moten captures as: "Toussaint's expansive vision and practical failure and, on the other hand,

Lieutenant Dessalines's limited vision and practical success")[81] are ultimately surpassed in *Monsieur Toussaint's* synchronic landscape. The play is "*a prophetic vision of the past*. For those whose history has been reduced by others to darkness and despair, the recovery of the near or distant past is imperative." Glissant's goal is "to renew acquaintance with one's history, obscured or obliterated by others, [it] is to relish fully the present, for the experience of the present, stripped of its root in time, yields only hollow delights."[82] Glissant's explosion of the alleged chasm separating Dessalines and Toussaint in popular memory and scholarship becomes apparent in the preface to the 2005 edition of the play:

> The 200th anniversary of the declaration of Haitian Independence (in 1804, a few months after Toussaint's death) will perhaps witness the revival of the debate between those who consider Emperor Dessalines the true founder of the new nation and those who consider Toussaint its initiator and indisputable prophet. The whole movement of *Monsieur Toussaint*, the action and the driving force as it were, is unleashed and sustained by the struggle that Toussaint undertakes in the icy solitude of his cell—a struggle against the dead who visit him, and against the living who are powerfully summoned to witness his final agony. In truth, Toussaint and Dessalines, and all the actors in this epic, are inseparable. The realization of such a historical event (the first successful resistance against all forms of colonialism; the first black state in the Americas; the advent of Africa, source of inspiration, on the New World scene) could not have rested on the will of a single individual. The grandeur of Toussaint's vision and the decisive actions of Dessalines complete each other.[83]

Another way of thinking this lauding of firsts is as a proliferation of use. Separation of the "actors in the epic," constructing a schematization of legitimacy that privileges Toussaint over Dessalines conflict with Glissant's main task: to provide a framework to think the revolutionary whole. In a 1978 author's note, Glissant states that in 1961 he could not imagine the present stay of Antillean theater "with regard to the experimental popular theatre which now brings forth a critical view of Antillean reality and authentic use of the Creole tongue."[84] Rather, the work was imagined as an aesthetic and historical intervention, which "proposed the presentation of a historical datum in its totality." This totality includes living and dead Haitian combatants: "It may be useful to point out that Toussaint's relations with his deceased companions arise from a tradition, perhaps peculiar to the Antilles, of casual communication with the dead."[85] This resonates with his essay "Theater, Consciousness of the People." Both this essay and the play desire a "total" constitution of the nation—a forceful, ameliorative thrust against the state of depersonalization as both imperialist tactic and legacy. A transcendence that can only occur via the plunge into the gully, that grand rupture that is the African slave trade as revolutionary futurity. From "Section II. ALIENATION AND REPRESENTATION (Unperceived and un-assumed in our unexpressed history)":

> (Let us leave History and go down into the gully course that is our future— our difficult becoming. Hegel does not enter with us.) The rupture of the slave trade, then the experience of slavery, introduces between blind belief and clear consciousness a gap that we have never finished filling. The absence of representation, of echo, of any sign, makes this emptiness forever yawn under our feet. Along with our realization of the process of exploitation (along with any action we take), we must articulate the unexpressed while moving beyond it: expressions of "popular beliefs" are a nonpossession that we must confirm; to the point where, recognizing them as a nonpossession, we will deal with them by abandoning them.[86]

Perhaps Hegel does enter with us. In 2005, the technical mastery and conditions of production for Caribbean theater have elevated so that now it has a chance to function as the reflective type of theater in Creole desired by Glissant. Finally one can write "at last a language *as one hears it.*" Glissant's statement on theater traces the journey from what he refers to as the "folkloric" capitulation of the popular street scene to an advanced stage, in which theater is offered to critically engage spectators in a further apprehension and comprehension of the problematic in order to secure an endgame of total liberation.

Glissant stakes his position on tragedy in "Note Concerning modern tragedy that no longer requires the sacrifice of the hero," an essay that converges with Freirean theorist-practitioner Augusto Boal's notion that tragedy cannot exist in a time of revolution. Rather, the time of tragedy *vis-à-vis* revolution is either prior or after:

> The structure of the system may vary in a thousand ways, making it difficult at times to find all the elements of its structure, but the system will always be there, working to carry out its basic task: the purgation of all antisocial elements. Precisely for that reason, the system cannot be utilized by revolutionary

groups during revolutionary periods. That is, while the social ethos is not clearly defined, the tragic scheme cannot be used, for the simple reason that the character's ethos will not find a clear social ethos it can confront.[87]

I am interested in the implied temporal questions of timeliness and untimeliness in that the tragic hero needs a clear-cut social order to strike out against—in other words, a well-defined field to transgress. In the flux-time of revolutionary upsurge, calculating this clear-cut field is a Herculean task. Note the tension here between tragedy as "structure" verses tragedy as "scheme." Between these two configurations (structure and scheme) is where to look for what I am calling the Black Radical Tragic. Structure here implies a structural continuity (the oppressive structural continuity that Black radicalism positions itself against but cannot be limited to); scheme implies a more generalized emplotment strategy in which its ambition lacks the totalizing force of tragedy-as-structure yet constantly strives to be its negation.

I advocate for a literal translation of Glissant as the way to do justice to the complexities of his theoretical work and categories. Here is Glissant in the original French:

> Le motif central de cet ouvrage est précisément que, de même que le réel martiniquais ne se comprend qu'à partir de tous les possibles, avortés ou non, de cette Relation, et du dépassement qu'on en réalise, de même les poétiques multipliées du monde ne se proposent qu'à ceux-là seuls qui tentent de les ramsser dans des équivalences qui *n'unifent pas*. Que ces poétiques sont inséparables du devenir des peuples, de leur loisir de prendre part et d'imaginer.[88]

Consider this more literal translation:[89]

> The central motif of this work is precisely that, just as Martinican reality can only be understood from the perspective of all the possibilities, aborted or not, of this Relation, and of the moving beyond that is realized with them, so the multiple poetics of the world are only granted to those who attempt to gather them in the forms of *equivalences that do not unify*. That these poetics are inseparable from the becoming of a people, from the time they have to take part and to imagine.[90]

I want to think about the culminating thematic phrase in this passage: "qui tentent de les ramsser dans des équivalences qui *n'unifent pas*." I maintain Glissant's original provocative sense of "equivalences that do not unify." The emphasis is on "equivalences," not "similarities" or "standardization." Equivalence denotes things that cannot be put in a hierarchy or ranked in a temporal progression but nonetheless can be set alongside each other in Relation. The central motif of Glissant's work is that the Martinican real can only be understood from the perspective of all the possible implications, aborted or not, of Relation and the moving beyond that is realized with them. So too the multiplied poetics of the world can only offer themselves to those who try to gather them among equivalences that do not unify. "Multipliées" (the past participle of the transitive verb "to multiply") as *multiplied* is peculiar—it is as if someone has gathered up poetics and multiplied them. Yet this imparts an active voluntarism onto his project. Such poetics are inseparable from (what Deleuze and Guattari might emphasize as)[91] the *becoming* of people, from their pleasure in "taking part"[92] and imagining difference. Equivalence is not a simple dance of ranked and prioritized equals. Related to this, abstract equivalence does not meld likeness; it melds difference and articulates such difference in the form of a common measure. In this sense, fidelity to Glissant's "equivalents that do not unify" slows down the equivalence logic of capital. His *Monsieur Toussaint* explodes leader/mass equivalence whereas his theoretical work demands that the negation of unity results in maintaining the nature of leadership as a problem.

Toussaint has to be sacrificed in Glissant's play. But such a death does not signify transcendence, since in Glissant's dramaturgical landscape the dead speak as well. John Berger offers up the following summation in his "Twelve Theses on the Economy of the Dead." Perhaps he learned this insight not just by decades of thinking about the intersections of visual arts, narrative, and revolutionary politics but also as translator of Glissant's elder countryman Césaire's *Cahier d'un retour au pays natal.*[93]

> How do the living live with the dead? Until the dehumanization of society by capitalism, all the living awaited the experience of the dead. It was their ultimate future. By themselves the living were incomplete. Thus living and dead were interdependent. Always. Only a uniquely modern form of egoism has broken this interdependence. With disastrous results for the living, who now think of the dead as the eliminated.[94]

For Glissant, there is a certain unwanted loss when one tries to ultimately transcend such oppositions, as opposed to maintaining their more messy sense of relation. This is bound up in his desire for the Caribbean to harness its past in service of a revolutionary future—without conflating the two temporalities in some sort of easy unity. A poetics of relation is one of the hallmark concepts of Glissant's analysis. "Equivalences that do not unify" complicate an effort to enact an easy bridge between leader and masses. It highlights an enduring problem. A moving beyond is brought about by the dissolution of the medium (the death of Toussaint), which resolves a condition of mediation yet defied every time the work is performed anew. For Glissant, relation is a desired and constitutive phenomenon in the world, not a methodological tool or conceptual apparatus to be done away with. Differences do not in the last instance "unify." In Glissant, there is an expanding of the tragic gap in C.L.R. James that allows him to think together the dead with the living, exorcising the need to unify such opposite states. The dead are a very different kind of chorus than in James. Yet there is still the need to raise the question of strategic mastery embodied in Toussaint coupled with the constant need to communicate one's goals. From the conclusion of *Monsieur Toussaint's Act IV, Scene V*:

> *Toussaint*: (*laughing in delirium*): Bad strategy, solider! . . . I can barely write, your captain was well aware. I write the word "Toussaint," Macaia spells out "traitor." I write the word "discipline" and Moyse without even a glance at the page shouts "tyranny." I write "prosperity"; Dessalines backs away, he thinks in his heart "weakness." No, I do not know how to write, Manuel.
> *Manuel*: He's delirious, Jura fever. Those people don't exist, Toussaint, they don't exist.
> *Toussaint*: Go behind the wall. You will find them, the living and the dead. Those waiting impatiently for me, and those who can wait no longer. If your eyes are open, you will see them. Go, Manuel, go. You will come upon Toussaint's first defeat. . . . Protect yourself from the dead, they are trickier than we are![95]

The conceptual work done by Toussaint's proper name is replaced by a value-laden pejorative signifying betrayal. The proper name morphs into a judgment on his strategic efficacy and fidelity to revolutionary principles. Actors in Glissant's drama are named by what they do. The above excerpt is not an episode in delirium or a meditation on the ambiguities surrounding transcription. It works to connect what I have attempted to argue about the tragic turn and in the Black Radical Tradition. It intersects with James's notion articulated in his appendix to the latter edition of *The Black Jacobins* in which he states, "Within a West Indian island the old colonial system and democracy are incompatible."[96] Just as the aesthetic mandate to answer the revisionist distortion of a Black radical continuum with a figuration of totality is a tall order, the strategic calculus necessary to bring about nothing less than democracy is equally broad. The exclusionary system of bourgeois governance impacts African people with overarching uncompromising brutality, demanding a political strategy flexing comparable expanse. Such a strategic widening runs the risk of tragic failures in transcription, translation. Through James's drama of mediation and Glissant's effort to explode such mediation, the Black Radical Tragic is explored as both a condition of possibility and mandate corresponding to the material conditions of a colonized people. It constitutes both its greatest strength and its greatest possibility for unraveling. It is nothing less than the precarious balancing act of the particular and the universal. As Aimé Césaire cautions the general secretary of the French Communist Party in his 1956 letter of resignation: "There are two ways to lose oneself: walled segregation in the particular or dilution in the 'universal.'"[97]

Paul Robeson as "Sporting Hero"

Historian Robert Hill asserts that "It is the contention . . . that *The Black Jacobins* would have been significantly different in quality in the absence of James's relationship to Robeson."[98] Hill attributes Robeson's intellectual range combined with his corporal stature as the force for James's shattering a British colonial conception of Black masculinity. Perhaps Robeson's total being dismantles what George Lamming, in another context, called "the colonial structure of awareness which has determined West Indian values."[99] Hill writes, "At a very profound and fundamental level, Robeson as a man shattered James's colonial conception of the Black physique. In its place the magnificent stature of Robeson gave to him a new appreciation of the powerful extraordinary capacities which the African possessed, in both head and body. Robeson broke the mold in which the West Indian conception of physical personality in James had been formed."[100] James refutes Hill's prescient observation in the typescript of his autobiography subtitled *Robeson*: "Hill is quite wrong when he says that Robeson shattered my West Indian conception of physical personality. We had people taking part from Guyana in Olympic Games and winning."[101] It is not my task to adjudicate between these statements but to point out that the gap between assertion and correction is generative, like the distance separating a sketch of a loved one and his/her actual self. Via a quick detour fragment (Bertolt Brecht's *Stories of Mr. Keuner*),[102] I want to attempt to think through Hill's insight by contrasting two pieces of writing by James on his exemplar of Black heroism, Paul Robeson: a private letter dated 5 January 1944 to Constance Webb[103] and James's Robeson tribute published in *The Black World*.

This is one of the aphoristic, didactic *Geschicten* (stories) in the Brecht collection:

> *If Mr. K. Loved Someone.*
> "What do you do," Mr. K. was asked, "if you love someone?"
> "I make a sketch of the person," said Mr. K.,
> "and make sure that one comes to resemble the other."
> "Which? The sketch?" "No," said Mr. K., "the person."

Brecht's insight introduces a discussion of the discrepancy in judgment witnessed when contrasting James's semiprivate criticisms of Robeson (in his letter to Constance Webb) with the open and aboveboard appreciation essay. At stake here is not only a representative revolutionary masculinity couched in James's description of his friend but also a matter of emblematic representation. To apply Brecht's insights to James and Robeson also raises the question of romantic love as it exists in the fragment. It is not a question of implying some sort of physical intimacy between the two individuals; rather, it is to note erotics scripted into James's remarks. Brecht posits a theory of ideal types and how one should take idealizations of a desired love object seriously as a material force in one's perception of the actuality of that figure. The sketch for Brecht (in what on the surface seems like a counterintuitive reversal) holds the weight of transformation here. I take this premise seriously when examining James's assertion that "Paul Robeson was and remains the most marvelous human being I have ever known or seen."[104] James commences his appreciation with a testimonial to the magnitude of the man. James lauds this "sporting hero" in the sketch for the wide range of his professional pursuits, his immense strength and stature, and his active listening ability. He underscores Robeson's "immense power and great gentleness"[105] and notes that Robeson always listened attentively to the criticisms and suggestions voiced by him and Stage Society producer Peter Godfrey.

His active listening skills did not, however, detract from his ability to assert leadership. James once again underscores its centrality by introducing the Raynal speech (quoted in his article at length, proliferating its use from play, to history, to the Robeson sketch under discussion) to recall when Robeson actively suggests where to cut the monologue. Robeson becomes for James the new "absolute standard[s] of physical perfection and development."[106] I want to highlight how the appreciation lauds Robeson as idealized sketch and reproduces indirectly James's main point on Toussaint's tragic degeneration. The Robeson of James's essay is scripted as the exact opposite of a Toussaint who no longer "would leave the front and ride through the night to enquire into the grievances of the labourers, and though, protecting the whites, make the labourers see that he was their leader."[107] James uses the emphatic "Gone were the days" to drive home this point. James's focus on Robeson's physical stature, repetitive emphasis on his subject's combination mode of self-effacement and assertion, and his ability to engage generously with the thought processes of others, is the sort of Brechtian sketch that outlines the idealized promise and potential of the desired object, in this case Robeson. In James's rhetorical universe, both Robeson and Toussaint work as a subtle synecdoche for the promise and potential of a liberated Black Nation. The essay in its flattering tone is out of sync with other appreciations James penned on comparable leaders of the Black liberation movement.[108] Compare the public appreciation with the semiprivate musings in James's modality as Il Postino (the amorous letter writer as political educator, Neruda in Michael Radford's 1994 film), via a letter to Constance Webb, an actress he courted for a decade in a series of correspondence ripe with political and aesthetic insights.

The occasion for this letter from James to Webb is the actress's interest in pursuing the role of Desdemona. Again, James resorts to the sort of older gentleman/schoolteacher tone when counseling Webb on the aesthetic and political implications of Shakespeare: "I think I understand something about Sh[akespeare]. I want you to know what I think."[109] James, as a Marxist confident in his mastery of Shakespeare, argues that the English playwright is seldom understood. For James, the mastery of rhythmic discipline as well as tonal control and the innovation demonstrated by the aesthetics of both Beethoven and Shakespeare are subject to the insult of attempts by the novice. Compared to the public sketch, the letter's tone referring to Robeson's performance of *Othello* (opposite Uta Hagen)[110] is uncompromisingly hostile:

> You see, I saw the Othello. It created a tremendous stir here. In my opinion in, particularly Paul R, was lousy. Not one of them, except at odd moments, had the Shakespearean rhythm—not one. I was shocked because Margaret Webster and Uta Hagen were both trained in England. To hear John Gielgud or Edith Evans is to hear a miracle of rhythmic beauty *and* naturalness. Without the first, there is no Shakespeare.
>
> Robeson was rotten. He is a magnificent figure, a superb voice, and as usual with him, at moments he is overwhelming. But in between his lack of training, his lack of imagination, were awful. For long periods he stood in one spot and *said* the lines, just said them. Dynamic development of the part, there was none except the crudest. And Shakespeare is dangerous for the amateur. Without strong feeling you slip immediately into melodrama. A great actor gives a standing sweeping performance in effect, but every line means something. Every phrase can stand for itself. It is built up into a whole. For long periods Robeson lacked grip. I knew he was just going on, to shout at the climax. I wish I could see it with you two or three times. How I would love to. Then I'd tell you what I think and you'd help put me right.[111]

James faults the actors for failing to decouple lines and in their individual iteration of such lines show how they build off one another. Phrases standing alone, yet "built" into the whole," is a significant aesthetic analogue to his overtly political concern pertaining to what individuals and combination of social forces make radical change possible. It is striking to note that in his point about diction and performance, James foregrounds the question of genre. He faults the actors for denigrating generically the play to the status of melodrama. James proceeds to laud the political import of the play in its bold depiction of love between a black man and a white woman: "*Politically* it is a great event. It was also very interesting, I could see it often again. It was a distinguished performance, and Robeson's remarkable gifts and personality were very much worth watching. But the play on the whole fell short." In the private correspondence, James's language betrays a certain intention to court Webb more than to offer a critique of the performance. How else to make sense of the combination of such a bold declaration of his knowledge of the subject and advice to the young actor coupled with this throwaway line about how if she were able to view the production with him perhaps she might "help put me straight"? That is pure flirtation rather than the request for an intellectual interlocutor. His entire tone of the piece is not of a thinker looking for further clarification. The letter's momentum turns on a notion of expertise, the mastery of rhythm for the Shakespearean actor, an expertise according to James desperately lacking in Robeson.

In the public appreciation sketch, Robeson's magnitude is built up via reflections on his stature, awesome intelligence, and largesse of generosity, wherein the semiprivate rumination a narrow assessment of skill rules the day. In this regard, coupling these two meditations on Paul Robeson work to help illuminate a sort of indirect relationship to the "tragic" iterations on the liberation of San Domingo. The awesome potential in the appreciation pushed up against the lament of failed technical mastery balances the sort of precarious footing occupied by Toussaint. Seemingly, Toussaint must assert his power in relation to the French and the planter class on the island while still being dependent on their technical skill. For the James that sees the conditions of socialism already in the factory, one might concur that whatever mastery needed to succeed is within the grasp of the exenslaved Africans and can expand infinitely once the fetters of colonialism are forced off and independence seized. It is odd to witness James pen a sort of rigid projection about the specific skill set needed to accomplish a given task—whether revolution or Shakespeare, especially since this skill set as conceived by James is so dependent upon Europe. He is shocked at Webster and Hagen's mediocre performance since they were both trained in England. I am not trying to argue for a dismissal of James's semiprivate writing on the grounds of a rigid Eurocentric elitism. Anthony Bogues offers the following helpful insights on Hill's observations:

> It is here that the intricate connections between a philosophical framework grounded in one tradition and a critique of that tradition burdened by many assumptions of the dominant discourse are strikingly revealed. For even Marxism as a radical social and political critique of colonialism and imperialism encoded assumptions about personhood that were rooted in the European Enlightenment. Therefore when James becomes a Marxist his conceptions of personhood were inherited from this tradition—one in which the distinction between "primitive" and "civilized" persons had already been embedded. James had a long way to go to come to terms with the distinctive African contributions to human civilization.[112]

The aesthetic ruminations on Robeson specifically and the Shakespearean acting craft in general work to both double the thematic concerns constituting James's Haiti period and complicate a sense of James's development in thinking as going beyond the need for revolutionary leadership (his line on the vanguard party, for example). Instead of synthesis, it is more precise to say that the gap between the two perceptions might be read as a stand-in for the sort of tragic gesture captured in both the historical study and play version of *The Black Jacobins*. A Glissantian gap, if you will. Instead of trying to resolve this issue, it seems more productive to see how for James it always hangs in the balance when reflecting on questions of leadership in the revolutionary process, when thinking through firsts and repetition of beginnings.

Firsts/Repetition

> The problem of beginnings is one of those problems that, if allowed to, will confront one with equal intensity on a practical and on a theoretical level.
>
> Edward W. Said

> Leopards break into the temple and drink all the sacrificial vessels dry; it keeps happening; in the end, it can be calculated in advance and is incorporated into the ritual.
>
> Franz Kafka

The literature on beginnings and repetition is too vast to attempt summary.[113] Not surprisingly, my thoughts on the matter are deeply indebted to the interventions of African American literature scholar James A. Snead: specifically, his essay "Repetition as a Figure of Black Culture." Snead develops Black culture in its figural repetition and proclivity toward incorporating accident and rupture. In other words, Black culture's rhetorical tropes and philosophical pedigree possess thoughtful strategies to deal with leopards and the empty vessels left in their wake:

> The discourse used in capital in European economic parlance reveals a more general insight about how this culture differs from black culture in its handling of repetition. In black culture, repetition means that the thing *circulates* (exactly in the manner of any flow, including capital flows) there

in an equilibrium. In European culture, repetition must be seen to be not just circulation and flow but accumulation and growth. In black culture, the thing (the ritual, the dance, the beat) is "there for you to pick it up when you come back to get it." If there is a goal (*Zweck*) in such a culture, it is always deferred; it continually "cuts" back to the start, in the musical meaning of "cut" as an abrupt, seemingly unmotivated break (an accidental *da capo*) with a series already in progress and a willed return to a prior series.

A culture based on the idea of the "cut" will always suffer in a society whose dominant idea is material progress—but "cuts" possess their charm! In European culture, the "goal" is always clear: that which always is being worked towards. The goal is that which is reached only when culture "plays out" its history. Such a culture is never "immediate" but "mediated" and separated from the present tense by its own future-orientation. Moreover, European culture does not allow "a succession of accidents and surprises" but instead maintains the illusions of progression and control at all costs. Black culture, in the "cut," builds "accidents" into its *coverage*, almost as if to control their unpredictability. Itself a kind of cultural *coverage*, this magic of the "cut" attempts to confront accident and rupture not by covering them over but by making room for them inside the system itself.[114]

"European culture" as abstract whole might not encourage thinking "a succession of accidents and surprises" but certainly savvy traditions of dialectical materialism build their whole conceptual edifice around such reversals and detours. As Said writes in *Beginnings*: "A revolutionary like Lenin is especially sensitive to left-wing communism because he knows reversibility as power and as limit, not simply as unconditional desire or phrase making."[115] Snead's felicitous phrasing—"a succession of accidents and surprises"—is a useful way to think revolution. Reversibility, accident, and zigzag are part revolutionary contingency and part studied resolve. They become inevitability only after the fact of their completion. What the various archival and performative turns toward the Haitian Revolution do is reactivate this generative dance of contingency and inevitability.

A 1967 typescript version of C.L.R. James's play *The Black Jacobins* includes a most illuminating epilogue in which "the scene is a private room in a hotel somewhere in an underdeveloped country."[116] James scripts a debate on revolutionary tactics between contemporary non-aligned leaders. He specifies that Speakers A, B, C, and so forth be played by the same actors who played Toussaint, Christophe, Dessalines, and so forth. Their respective pronouncements apply to a twentieth-century Bandung-like context but reverberate the positions of their Haitian combatant precedents. The most lucid and most militant character sports an eye patch (signaling Moïse). Echoing Brecht's suggestion that his actors disaggregate their own individual identities from the role they are playing and make such disaggregation visible to their audiences, James forces us to think the connection between the protagonists of the preceding Haitian revolutionary drama alongside the epilogue's non-aligned voices. Neatly conflating Speaker A, B, C with Toussaint, Christophe, Dessalines would problematically short-circuit the interpretive operation James insists. He scripts Speaker A, B, C, not Toussaint2, Christophe2, Dessalines2, Moïse2. The repetition here claims resonance and relation between the views of Haitian combatants and non-aligned leaders, yet that relation is precisely not one of accrual. The repetition-repertoire that is the Haitian Revolution both assumes and problematizes a sense of origin and beginnings. Taken as a whole, such a sequence of repetitions does not "accrue" in the same way financial portfolios accrue. It is the strength and clarity of Snead's thought that provide a framework to think repetitions of the Haitian Revolution that amass and not only refuse to accumulate and interrogate the very logic of capital accumulation. Perhaps this is what Michelle Cliff's *Abeng* is getting at in her ethical imperative: "only to be gathered not sold."[117]

* * *

In summation, Robeson's body in performance carries the weight-shattering colonial mythologies of Black docility challenged in both dramatic and historiographic versions of *The Black Jacobins*. The body onstage of a singular Black radical intellectual helps solidify the strategic priorities and theoretical commitments of a key text analyzing a Caribbean past in order to think about a radical future for the African continent. Both the play's subject matter and its conditions of performance mirror the commitment to Black internationalism of James's Pan-Africanist London milieu. The play undermines its main actor's virtuosity by staging his actions as constitutive of a collective. It is not only the figure and intellectual weight of Paul Robeson that dictated the final outcome of James's landmark historical study. The vocabulary and challenges of dramatic staging spill into the history and influence the key constitution of its categories. James's London play signals a lifelong attempt of its author to show how the representation of individual revolutionary strivings is only intelligible as part of a collective movement.

3

Tragedy as Mediation
The Black Jacobins

Mr. C.L.R. James, and through him I learned how an underground movement worked.

Kwame Nkrumah

For Lenin, on the other hand, *compromise is a direct and logical consequence of the actuality of the revolution.*

Georg Lukács, Lenin: A Study in the Unity of His Thought

C.L.R. James Looks at St. John the Baptist Preaching

Sometimes the building blocks of what Cedric Robinson calls Black radicalism's "ontological totality"[1]—"the collective consciousness informed by the historical struggles for liberation"—are constructed from stone and marble. In 1932 when C.L.R. James departed for his first trip to the United Kingdom,[2] he was tasked to write a series of vignettes on British culture and society for *The Port of Spain Gazette* (Trinidad). In London's Victoria and Albert Museum he saw Auguste Rodin's sculpture *St. John the Baptist* (Fig. 3.1). James writes: "I sat and watched it and when the body is still the mind moves."[3] James's concedes here to intellectual work the radical force of motion, somewhat separate but still tethered to the still body. *St. John* is a bronze work, sculpted larger than life, that Rodin initially began to model in 1877. A naked and svelte St. John the Baptist stands atop a small bronze pedestal, walking *still*, right arm bent/finger pointing slightly up, perhaps evoking French Jacobin painter-theorist Jacques Louis David's death-defiant philosopher in his 1787 oil canvas *The Death of Socrates*. This encounter with Rodin provokes questions of temporality, embodiment, and identification that for James sustain decades of political praxis. Rodin's sculpture is larger than life. This flies in the face of the compression fate of many Rodins. Art historian John Berger writes

Figure 3.1: Rodin, *St. John the Baptist*, 1881. Presented to the Museum by a Committee of Subscribers. © Victoria and Albert Museum, London.

of "the compression ... [Rodin's] figures suffer."[4] Rodin's technique of bodily compression and hyperextension, analyzed in the writings of his assistant Rainer Maria Rilke (both his study *Auguste Rodin* and novel *The Notebooks of Lauridis Brigge*), resonate with C.L.R. James's reflections on his lead actor Paul Robeson, who for James is an embodied synecdoche of Black revolutionary aspiration. In the larger-than-life figure of Robeson, a whole philosophical and aesthetic register of Black radicalism is compressed. Hazel Carby's scholarship is a conceptual bridge linking the question of scale in Rodin to a 1925 series of Robeson photographs. Nickolas Murray's photographic images in Carby's analysis attempt to capture a naked Robeson in cramped, compressed spaces.[5] James's early perception of *St. John the Baptist* introduces the problem of arranging bodies and staging the interdependence between an individual and a mass of bodies imperative to the problem of leadership in the Haitian Revolution. The figurative violence done to bodies in Rodin's sculptures (the violence of compression and hyperextension) is a thought catalyst for a young Trinidadian intellectual who charts his own radical political roadmap by dramatically staging the philosophical calculus of acts of violence against and on behalf of Haitian revolutionary bodies. A seed is planted for James that dialectically links sculptural compression (the force of reduction) with the multiplicity of uses of the Haitian Revolution (the force of proliferation). Despite *St. John's* compositional, formal largesse exceeding the human body's proportions, Rodin compresses a theory of mental labor in his sculpture. A long nineteenth-century explosion of freedom in the French colony of San Domingo distills and sharpens the Rodin sculpture for James, who translates its affect into a play. I present James looking at St. John's naked body in discussion with a cluster of radical thinkers (John Berger, Franz Fanon, and Hazel Carby) who take seriously nakedness as a site for political thought.[6] C.L.R. James's observance of Rodin's *St. John* has no easy, formative relationship to his Haitian Revolution work. Rather, what follows is speculative—an inventory of resonances between a brief encounter with a sculpture and a lifetime preoccupation with a revolution.

"Naked Declivity" Versus "Nude"

Rodin's *St. Jean-Baptiste Prêchant* (1878)[7] defies mimetic representation by design. It is fashioned larger than life in response to critics who accused Rodin of using body-casts for his sculpture *The Age of Bronze* (1876). Corporal aggrandizement in *St. John* makes legible in sculptural representation mental gears turning. Compressed in its sculptural largesse is a whole theory of thought in motion. Rodin explained to his friend Paul Gsell that the paradoxical still movement in his figure's steps signifies attitudinal flux: "Note, first, that movement is the transition from one attitude to another."[8] This resounds with what C.L.R. James calls in his *Notes on Dialectics* ideological leaps.[9] Rodin notes: "It is, in short, a metamorphosis of this kind that the painter or the sculptor effects in giving movement to his personages. He represents the transition from one pose to another—he indicates how insensibly the first glides into the second. In his work we still see a part of what was and we discover a part of what is to be."[10] The quick transitions and glides are a result of rehearsal and constant preparation. When James visited the Victoria and Albert Museum's Rodin exhibit, his perceptions of Rodin's sculptures were most likely curated by captions from Rainer Maria Rilke. In his 1903–1907 study of Rodin, Rilke offers a way to think about dramatization of revolutionary pasts that thematically intersects with the endeavors of James's Haiti writings. Rilke's musings are Deleuzian in their language of becoming and emphasis on the proliferation of use: "This simple becoming-concrete of its longings or its apprehensions. . . . An artistic whole must not necessarily be identical with the usual thing-whole, that, independent of it, there arises within the picture itself new unities, new associations, relationships and adjustments."[11] "Longings" recall how far desire propels artist-intellectuals mining Haitian revolutionary pasts for their own use. Indeed, complex staging and restaging of the Haitian Revolution produce "new unities, new associations, relationships and adjustments." Yet it is perhaps problematic to use insight from sculpture (a fairly permanent and stable aesthetic form) to illuminate the work of drama (in its fleeting performative register). Shifting between the specific protocols for thinking these different artistic genres presents a challenge that requires a theory of mediation to avoid short-circuiting the complexity of such a task: "Rodin has always shown this power of lifting the past into the realm of the permanent when historical characters or facts seek to live again through his art."[12] The arrangement of bodies onstage helps bridge the gap between the ephemeral and the permanent constituting the relationship between performance and sculpture arts. This gap or lacuna also holds true for Haitian revolutionary drama and how it negotiates pasts and presents. A permanence of reference, a historical reserve, the Haitian Revolution is re-accessed, its fleeting nature as performance defied each time an artist stages its historical becoming. Here is what Rilke had to say about the sculpture that caught James's attention:

One might describe this movement by saying that it rests enclosed in a tight bud. Let thought be set on fire, let the will be swept by tempest, and it will open. And we have that *John* with the eloquent, agitated arms, with the great stride of one who feels another coming after him. This man's body is not untested: the fires of the desert have scorched him, hunger has racked him, thirst of every kind has tried him. He has come through all and is hardened. The lean, ascetic body is like a wooden handle in which is set the wide fork of his stride. He advances, advances as though all the wide spaces of the world were within him, as if he were apportioning them with his spread, seeming to make the sign of striding forward in the air. This *John* is the first pedestrian figure in Rodin's work.[13]

Here is what C.L.R. James said about the sculpture:

John the Baptist Rodin called it, but it is no more John the Baptist than I am John the Baptist. It is a statue of a naked man walking, that's all, neither more nor less, and Rodin was persuaded to call it *John the Baptist*. But all that is irrelevant. The only thing that matters is the statue. In the basement of the British Museum are plaster-casts of the *Apollo Belvedere* and the *Venus de Milo*, but on the Day of Judgement, the twentieth century will be able to look the old Greeks in the eye and say, "We admit that yours are the best, but . . . " and then produce the Rodin. No one who sees it can pass it by. That is one thing with the plastic arts. You need some training in literature, and more in music, but any fool who will take the trouble to look can see a picture or a statue. I was dreadfully tired out but the thing made me fresh again.

Ours is not the only age of scientific enterprise and multitudinous organization. . . .

Browning was speaking of a girl, but there are other things than girls that make the blood burn. The Rodin statue is one. I sat and watched it and when the body is still the mind moves. I reflected that a Greek who lived two thousand years ago could have sat with me and watched. He would have seen it with much the same eyes and feelings that I did. But the Schneider plane would have been meaningless to him. Three thousand years from now, some wanderer from the West Indies will walk down Exhibition Road. He will go into the Science Museum and see the latest thought-plane. (That vanished type of conveyance, aircraft, will be represented by models.) Will he see Lieutenant Stanforth's plane? Only as one of a crowd of obsolete designs.

But in the Art Museum he will see the statue of the man walking. It will be to him as it is to me. It cannot grow old. It cannot go out of date. It is timeless, made materially of bronze but actually, as has been said of great literature, the precious life-blood of a master spirit.

That is why though I shall sometimes visit the Museum of Sciences it will always be on my way to the Museum of Art.[14]

C.L.R. James evacuates Rodin's *St. John* of all its particularity—the joke is on us and for James "it is no more John the Baptist than I am John the Baptist." Such evacuation happens on the level of proper name. The sculpture represents an almost transhistorical representation of "man" on the move, a representation that by way of its formal qualities is accessible to all. No training needed. Its accessibility, its universality trumps technological innovation. The Schneider plane is "meaningless" to the two-thousand-year-old Greek but the Rodin "make[s] the blood burn." Rilke's exposition links earthly suffering with the formal detail of the finished product: tests by fire and hunger are legible on the figure's body itself. The chisel writes on the figural body an archive of world-historical suffering. Such suffering is emplotted in the bronze. The artisan-cutter is often thought of as exhibiting radical (albeit individualist negating) agency, enacting the ultimate legibility, a high-stakes sort of writing on the body. Rodin's chisel writing on the body is subject to a series of misinterpretations in terms of its attribution. It is neither the after-effects of the artistic master nor the possessive individualist property of the sculpted figure itself. It is rather a ledger of world-historical suffering misread as either artistic genius or individualist destructive resolve. This world-historical attribution, in the last instance, does not negate the individual genius; it *confirms* it. The chisel writing on the figural body is penned by the world but never recognized as such. So—it flees. *St. John* is more maroon than Walter Benjamin's flaneur. His stride is not light and easy. His stride anticipates the chase, anticipates the flight from those in pursuit. "The first pedestrian figure in Rodin's work" registers a litany of earthly suffering, tragic suffering if you will, and that litany is captured, heightened, and reflected by the formal mastery and care of the sculpture-artist. The earthly suffering in this formulation mandates formalist attention. It is the foregrounding of process in Rodin, the unwillingness to cover up the blips, the re-routings, the so-called mistakes and dialectical zigzags along the way. As Rosalind E. Krauss states, Rodin's sculptures are "riddled with the accidents of the foundry."[15]

This intersects with Hazel Carby on the aforementioned photographs of Paul Robeson: "Though the body is in repose, the tense muscles, the enlarged veins of the right arm and hand, and the light playing on his heels and curled toes indicate that, at any moment, this man could spring into action and become a force that could not be contained."[16] *St. John*'s stillness of body signifies intellect in motion. This is a helpful reminder when considering how Modernist representations of Paul Robeson analyzed by Carby want to lock his subject's meaning in a bodily frame. Yet the body and mind escape. My interest in Robeson's stature is not to reinstate the body as prime site of significance, at the expense of intellect. Rather, it is to emphasize that even sculptural, portraiture, and photographic form signify movement in all their glorious stillness. Coupling John Berger's gendered opposition between naked and nude with Charles Lam Markmann's translation of Fanon's formulation "naked declivity" clarifies.

Frantz Fanon writes in *Peau noire, masques blancs*: "Il y a une zone de non-être, une region extraordinairemeent sterile et aride, une rampe essentiellemnt dépouillée, d'où un authentique surgissement peut prendre naissance."[17] Markmann translates this as: "There is a zone of nonbeing, an extraordinarily sterile and arid region, *an utterly naked declivity* [emphasis added], where an authentic upheaval can be born. In most cases, the black man lacks the advantage of being able to accomplish this descent into a real hell."[18] *Une rampe*, a ramp, slope, or incline; *essentiellemnt*, basically, mainly, essentially; *dépouillée*, meaning bare translates as "naked declivity." I will restrict my observations here while acknowledging that there are surely pages to glean from this formulation. First, it is unclear that the descent is unwanted, as much as it is unclear the nature of the impediments blocking the plunge into such a fiery descent. Perhaps the morbid conditions Fanon analyzes in the pages that follow account for such a lack. Descent is desirable since that is where "an authentic upheaval can be born." Surely there is much in *Black Skin, White Masks* that requires upheaving. Naked is the precondition of upheaval and revolutionary reorganization. Nakedness is the precondition for escaping the overdetermined Modernist racial calculus that confuses *photographically* capturing Robeson's body with *actually* capturing his body. I relate this to John Berger's meditation on gendered perception in the fine arts; whereas to be naked is to be without clothes for oneself and to be [implied female] nude is to be naked for the pleasure of the [implied male] gaze:

To be naked is to be oneself.

To be nude is to be seen naked by others and yet not recognized for oneself. A naked body has to be seen as an object in order to become a nude.
(The sight of it as an object stimulates the use of it as an object.) Nakedness
reveals itself. Nudity is on display.

To be naked is to be without disguise.

To be on display is to have the surface of one's own skin, the hairs of
one's own body, turned into a disguise which, in that situation, can never
be discarded. The nude is condemned to never being naked. Nudity is a
form of dress.[19]

For Berger, objectification and display are preconditions for use. Refusing to decouple Fanon with Berger acknowledges that both radical
thinkers privilege nakedness as a site of critical thought. Certainly to
be for oneself and not *solely* for another constitutes a requirement for
authentic upheaval. Carby's analysis of escape in the Robeson nudes
should remind Berger that optimism is never entirely foreclosed and
condemnation is never entirely final. Coupling Fanon's gendered male
champion of nakedness as prerequisite for revolt with Berger's gendered
schema in which women are locked into a prison of their nudeness at the
expense of their nakedness requires a theory of mediation. This theory
of mediation, or articulation, must think through the intersecting regi-
mens of race and gender, viewer, and viewed. On this problem in C.L.R.
James, Hazel Carby writes: "In Captain Cipriani as well as in his cricket
journalism, [C.L.R.] James sought to develop a theory of a direct, unmediated relation between the heroic male figure and the people, a theory
which used a cultural aesthetics of body lines in direct opposition to the
modernist strategies of cultural producers like Muray or Macpherson,
who regarded themselves as necessary mediators and interpreters of
art."[20] Thinking alongside and against this assertion of desire for unmediated relation poses the problem of mediation and revolutionary leadership as an open and central question animating C.L.R. James's Haiti
writings.

James famously writes in the preface: "In a revolution, when the cease-
less slow accumulation of centuries bursts into volcanic interruption, the
meteoric flares and flights above are a meaningless chaos and lend themselves to infinite caprice and romanticism unless the observer sees them
always as projections of the sub-soil from which they come."[21] How can
such projections that emanate from the subsoil speak to the dynamism of

sculpture and pedestal, sculpture and relief? Here is Rosalind Krauss on sculpture and relief:

> Relief, as we have seen, suspends the full volume of a figure halfway between its literal projection above the ground and its virtual existence within the "space" of the ground. The convention of relief requires that one not take literally the fact that a figure is only partially released from its solid surrounds. Rather, the ground of relief operates like a picture plane, and is interpreted as an open space in which the backward extension of a face or a body occurs.[22]

"Partial release" is a problem. Encountering sculpture in general, and Rodin in particular, for James is a productive laboratory to think the dialectical interdependence of binding and escaping, grounding and transcendence, base and superstructure, suspension and independence, virtual and actual. Krauss's "partial release" resonates with Hazel Carby's concern about Paul Robeson's ability or inability to escape a Modernist racialist representational calculus. Sculpture's base and figure foregrounds a heightened attention to the politics of spatial topography central to James's Marxist method. An interpretation of mediation in Rodin is in tension with James's thoughts.

On Rodin's 1880 bronze sculpture, *Adam*, specifically its "unintelligibility" related to discourses on the self, Krauss theorizes: "a belief in the manifest intelligibility of surfaces . . . that entails relinquishing certain notions of cause as it relates to meaning, or accepting the possibility of meaning without the proof or verification of cause."[23] She expounds on how meaning occurs within experience as a framework to think about what Rodin is up to. For Krauss, the antimimetic properties of Rodin's body sculptures prohibit an immediate identification between subject (viewer) and object (sculpture) that corresponds with the anatomical parity between observer and observed object. Rodin's enacted critique of mimesis does not allow for an understanding of meaning that precedes experience. Rather meaning happens within and alongside experience:

> If this observation is transferred to the realm of sculpture, it would seem that a sculptural language can only become coherent and intelligible if it addresses itself to these same underlying conditions of experience. I know that certain contractions of muscles in my face occur when I experience pain and therefore become an expression of pain, a representation of it, so to

speak. I know that certain configurations of the anatomy correspond to certain acts I perform, such as walking, lifting, turning, pulling. Thus it would seem that the recognition of these configurations of the anatomy correspond to certain acts I perform, such as walking, lifting, turning, pulling. Thus it would seem that the recognition of those configurations in the sculptural object is necessary for the meaning of that object to be legible; that I must be able to read back from the surface configuration to the anatomical ground of a gesture's possibility in order to perceive the significance of that gesture. It is this communication between the surface and the anatomical depths that Rodin aborts. We are left with gestures that are unsupported by appeals to their own anatomical backgrounds, that cannot address themselves logically to a recognizable, prior experience within ourselves.[24]

This is a helpful lens to think a fundamental tension in C.L.R. James's thinking—a tension visible in his newly arrived in London commentary on Rodin's sculpture. James's understanding of *St. John* as universal man walking short-circuits mediation. There is almost a willed immediate identification here. His commentary refuses to concede to the antimimetic aspects of Rodin's sculptures of bodies in motion, vying instead for a sort of radical political humanism, an almost transhistorical representation of man on the move. This signals a lifelong tension in James's thinking: he wavers between insisting on a dialectical complex inventory of the various mediating levels that inform phenomena and a countermove insisting on immediate (unmediated) significance. Sometime he encourages thinking the various forms of political and aesthetic meaning, other times he short-circuits his dialectical savvy and claims immediate identification: *St. John* is "just a man walking."

Mediation and Immediacy in C.L.R. James

Mediation "in a literal sense . . . refers to establishing connections by means of some intermediary."[25] "The contrast between mediation and immediacy is itself an opposition that requires mediation, and the result of this, Hegel argues, is that nothing is purely immediate or purely mediated: everything is both at once."[26] Consider this example of the acorn and the oak:

> An acorn is mediated, as well as immediate, since it is the result of a previous cycle of growth, and the oak is immediate, as well as mediated, since it has a definite present character that can be described without explicit

reference to its relations with other things or to the process that led up to it. Something that lacked all immediacy would be nothing but a cross-section of a process or the intersection of a set of relations, with no intrinsic nature of its own. Something that lacked all mediation would have nothing but an intrinsic nature, with no relations to anything else and no process leading up to it; it would not even have an intrinsic nature, since all DETERMI-NACY depends on mediation.[27]

This metaphor is pedagogically lucid. Oaks and acorns recall Brecht and Kafka's forest variety of tree trunks. My own sense of mediation comes from Georg Lukács's 1926 essay "Moses Hess and the Problems of Idealist Dialectics." Lukács's task is to put forward a critique of philosopher Moses Hess and fellow travelers, a circle of militants called the "true socialists." He faults Hess's attempt to move beyond Hegel's alleged analytical caveat to stay rooted in the present. Hess's attempt to go beyond Hegel only places him in a position where he trails behind. This is not a judgment on his fidelity to proletarian struggle; rather, it is a judgment on the coherency of his philosophical categories. By overstating the claims of Hegel's quiescent accommodation with the present and by desiring to transcend it, Hess abandons the philosophical rigor that insists on some kind of mediated relationship between present and future—a mediation that Hegel, even in his limitations, was well poised to notice. Lukács understands Hegel's temporal definition of philosophy ("time translated as thought") as a deep reckoning with *what is*:

> That Hegel stops at the present is related, as I have already indicated, to the most profound motives of his thinking—to be precise, in his (in the correct sense) historico-dialectical thinking. For instance, in the preface to his *Philosophy of Right* he writes: "The task of philosophy is to comprehend *what is*, for *what is* is reason. As for the individual each is *child of his time* anyway; philosophy, too, is *its time translated into thought*. It is just as stupid to imagine any philosophy can transcend its contemporary world as that an individual can jump over his time, jump across the Straits of Rhodes."[28]

This is of paramount importance for thinking about the relationship between *actual* presents and ameliorative futures. In James one finds a constant calibration and recalibration, a constant toggling between the possible and the impossible, the actual and the speculative.

Throughout his life, the only two choices for James would remain either socialism or barbarism. However, the tasks needed to realize the more favorable of the two options, as well as the agents privileged to get it done, are constantly rethought. His "Dialectical Materialism and the Fate of Humanity" (1947) introduces this concern for the dialectic and the concept of mediation. Written nine years after the release of *The Black Jacobins*, it represents the twilight hour on James's faith in successful radical mediation between leader/party and mass (not the same as an abandonment) yet, simultaneously, an apex in his faith in the masses to transform their lives. Composed during his "American period," the combination of witnessing the creative spontaneity of the American working class with the collective theoretical labors of his breakaway renegade Trotskyist group, the Johnson Forest Tendency, pushes James toward almost repudiating the need for mediation all together. I want to back up a little to preserve mediation as a generative problem:

> Toward the end of the 1940s the members of the Johnson Forest Tendency began to publish the results of their intensive collaborative exercise. The lengthy essay, *Dialectical Materialism and the Fate of Humanity* (1947) was James's attempt to sort out some of the muddles in Trotskyite thinking—in particular the problem of thought and its relationship to the dynamic of history. He was seeking to clarify the dialectical method—the process by which, what Hegel called the abstract universal becomes concrete; and to demonstrate, through its use as a methodological tool, the progressive movement of society. It is one of the very few places, too, that James offered a definition of socialism—the complete expression of democracy—mindful as he always was of its distortion through identification with Stalinism.[29]

The Stalinist terror his piece decries is proof of the Russian Revolution's specific effectiveness and confirmation of the radical insistence on universality by the masses of Russian workers and peasants. The masses' forward movement is both simultaneously complete and partially realized such that only a counteroffensive as grisly as the Moscow trials could hope to quell its energies by way of party structure mediation. The essay gives an account of how James views both Hegel and Marx's formulation of the dialectic and how that concept gets employed by James as an analytic capable of capturing revolutionary movement in history. Here we see an introduction of terms that will remain pivotal in the formulation of James's analytic toolbox: negation, the whole, the universal, the real, totality, and, most important for our sake here, mediation. The revolutionary process is captured the following way: "The history of man is his effort to make the abstract universal concrete. He constantly seeks to destroy, to move aside, that is to say, to negate what impedes his movement towards freedom and happiness. Man is the subject of history . . . the fact that man as such is 'pure and simple negativity' . . . is a cardinal principle of dialectical movement."[30]

James applies his sketch of Marxian and Hegelian dialectics to the example of the rise of the institutionalized Christian Church in Europe, its consolidation as a mediating institution that pacifies the demands of its radical toilers: "The Christian revolutionaries, however were not struggling to establish the medieval papacy. The medieval papacy was a mediation to which the ruling forces of society rallied in order to strangle the quest for universality of the Christian masses."[31] The Church mediated the more radical demands of the mass and in doing so demonstrates how such mediation contained and diluted their radical energy. Such insights on the development of religious institutions ring true for secular politics whereas "democratic politics, like religion, was a form of mediation by which men gained the illusion that they were all members of one social community, an illusion of universality."[32] The series of revolutions charted in the work signify the ongoing effort of the people to realize the universalism latent and manifest in the theological/philosophical promise of a Christian Kingdom of Heaven on earth. In this framework, "man" constantly negates a particular, actual set of oppressive conditions and in this action achieves a new universality in terms of realization of true freedom. As E. San Juan Jr. writes, James "holds that the dialectic of concrete and abstract embedded in the logical principle of universality has been short-circuited by Hegel's idea of mediation. These mediations are symptoms of the failure to grasp the truth as the whole: not only in human actions but also in people's needs and aspirations."[33] For James, this is an ongoing, permanent process of movement. Mediation works as a device to convey a certain lack captured in the disjuncture between the stated goals of universal freedom for all and the limitation of such universal freedom to a small, privileged class. James states his understanding of mediation in the writing of Hegel as the following: "The new state established after the revolution, the ideology which accompanies it, are a form of mediation between the abstract and concrete, ideal and real, etc." In cataloguing this revolutionary process, for James the agency of the masses frustrates the need for mediation whether in the form of the state and its accompanying bureaucracies or in the form of the revolutionary party: "The quest for universality, embodied in the masses, constituting the great mass of the nation, forbids any mediation."[34] For James mediation is defined as a bridge concept that paradoxically links while simultaneously expressing a gap between the ideal statement of a revolutionary vision and its concrete actuality—the gap between Brecht's *amour* and his sketch-drawing.

The Black Jacobins represents a more nuanced hope for the possibility of effective mediation. The text's formal construction as well as its theme render it more optimistic about the positive effects of mediating forces in revolutionary processes. The narrative structure of *The Black Jacobins* in its formulation of the tragic backs up a bit from his essay's aversion to mediation to tell the story of how this specific protracted revolutionary process turns on Toussaint L'Ouverture, a key figure mediating the wants and creative energy of the Haitian people, strategic expediency, and long-haul vision. *The Black Jacobins* in the trajectory of James's political thought is an early major attempt to theorize the relationship between leader and base. It is such blockages between these two forces, the failure to harmonize mass sensibilities and positions with the revolutionary strategy as dictated from above that is the source of the exploration on the tragic as mediation in this work.

It is helpful to gloss Raymond Williams's discussion of mediation in his study *Keywords: A Vocabulary of Culture and Society* (1983). Williams's work examines, through an alphabetic presentation of a "vocabulary" of cultural and sociological analysis, how "the most active problems of meaning are always primarily embedded in actual relationships, and that both the meanings and the relationships are typically diverse and variable, within the structures of particular social orders and the processes of social and historical change."[35] Hence the study is referred to as a "vocabulary," not a dictionary. Speaking on the complexity of the concept of mediation in its current usage, Williams charts its variants: "(1) the political sense of intermediary action designed to bring about reconciliation or agreement; (2) the dualist sense, of an activity which expresses, either indirectly or deviously and misleadingly (and thus often in a falsely reconciling way), a relationship between otherwise separated facts and actions and experiences; (3) the formalist sense, of an activity which directly expresses otherwise unexpressed relations. It can be said that each of these senses has a better word: (1) *conciliation*; (2) IDEOLOGY OR RATIONALIZA-TION . . . (3) *form*."[36] Tragedy is a form that speaks to the intermediary role of leadership in framing an agenda for radical transformation.

James's method of analysis, its understanding of tragedy, is too attuned in its understanding of "what it is" to be dogmatically or Romantically swept away with the "what it can become." At the same time, *The Black Jacobins* is a dexterous presentation of the interdependence between leadership and a mass base that subverts both a heavy-handed authoritarian revolutionary leader prescription and the inverse—an anarchistic, idealistic notion that leadership is not crucial to bridge and mediate the gap between what *is* and what *is possible*.

For James, tragedy from the onset is always informed by mass struggle in both its conditions of performance and content. Tragedy in James's formulation is interesting precisely because of its root as a key ritual of Athenian democracy involving the direct and active participation of the masses. Even before its use is underscored in the revisions of his text on Haiti,[37] tragedy is lauded for its mass affiliation. James emphatically states this point in a June 1953 letter to a literary critic:

> A tremendous popular production in which the people themselves were vitally interested and settled who should win the prizes. I would like to mention, by the way, that Plato for certain, and I think Aristotle also, fumed with rage at the role the masses of the people played in all this. If they had had things in their hands, they would not have organized anything like the masterpieces that have come down to us. The power came from the Athenian democracy. When democracy declined the great Athenian drama declined with it.[38]

The great tragic tradition in Elizabethan drama collapsed as soon as the price of admission increased from a penny to a six-pence. The price increase relates to the newness of such modern artistic technological innovations as film:

> In the early days of modern film, in the days of Chaplin, D. W. Griffith and the early Keystone comedies, you had a new art being shaped and its foundations laid in much the same manner that the Greek and Elizabethan tragedians laid the foundations of their drama. The movies were new, as new as Aeschylus was new. They were a genuine creation—they had no models to go by. To succeed they had to please the people.[39]

Expertise in judgment is not coupled with education level in James's understanding of the intimate relationship between dramatic tragedy and the masses of people. He proposes the following challenge to his interlocutor: "How educated were the Greeks who shouted and stamped and gave

Aeschylus the prize thirteen times?"[40] Tragedy for James couples mass approval with aesthetic judgment. The linking of developments in film technology with Greek and Shakespearean tragedy highlights the other key component of tragedy: newness. In a 1953 essay entitled "Notes on *Hamlet*," James underscores the effectiveness of tragedy to foreground the struggle between new and old:

> A recent critic has said that Shakespearean criticism is a jungle, a wilderness and a forest; and the wildest part is the jungle of modern criticism on *Hamlet*. Mr. Redgrave says that of the great tragedies *King Lear* is the only one in which two ideas of society are directly confronted and the old generation and the new are set face to face, each assured of his own right to power. This is false. All the great tragedies deal with precisely this question of the confrontation of two ideas of society and they deal with it according to the innermost essence of the drama—the two societies confront one another within the mind of a single person.[41]

In one warring body and mind, Toussaint attempts to reconcile the emergent new promise of revolutionary France with France's persistent colonial legacy of betrayal and enslavement. The aspirations and upsets of Jacobin France combine with the aspirations for a liberated San Domingo and wreak havoc in the mind of James's historical protagonist. The combination sparks a tragic wavering and waffling. Toussaint's Prince of Denmark affliction is not an idealistic symptom restricted to the mind; it is a response to a concrete changing political landscape in which the failed promise of revolutionary France collides head-on with the aspirations of Toussaint's Black Jacobins. In James's analysis of Shakespearean tragedy, the arc of the form dictates that the drama of two confronting societies plays out in a specific individual.

James in his attention to the particularity of the Haitian revolutionary struggle identifies a key problematic of Black radical aesthetics and thought. Consider these two assertions about the relationship between temporality and revolution. The first is what I see as a central tenet in Fred Moten's work that thinks the transformative resources of Black radicalism = Black Art. The second is a prescription on Marxian temporality and the new by Fredric Jameson: (1) We already have everything we need. (2) "If there is to be a new form of life it must be happening all around us right now. It has to be disengaged from the things that limit it."[42] Two theorizations of the future in the present that resonate with the set of reading protocols implied in James's Haiti writings—the Haitian Revolution as theatrical labor and feats of formal mastery that surpass the limitations of the Kantian "ought."

The study and practice of literature sometimes prefigured but always informed C.L.R. James's political praxis as a revolutionary Marxist. Constitutive of this political journey is a progressively heightened faith in the capacity for everyday working people to radically transform their lives, without reliance on intermediary forces. A protracted study of Greek and Shakespearean dramatic tragedy and the English novel tradition both helped James to consolidate such priorities. Quiet at study in Queens Royal College's Masters Room, young Trinidadian scholar Cyril Lionel Robert James read the complete work of William Makepeace Thackeray. In her reflection on her colleague James's intellectual development, Anna Grimshaw credits the work of Thackeray as "the central feature of his mature political vision, as he moved away from any attachment to notions of specialized intellectual or political leadership and increasingly recognized that people themselves were the animating force of modern civilization."[43] The illustrated novels of Thackeray, according to Grimshaw, helped solidify what critic E. San Juan Jr. calls "the mass line in C.L.R. James's works."[44] With equal zeal, both Greek and Shakespearean tragedy constituted James's literary diet. Cedric Robinson cites James's reminiscence: "I laughed without satiety at Thackeray's constant jokes and sneers and gibes at the aristocracy and at people in high places. Thackeray, not Marx, bears the heaviest responsibility for me."[45]

James's engagement with literature and sport demonstrated a consistent care to attend to the desires and potentialities of the masses of people—whether in a Trinidadian, Pan-Africanist, or North American context. *Beyond a Boundary*,[46] his cricket study published the same year as the reissue of *The Black Jacobins*, phrases this most significant question for James the revolutionary as "What do Men Live By?" Traces of a tragic form negotiate the tension between the leader and the base in his study of the Haitian Revolution—*The Black Jacobins: Toussaint L'Ouverture and the San Domingo Revolution*. He adds further tragic emphasis in his additions to the 1963 iteration of his text via an Aristotle-inspired concept of the tragic modified to signify the communicative degeneration between leader and base in a revolutionary upsurge. Toussaint is scripted by James as a figure of mediation balancing the radical demands of the Haitian people striving to be free with the strategic vision needed to realize such demands. As such, his leadership is compromised by not sufficiently communicating policy and rationale directly to his base, thus placing his saliency as a leading organizational force in jeopardy. If a mass insistence on universality is mediated through the actions and directives of individual leadership, the constant communicative dialectical push and pull between leader and base must be maintained. The baggage of various choices in narrative emplotment is imperative here—a point that David Scott's scholarship brings to bear on an understanding of James.

On David Scott's Conscripts of Modernity: The Tragedy of Colonial Enlightenment

> "I have noticed," said Mr. K., "that we put many people off our teaching because we have an answer to everything. Could we not, in the interests of propaganda, draw up a list of questions that appear to us completely unsolved?"
>
> Bertolt Brecht, *Stories of Mr. Keuner*

David Scott argues that the 1963 reprinting of *The Black Jacobins* replaces its Romanticist-vindicationist narrative mode with a more sober tragic narrative emplotment. I propose that perhaps the tragic existed in James all along, existing in motion and in history—a suggestion made possible by Scott's own rigorous work. What Scott calls the "problem-space"—the tension between leader and base—is still relevant to the task of breaking the double bond of imperialism and monopoly capitalism. The elite poetics/mass politics contradiction of the text helps James formally reproduce and emphasize Toussaint's challenge. It is the hinge that connects *The Black Jacobins'* form and content. Scott's, via Talal Asad's "conscripts of modernity," is a lasting bind constitutive of the Black Radical Tradition.

For Scott, "Toussaint is imagined not only as a newly languaged Caliban, but as a modernist intellectual, suffering like Hamlet, the modern fracturing of thought and action."[47] I propose that Hamlet's paralysis is actually a question of Hamlet's radical thought—active and in motion. As Lacan intones, "Hamlet's strange apathy belongs to the sphere of action itself."[48] *The Black Jacobins* "takes Shakespeare's Hamlet to stand as a paradigm of tragic figuration. If for James that melancholic and obsessively self-regarding Prince of Denmark symbolized the emergence of a new kind of individual, the modern intellectual, I suggest similarly, for James, Toussaint inaugurates a new kind of individual, the modern colonial intellectual."[49] Scott does not evoke the Hamlet of Malcolm X's Oxford Union Presentation address on the need for revolutionary violence to rupture a status quo of suffering: "Taking up Arms Against a Sea of Troubles." He instead looks to a Hamlet that observes that our concept of time "is out of joint." This is congruent with Scott's desire to make a specific argument about narrative, choice, political will, and temporality: that the questions a study raises are only sensible within the specific time of their posing. James's original preface's reliance on a Coleridge's/Wordsworth's Romantic sensibility, his 1963 additions to the text underscoring Toussaint's "tragic" mistake, and his 1963 appendix "From Toussaint L'Ouverture to Fidel Castro" all rest on a set of temporally specific concerns of the author participating in his historical moment both as narrative presentation and historical transformation. A passé problem-space poses a challenge, a thoughtful provocation for those who still desire some sort of Pan-Africanist (anti-imperialist) and proletarian radical transformation. This logic of problem-space (not necessarily Scott's study) implies that the revolutionary centered horizon modified from Sartre is yesterday's business. Yet to be defeated does not equate to being surpassed. The historicizing rigor of Scott's political periodization—in other words, the problem-space—does not carry over into his literary periodization: the opposition between romance and tragedy. In a sense it's a problem of mediation. Michael McKeon's insight into the work of Northrop Frye resonates here: "So far from enabling a theory of literary history, Frye's modal periodization freezes history into an immobile 'literary structure.'"[50] Literary modes are transhistorical; genres are historical. Genres can rise and fall and come and go—like empires or dinosaurs. Genres subtly refract and capture the interplay of residual and emergent properties and developments. Scott's problem-space foregrounds the specificity of discrete political conjunctures with great sensitivity but his aesthetic categories (Romance and Tragedy), in their transhistorical status as literary modes, undermine such a thoughtful procedure. Perhaps it is this contradiction that makes *Conscripts* so awesome in its generativity.

Problem-space is identified as the "discursive context" for scholarly intervention: "A problem-space, in other words, is an ensemble of questions and answers around which a horizon of identifiable stakes (conceptual as well as ideological-political stakes) hangs."[51] Problem-space is a "necessarily temporal concept." Scott criticizes postcolonial scholarship's engagement with James for how it anachronistically claims questions from an earlier anticolonial period—questions and answers cannot be successfully uncoupled. This is surely a hallmark of dialectical method. Evoking Hayden White he notes that "forms of narrative . . . have built into their linguistic structures different myth-models or story-potentials . . . different stories organize the relationship between past, present, and future, differently."[52]

For Scott, James in *The Black Jacobins* employs two ways of storytelling: Romantic Vindicationist and a later tragic emplotment. Tragedy "sets before us the image of a man or woman obliged to act in a world in which values are unstable and ambiguous. And consequently, for tragedy the relationship between past, present, and future is never a Romantic one in which history rides as triumphant and seamlessly progressive rhythm, but a broken series of paradoxes and reversals in which human action is ever open to unaccountable contingencies and luck."[53] Scott argues that "*The Black Jacobins* is, above all, a literary-historical exercise in revolutionary Romanticism. . . . A modernist allegory of anticolonial revolution written in the mode of a historical Romance."[54] It employs writing as vindication and is tasked to reclaim and demonstrate the agency and ability of masses defamed by racist historiography. In the text's reprinting, James tempers Romantic vindication with a more tragic tone, one more conducive to subtle meditations on the relationship between agency and necessity, the way that actions are limited by conditions. He borrows the title object from Bernard Yack's *The Longing for Total Revolution* and labels as such the main motif of anticolonial Romance, a category that includes both James's *The Black Jacobins* and Fanon's *The Wretched of the Earth*. Scott signals the addition of seven beginning paragraphs in the latter version of *The Black Jacobins*' chapter 13, "The War of Independence," as constituting the new tragic tone. Note the contrast between Romantic and Tragic modes of storytelling:

> Where the anticolonial narrative is cast as an epic Romance, as the great progressive story of an oppressed and victimized people's struggle from Bondage to Freedom, from Despair to Triumph under heroic leadership, the tragic narrative is cast as a dramatic confrontation between contingency and freedom, between human will and its conditioning limits. Where the epic revolutionary narrative charts a steadily rising curve in which the end is already foreclosed by a horizon available through an act of rational, self-transparent will, in the tragic narrative the rhythm is more tentative, its direction less determinative, more recursive, and its meaning less transparent. I mean to suggest, in other words, that tragedy may

offer a different lesson than revolutionary Romance does about pasts from which we have come and their relation to presents we inhabit and futures we might anticipate and hope for. If one of the great lessons of Romance is that we are masters and mistresses of our destiny, that our pasts can be left behind and new futures leaped into, tragedy has a less sanguine teaching to offer. Tragedy has a more respectful attitude to the past, to the often-cruel permanence of its impress: it honors, however reluctantly, the obligations the past imposes. Perhaps part of the value of the story-form of tragedy for our present, then, is not merely that it raises a profound challenge to the hubris of the revolutionary (and modernist) longing for total revolution, but it does so in a way that reopens a path to formulating a criticism of our present.[55]

There is a vindicating thread that runs through the narrative arc of the text. As James made abundantly clear, there was an entire school of racist historiography that he was challenging in his study on Haiti as a trail-blazer of Pan-African resistance. It would be a tough sell to completely dismiss the need still for this critical spirit. Moreover, all versions of *The Black Jacobins* present Toussaint and the Haitian masses as calculating, pragmatic, and strategic in their resistance, tempered in their political judgment. This is hardly a sort of pure Romanticist plot of swooping victory of good versus evil. Furthermore, is not obvious that Romanticist plotlines are themselves that simple. James and Toussaint are always attuned to the actuality of the situation at hand—and in their own fits of gothic flourish, many Romantics were as well.

James's study is not a study in search of Total Revolution as its desired object—it posits a specific theory on a specific struggle and relates it to his present concern for a radical future for a decolonized Africa (1938) than disappointment in the failure of the newly Caribbean nations to success-fully join in Federation (1963). Indeed this is Scott's argument. It posits a tragic problematic, the interdependent relationship between leader and base. Scott's theoretical and textual acumen is the condition of possibility for these assertions. It is almost as if Yack's liberalism, the force of its nar-rative emplotment (the baggage of Yack's liberalism), results in an overem-phasized differentiation between Romanticist and Tragic modes in James. A framework reliant upon transhistorical literary modes will find "total revolution" as an object. Their likeness aligns—the modal and the total.

Donald Pease offers a concise assessment of Scott's project: "We inhabit a historical conjuncture in which the modern national-liberationist project is no longer hegemonic. But the paradigm that would supplant it has not yet appeared."[56] If indeed we are in a sort of *Il Gattopardo* Gramscian interregnum space where the old has not died and the new has not yet been born, minimizing the complexity of the old will not hasten the arrival of the new. Only a dialectically rigorous and unrelenting revisiting and reuse of the old has a winning chance in generating something new—aesthetic categories need to be historicized concurrent with political-historical context and content. Relevant to this task, Edward W. Said applies a Gramscian lens to Lampedusa's novel *The Leopard*: "'If we want things to stay as they are,' we have already heard Tancredi saying to his disapproving uncle, 'they will have to change.' Tancredi is very much like Napoleon's nephew in Marx's *Eighteenth Brumaire*, a man whose ascendancy depends on the exploitation of a class of people like Tancredi's father-in-law, Calogero: people who want the association with aristocracy as an entrée to power."[57] Radical traditions should be supplemented by critique and generously engaged in order to retain what is useful and to discard what is not. "In the interests of [Brecht and Herr Keuner's] propaganda," David Scott's meticulous scholarship generates a useful list of questions. My only wish, evoking his study's categories, is that we both could occupy an earlier problem-space where we could argue these questions in a fraternal space of radical organization.

"To Make the Natives Buy Lancashire Goods": *The Fold in Defense of Abyssinia*

Caribbean specialist Alex Dupuy asserts that *The Black Jacobins* retains "its status as the classic Marxist statement on the Haitian Revolution as one of the most authoritative interpretations of that momentous history from any perspective."[58] Through his participation in George Padmore's International African Service Bureau, James joined an ensemble of Pan-Africanist activist-intellectuals to condemn Mussolini's 1935 invasion of Ethiopia.[59] Championing Ethiopia's self-determination is a key issue in which James coalesces around an intellectual and activist milieu that includes George Padmore, Paul Robeson, J. B. Danquah, and Amy Ashwood Garvey. This is the intellectual community and action-based milieu for which James pens *The Black Jacobins*. James embraces armed struggle as tactical preference for his Pan-Africanist colleagues. The composition of the book, from the outset, is part of a collectivist struggle, which attempted to intervene in defense of an Abyssinia threatened by fascism. The book helps clarify the political vision of the International African Friends of Ethiopia and provides a theoretical foundation for their agitation. Robert Hill makes this point explicitly in speaking about the initial version of the text:

> Within the specific context of the changing balance of political forces in the world at the time, the International African Service Bureau was debating the political course which the African struggle would follow. *The Black Jacobins* was probably the most important factor in the evolution of the strategic perspective of the group, which became the premise that *armed struggle* would be the form of the African revolution.[60]

C.L.R. James situates Toussaint in the midst of the French and American revolutions. As he states in the bibliography of the revised edition: "It is impossible to understand the San Domingo revolution unless it is studied in close relationship with the revolution in France."[61] He designates French Revolution scholarship as the "greatest schools of Western civilization, [combining] scholarship with the national spirit and taste, and with respect for the Revolution without which the history of the revolution cannot be written." James inserts himself into a larger continuum of French radical historiography that includes Michelet, Lefebvre, Aulard, Mathiez, and Jaures. Michelet, referred to as "the spirit of the Revolution," is designated by James as "the best preparation for understanding what actually happened in San Domingo."[62] By inserting himself into a preconstituted tradition of French historians, James establishes himself as inheriting a previous school of historiography and, more important, mimics the transatlantic movement via scholarship that Toussaint and his colleagues experienced in praxis. This layering of traditions is in effect a kind of layering of folds: Toussaint and his comrades act upon and reverberate throughout the Atlantic world, James retroactively enlists and extends classical dissident French revolutionary historiography. Just as the French Revolution and Haitian Revolution are coupled for Toussaint, James refuses to separate himself from French schools of historiography to pursue his exposition on Haiti. A heavily annotated ten-page bibliography charts his historical antecedents. Footnotes from Lefebvre's two-volume study of the French Revolution make up a large part of James's text. Lefebvre and Michelet are James's descendants in actuality, but this is only so if and when James claims them. Perhaps this is the feat of fold that the Black

Radical Tragic enacts in the book: one that links with aplomb actuality with a kind of archival voluntarism. *The Black Jacobins* mediates between two activist intellectual communities: the ensemble of Pan-Africanists struggling in London against Italian fascist incursions into Abyssinia and the school of mostly socialist French historians pivotal to James's study. Such mediation generates branches of mediation, linking struggles in the Soviet Union to the Caribbean to Franco's Spain to republican revolutions in Europe to anticolonial wars vying to clarify a radical understanding of democracy. If triangulation is a way to geometrically map the narrative structure of *The Black Jacobins* (wherein the three points connect Haiti, Jacobin France, and the Soviet Union), a consideration of the African decolonial contexts of the text encourages proliferations. This formal layering effect partially accounts for not only the work's enduring influence but also the work's enduring use. A multiplying effect of triangulated folds.

The Eighteenth Brumaire *of C.L.R. James*

Getting together in London and meeting over a period of two to three years on a fairly regular basis afforded me the opportunity that I, and a number of other people were seeking—to acquire a knowledge of Marxism, a more precise understanding of the Russian Revolution, and of historical formation.

One of the most important things which I got out of that experience was a certain sense of historical analysis, in the sense that C.L.R. James was really a master of the analysis of historical situations. It was not enough to study Lenin's *State and Revolution*. It was important to understand why it was written and what was going on in Russia at the precise time. It was not enough to study Lenin's *What Is to Be Done*. One must understand the specific contextual nature of the discussions that were going on in Russia at this time. This comes to my mind because I feel that a lot of the debates that do go on about Marxism are definitely out of context. People pull from texts without knowing the history of those texts and the [context] of the debates in which they were located. One thing is certain about C.L.R. James—he has mastered a whole range of theory and historical data and analysis. This explains why he was very good at focusing in. The group might do some reading and try to

understand what a text says. But James gave it that added dimension
which nobody else in the group could easily acquire in being able
to say: this is what Lenin was about; this is what Trotsky was doing;
he had just come from this conference or this debate, or this was his
specific programmatic objective when he was writing, and so on.

                                                      Walter Rodney

In his discussion of Haitian president Faustin Soulouque (1782–1867)
and the allusion to him in Karl Marx's *The Eighteenth Brumaire of Louis
Bonaparte and his "shady characters,"*[63] Laurent Dubois deconstructs the
farcical fashion in which Soulouque is framed in many accounts of Haitian governance, including Marx's essay.[64] *The Eighteenth Brumaire*[65] is a
masterful piece of philosophically infused political reportage analyzing
Napoleon III's coup d'état of December 1851. It is a rejoinder to two other
accounts: Victor Hugo's *Napoléon le Petit* and Proudhon's *Coup d'État*. Its
form as political reportage demands conjunctural specificity and detail.
Its close readings, its philosophical insight, its dialectical reversals, the
acrobatic shifts in form and content, its piercing of pomp and artifice
in service of demonstrating the actuality of petit-bourgeois class bias all
come to fruition by way of Marx's unrelenting historicizing.

As Brian Meeks argues,[66] James directly cites Marx's *Eighteenth Brumaire* only once in *The Black Jacobins*. This is when James explains the
"common derivation of prejudice, small whites, big whites, and bureau-
cracy [that] were united against Mulattoes."[67]

> Upon the different forms of property, upon the social conditions of exis-
> tence as foundation, there is built a superstructure of diversified and char-
> acteristic sentiments, illusions, habits of thought, and outlooks of life in
> general. The class as a whole creates and shapes them out of its material
> foundation and out of the corresponding social relationships. The individ-
> ual in which they arise, through tradition, and education, may fancy them
> to be the true determinants, the real origin of his activities.[68]

Dr. Walter Rodney's gloss of C.L.R. James's study group's pedagogic and
critical reading strategy poses an interesting challenge when thinking
about how James engages *The Eighteenth Brumaire of Louis Bonaparte*.
Unlike his usual method of dialectical historicization and contextualization, James vis-à-vis *The Eighteenth Brumaire* employs a rhetorical tactic
of unmediated application and direct substitution.

James directly employs Marx's theory of individual agency versus histori-cal necessity from *The Eighteenth Brumaire of Louis Bonaparte* (1851–1852)[69] when he states in the 1938 *preface to the first edition* of *The Black Jacobins*:

> Great men make history, but only such history as it is possible for them to make. Their freedom of achievement is limited by the necessities of their environment. To portray the limits of those necessities and the realiza-tion, complete or partial, of all possibilities, that is the true business of the historian.[70]

Through his extended musings on Toussaint, "the first and greatest of West Indians," a careful reader can note the crystallization of James's entire critical method: "Yet Toussaint did not make the revolution. It was the revolution that made Toussaint. And even that is not the whole truth."[71] He will repeat this formula in his 1963 additions on tragedy in reflections on such Pan-Africanist luminaries as Kwame Nkrumah, Fidel Castro, and Kwame Ture/Stokely Carmichael[72] and direct his confidence in the revolutionary potential of men and women from the "sub-soil," rethinking both Leninist theories of organization and the struggle for Black self-determination. This balancing act between an individual pro-tagonist and his or her accompanying social base animates James's study. Further on:

> In a revolution, when the ceaseless slow accumulation of centuries busts into volcanic eruption, the meteoric flares and flights above are a meaning-less chaos and lead themselves to infinite caprice and romanticism unless the observer sees them always as projections of the sub-soil from which they came. The writer has sought not only to analyse, but to demonstrate in their movement, the economic forces of the age; their moulding of society and politics, of men in the mass and individual men; the powerful reaction of these on their environment at one of those rare moments when society is at boiling point and therefore fluid.[73]

The analysis is the science and the demonstration the art which is history.[74]

This is the heart of history's dialectical motion, which informs James's reflections and praxis on behalf of Black radical struggle. It helps him clarify the work of the tragic in his latter addition of the text: "He was now afraid of the contact between the revolutionary army and the people, an infallible sign of revolutionary degeneration."[75] The tragic for James is a mark of revolutionary degeneration. It marks the point when the leader loses touch and stops communicating with his base. At another moment in the *preface*, James writes of "The transformation of slaves, trembling in hundreds before a single white man, into a people able to organize themselves and defeat the most powerful European nations of their day" and abruptly shifts the focus by stating, "By a phenomenon often observed, the individual leadership responsible for this unique achievement was almost entirely the work of a single man—Toussaint L'Ouverture."[76] These lines act as primer on how to read the Haitian Revolution and (more important for our sake) how to underscore the formal considerations of James's text. James chides Romanticism as a mode of emplotment for revolutionary exposition from his 1938 vantage point. Furthermore, he chides it by name: the "infinite caprice and romanticism." Here we see the same kind of Raymond Williams prerogative to think the tension between colloquial and academic understanding of tragedy, this time applied to understandings of romanticism. The *preface* is a primer to understand the methodology in the formal presentation that will follow in his book. San Domingo society, its class structuring, its landscape, its antagonisms, and, most important, its masses of people are the subsoil that the critic ignores at his or her peril. The chapter progression of "The Property," "The Owners," and "Parliament and Property" sets us up for a properly grounded understanding of the fourth chapter, "The San Domingo Masses Begin," and the fifth, "And the Paris Masses Complete." The entire subsoil prefigures the sixth chapter, "The Rise of Toussaint." Here is a mode of historical exposition in need of mediation, apparent in the organization of the work itself; yet such mediation curiously short-circuits when it comes to James's evocation of the methodological insights of Marx's text.

During one of James's Montreal lectures, his proposed suggestions for reading *The Eighteenth Brumaire* defy his own historicizing rigor. A logic of direct substitution trumps dialectical contextualization. There is no anxiety of influence about directly employing "poetry of the past" here. He glosses the document and contextualizes its insights, supplementing lines from the text with additional material from Marx, most notably his correspondences, demonstrating the readerly care signaled in Walter Rodney's appreciation. Yet in the conclusion of James's talk, entitled "Marx's *Eighteenth Brumaire of Louis Bonaparte* and the Caribbean," James favors overt crudeness. He directly substitutes the proper names of twentieth-century Caribbean politicians for Marx's nineteenth-century examples:

Well, I think, if you don't mind, ladies and gentlemen, we have covered the *Eighteenth Brumaire*. I haven't gone into it in detail—that would have been quite absurd. But I have selected certain points in which stand out, and I have rather crudely made the application to the Caribbean. It may sound a bit crude, but it isn't. Do you know why? Because in 1848 and 1851, France, a backward country—underdeveloped, so-to-speak—was making the transition to the modern state. We in the Caribbean are making the same transition, so that what he [Karl Marx] writes here has an extraordinary application to what is happening to us and you cannot understand what is taking place in the Caribbean in particular, and in various other underdeveloped countries, unless you have a proper view of economics, historical analysis, and political developments.[77]

But why turn to Marx for this triple-methodological threat of economics, historical analysis, and political analysis? Earlier in the talk James presents problematic sweeping dismissals of the caliber and actual existence of the methodological foundations of Caribbean intellectual thought. He asserts that "The West Indies have no method of history"[78] and that "The West Indian reactionaries today have no slogan."[79] Both of these assertions can be easily challenged and James knows as much. So what does he accomplish here? At a certain point in the talk James references a letter from Marx to an American friend that specifies the two central qualities of polemic as "both coarse and fine."[80] There is a way in which James models the very advice he cites from Marx. Coarse (and untrue) dismissals of Caribbean methodological insights and their rigor, blanket refusals to acknowledge how the Caribbean political field in the twentieth century constitutes its categories via its own slogans that exist alongside more nuanced (fine) contextualization of both French reactionary nineteenth-century landscapes and twentieth-century Caribbean politics. Use here for C.L.R. James trumps all. *The Eighteenth Brumaire's* dialectical savvy is utilized to frame the dialectical savvy of *The Black Jacobins*. James will repeat this logic of direct substitution in his 1977 study of Kwame Nkrumah, this time by way of another nineteenth-century source: Dostoyevsky's 1880 Moscow address on Pushkin. James offers extensive citation from this address with the following caveat: "The only thing to do is to quote various passages, and the reader is asked himself to substitute Africa wherever Dostoyevsky says Russia."[81] Fredric Jameson by way of Sartre's distinction between *category* and *notion*, a distinction that hinges on a question of temporality sheds light on this dual usage: "Althusser, like

Foucault, limits himself to the analysis of structure. From the epistemological point of view, that amounts to privileging the *concept* over against the *notion*. . . . The concept is atemporal. One can study how concepts are engendered one after the other within determined categories. But neither time itself nor, consequently, history, can be made the object of a concept. There is a contradiction in terms. When you introduce temporality, you come to see that within temporal development the concept modifies itself. *Notion*, on the contrary, can be defined as the synthetic effort to produce an idea which develops itself by contradiction and its successive overcoming, and therefore is homogenous to the development of things."[82] James's interpretive praxis flexes dialectical savvy and a notional attention to temporality, but when the day demands a *coarse* rule of direct substitution, conceptual use reigns supreme.

"Every Cook Can Govern"—James's Engagement with Aristotle

Tragedy mediates between the protagonist and the polis, the leader and the chorus, the individual and the base.[83] Kara M. Rabbitt brilliantly captures James's play on Aristotle: "James appears to make full conscious use [in *The Black Jacobins*] of Aristotelian tragic structure, allowing a mimesis of the historical events of the Haitian Revolution to point toward the universals regarding the fall of colonialism and repressive hegemonic systems that he will underline in his 1938 conclusion and the 1963 appendix."[84] Key to my entire project is this tension between what Rabbitt argues as "a materialist analysis of history and a portraiture of a powerful individual."[85]

Toussaint's tragic "revolutionary degeneration" does not involve a sort of convenient grafting of one set of terms from a different time period to make sense out of a latter phenomenon. James's employment of Aristotle marks a *repetition with a difference*. His working with Aristotle's categories modifies such categories. For Aristotle, the hamartia or tragic flaw as sketched in his *Poetics* relates to the requirements for his formulation of the tragic hero—"a man who is neither a paragon of virtue and justice nor undergoes the change of misfortune through any real badness or wickedness but because of some mistake . . . of great weight and consequence."[86] What constitutes tragedy in the last instance for Aristotle is its reception—tragedy is a recognition engine. It produces an identification with the hero (hence the hero cannot be too lofty) that produces a catharsis among the audience, a safety valve sublimating the polis's angst.[87] James's hamartia is not about a transgression of morality—rather, it is a tactical failure. The Aristotelian tragic structure outlined in *Poetics* differs from James's formulation that distinguishes between analysis as science versus art/demonstration as history. For Aristotle, poetics/art is superior to history since it is the narrative mode that speaks in universals and is most suited for speculative thought. James's sees dialectics as a process in which "you speculate, you create truth"[88] and shares an affinity with Aristotle's *Poetics*:

> It is also clear that the poet's job is not to report what has happened but what is likely to happen: that is, what is capable of happening according to the rule of probability or necessity. Thus the difference between the historian and the poet is not in their utterances being in verse or prose; the difference lies in the fact that the historian speaks of what has happened, the poet of the kind of thing that can happen. Hence Poetry is more philosophical and serious business than history; for poetry speaks of universals, history of particulars.[89]

James embraces both Aristotle's and Hegel's commitment to the project of systemic totality. James is critical of literary criticism for not integrating "piled up . . . mountains of information" into any "coherent system or method" and claimed unflinchingly that his "ideas of art and society . . . like specifically literary criticism, are based upon Aristotle and Hegel."[90] Its tragic configuration is *in excess of* Aristotle—since he "envisaged the entry of the chorus."

James's hamartia is less concerned with catharsis than it is with overcoming a problem in revolutionary organization that gets repeated across time:

> Toussaint had burnt his boats. With vision, courage and determination he was laying the foundations of an independent nation. But, too confident in his own powers he was making one dreadful mistake. Not with Bonaparte nor with the French Government. In nothing does his genius stand out so much as in refusing to trust the liberties of the blacks to the promises of French or British imperialism. His error was his neglect of his own people. They did not understand what he was doing or where he was going. He took no trouble to explain. It was dangerous to explain, but still more dangerous not to explain . . . it is no accident that Dessalines and not Toussaint finally led the island to independence. Toussaint, shut up within, immersed in diplomacy, went his torturous way, overconfident that he had only to speak and the masses would follow.[91]

Toussaint's state of being "shut up within himself" represents a challenge to conventional understandings of the role of radical leadership. Toussaint's error in judgment assumes a sort of static, mechanistic base that only awaits direction, in order to be mobilized. This stance presumes the sort of mass base that is powerless without mediation—an understanding James's study takes great strides to complicate. James's wording here marks his own rethinking of what constitutes the vanguard and his accompanying effort to move beyond such concepts. Toussaint is effectively silenced, incapable of speech at the point he fails to consult and consider his base. His pronouncements are inaudible without the masses as their condition of possibility. James confronts Toussaint's crisis in method:

> It was in method, and not in principle, that Toussaint failed. The race question is subsidiary to the class question in politics, and to think imperialism in terms of race is disastrous. But to neglect the racial factor as merely incidental is an error only less grave than to make it fundamental. There were Jacobin workmen in Paris who would have fought for the blacks against Bonaparte's troops. But the international movement was not what it is today and there were none in San Domingo. The black labourers saw only the slave owning whites. These would accept the new regime, but never to the extent of fighting against a French army, and the masses knew this.[92]

Tragedy is the frame that narrates the failed mediation between Toussaint and his base. It is historically realized in Toussaint's Haiti by his misdirected support for the white settlers:

> [Toussaint] still continued to favour the whites. Every white woman was entitled to come to all "circles." Only the wives of the highest black officials could come. A white woman was called madame, the black woman was citizen. Losing sight of his mass support, taking it for granted, he sought only to conciliate the whites at home and abroad.[93]

It is this strategic miscalculation that lays the path for the Dessalines's completion. Echoing his critique of Toussaint, James berates himself for errors in his own historiography's failure to negotiate the subtlety between revolutionary leader and base and sufficiently foreground the chorus. This has everything to do in this case with his criticism of his own use of the historical archive. James criticizes his use of the Swiss traveler Girod-Chantrans's description of a group of laboring enslaved

Africans. Instead of relying on secondhand sources in the historical archive, James in 1971 would "write descriptions in which the black slaves themselves, or people very close to them, describe what they were doing and how they felt about the work that they were forced to carry on."[94] He chides himself for reproducing the material from the perspective of "sympathetic observer" instead of a direct accounting from the subjugated masses themselves. Again a short-circuiting of mediation enacts a utopian desire to re-animate the Haitian revolutionary archive. James in a key summing-up moment of this talk revisits his use of a quotation from Pamphile de Lacroix, a soldier participating in General Leclerc's mission to San Domingo to restore slavery. Note how James uses repetition to drive home his point:

> But no one observed that in the new insurrection of San Domingo, as in all insurrections which attack constituted authority [as in all insurrections which attack constituted authority, all, ALL, A-L-L], it was not the avowed chiefs who gave the signals for revolt but obscure creatures for the greater part personal enemies of the coloured generals.[95]

The transcribers of these remarks typographically represent variations on the theme of all, ALL, A-L-L to further highlight James's rhythmic speech, his exacting, patient, yet slicing Trinidadian lilt. Through his repetition and explicit clarification ("Is that clear?") James declares the political stakes of his argument. James goes on to repeat again the key line in de Lacroix and extends the insight to a contemporary American setting, demonstrating its universal application:

> Now, I will read again from Pamphile de Lacroix: No one observed [but he did] that in the new insurrection of San Domingo, it was not the avowed chiefs who gave the signal for the revolt but obscure creatures. (They were not only in San Domingo obscure. They were obscure in Watts, they were obscure in Detroit, they were obscure in Newark, they were obscure in San Francisco, they were obscure in Cleveland, they were obscure creatures in Harlem.) They were obscure creatures, for the most part personal enemies of the coloured generals. Is that clear? And he says that in all insurrections which attack constituted authority comes from *below*.[96]

The Black Jacobins is first and foremost, in James's retrospective analysis, a tale of the ex-slaves as chorus—that force "in the Greek tragedy . . . decisive in the solution of the problem."[97] Tragedy is a device that not only accounts for Toussaint's failure to communicate and clarify his strategy to his base but also acts as a useful formal device in James's work. James's examination of Haiti presents a challenge of how to organize perception: What is the aesthetics of organization and the organization of aesthetics suitable to narrate Black radical movement? It is not enough to write a history privileging the entry of the chorus as foundation and anchor to make sense out of multiple perceptions. One has to create the organizational structure appropriate to actualize mass-driven systemic change. Through narrative choice and employment of a vocabulary of the tragic, James finds a vehicle to mediate between "The analysis is the science and the demonstration the art which is history." The peculiar syntax of this formulation captures how James is supplementing Aristotle. It is why in London James only stops into the science center en route to the art museum.

There is a tension between James's biographical presentation as a solitary "British intellectual" writing about revolutionary Haiti in London and spending hours in the Paris archives versus James as participant in a community of African activist-intellectuals intervening in such events such as the Italian invasion of Abyssinia. Santiago Colás beautifully illustrates James's tendency to process phenomena dialectically by weaving into a passage by Anna Grimshaw—the Hegelian dialectic of Sense-perception, Understanding, and Reason.

> First of all [this is the Sense-perception part], James has a remarkable visual sense. He watched everything with a very keen eye; storing images in his memory for over half a century, of distinctive personalities and particular events, which [now she moves to Understanding] he wove into his prose with the skill and sensitivity of a novelist. Although his passion for intellectual rigour gave a remarkable consistency to the themes of his life's work, his analyses were never confined. [finally, on to Reason] He was always seeking to move beyond conventional limitations in his attempt to capture the interconnectedness of things and the integration of human experience.[98]

James hones and sharpens his sense of revolutionary historical methodology through his extended study of Haiti. He acknowledges yet downplays this context for the work's production along with his pre-London radicalization. James treats his self-conscious political intervention inspired by a collective working toward African liberation as fortuitous oddity, a stumbling into the Parisian archives prompted by his grand literary designs: "I had made up my mind, for no other reason than a literary reason."[99] Santiago Colás captures the dialectical imperative articulated in James's formalist priorities:

> Dialectical thinking is thought to the second power, a thought about thinking itself, in which the mind must deal with its own thought process just as much as with the material it works on, in which both the particular content involved and the style of thinking suited to it must be held together in the mind at the same time.[100]

"Thinking about thinking" translates in *The Black Jacobins* as attention to the questions of form.

Sylvia Wynter's Pieza-Effect: The Production of Tragic Subjects

Thus far, we have been looking at the tragic in C.L.R. James's texts as a form of dialectical mediation. Primarily, the tragic is a modality that mediates the relationship in a revolutionary situation between leader and base. Sylvia Wynter's concept of "Pieza-Effect"[101] as it relates to James's *Beyond a Boundary* helps to further elaborate on James's uses of Aristotle's hamartia to explain the divide between leader and base. Wynter posits the Pieza, the general equivalence of value in the traffic and circulation of African slaves at the center of James "counter-poiesis." The Pieza was an enslaved African in optimal physical health that the traders from Portugal used as the abstract equivalent to judge the worth of other enslaved Africans at market. James's text in its organization and its constant mediations formally mirrors the gap between Toussaint and the Haitian masses. Sylvia Wynter posits an interconnection between aesthetic categories and political philosophy in James: "The Jamesian poiesis, taken as a system, the theoretics providing a reference for the esthetics and vice-versa, provides the condition of possibility for the emergence of a Jamesian doctrine, one that subverts its own center—the labor conceptual framework."[102] James's historical positioning as a British colonial subject in the Caribbean—"the ecumenicism . . . of being Caliban"[103]—produces and dictates the necessity of a pluri-conceptual frame to determine the question of who or what group constitutes a revolutionary agent: "Because of the multiple modes of coercion and of exploitation, the factory model was only one of many models. Thus there could be no mono-conceptual framework—no pure revolutionary subject, no single locus of the Great Refusal, no single correct line."[104] Wynter's piece fuses together politics with aesthetics. She highlights James's pluri-conceptual orientation and demonstrates how his categorical openness is dictated by both his aesthetic sensibility and his multiple historical groundings symbolized by the phrase "an intellectual wanting to play cricket."[105] "A pluri-conceptual theoretics, a universal-based on the particular [recall here Césaire] is the logical result and outcome of the Jamesian poetics."[106] Wynter helps to think about how the tragic underscores the sort of revolutionary subject constituting James's analysis.

Wynter commences her discussion of James's theoretical orientation through a detour on the literary production of subjectivity in the work of Pierre Macherey. *Pour une theorie de la production litteraire* (1966) extends Althusserian structural Marxism to argue for how production spills into all aspects of the society, creating autonomous laws of development specific to discrete objects of analysis: "The homology between the historical and the fictional universe is not realized at the level of a particular element but at the level of the system. It is the fictional system in its ensemble which produces an effect of reality."[107] For Macherey, Wynter argues: "the novel . . . is not the product of a doctrine, not the form-giving mechanism to an already pre-established content. It is, rather, the condition of possibility of the emergence of a doctrine." Aesthetic structures shape and determine the ideological matrix of the author's ideology. They do not reflect a one-to-one correlation between form and objective referent.

Here the Foucauldian insight that power creates subjects, instead of reflecting, is applied to literary forms. James, because of his specific theoretical tendencies and political concerns, does not go as far as Wynter, who advocates the "equiprimordiality of structure and cultural conceptions in the genesis of power" or that both (cultural/structural) aspects of power "serve as a code for the other's development."[108] James, as Wynter points out, cannot settle with a canonical labor-centric Marxian methodology. By unhinging a classical Marxist notion of production as the key turn for revolutionary agency and transformation, one is left with more room to theorize and narrate revolutionary movement and focus attention on subjects outside the classical Marxist kin of vision—women's struggles, Black self-determination, and so forth. The tragic not only narrates a pre-existing revolutionary problematic in James—mainly the degeneration of communication between leader and base—it also produces such a paradox formally in its very ideological structure, hence highlighting its urgency and priority. The Black Radical Tragic formal prerogative is a "quest for a [theoretical-informed, praxis-based] frame to contain them all"[109]—where "them all" constitute the multiple identities and competing subjective entry points of struggle particular for achieving Black self-determination. James does not share the post-structuralist suspicion of totality. His ecumenicism is wrapped up in his commitment to develop a sound method of categorization appropriate to adequately frame his particular research and praxis-based objects.

Wynter, like Immanuel Wallerstein's Worlds Systems approach, commences her analysis of the political economy by underlying her study with circulation/accumulation (of enslaved Africans objectified as commodities) instead of the classically Marxist notion of production that informs Macherey's analysis. The Pieza framework in Wynter accomplishes the following: it foregrounds the centrality of African labor in the development of European hegemony and opens up standard notions of what signifies production. Her article posits a single network of accumulation divided into three stages: (1) circulation for accumulation, (2) production for accumulation, and (3) consumption for accumulation. Each stage has its corresponding historical actors—African slaves, the working class, and the consumer. The international network of accumulation leads to a "differential ratio of distribution of goods and rewards with cultural legitimacy granted accordingly."[110] Such cultural legitimacy rations "also distort and minimize the contributions of various pieza groups to the process of global capital accumulation." Different Pieza groups mean different sites, opportunities, and actors of resistance to domination. Wynter grounds her theoretical claims in a historical interpretation wrapped up in twentieth-century Pan-African congressional politics. What she argues for as James's theoretical polyvalency informs her understanding of James's disassociation with the 1974 6th Pan African Congress in Dar Es Salaam. James's chiding of certain African revolutionary elites has to do with their eliding of questions of the popular in crafting their political agendas and making sense of the past. His "pieza orientation" helps James to align more with a sort of Fanonian identification with the peasantry. Wynter's text brings home the point that the poetic conception of James's study helps produce the very subjects his study chronicles.

My purpose in engaging Wynter here is to mark how James's framework signals an opening up that allows for the consideration of different subjects of focus in a revolutionary process. "The Counterdoctrine of Jamesian Poiesis" shares a critical spirit with Raymond Williams in that it opens up the received ideas that "no longer describe our experience." James's method makes room for the privileged entry of the chorus. His view from the "subsoil" allows him to register the Haitian masses in motion. In the tragic passages chronicled thus far in *The Black Jacobins*, it is demonstrated over and over again how James gives the masses of the Haitian people the privileged position of wisdom and revolutionary judgment, often outflanking the expertise of their leadership. However, in enacting this repeated phenomenon, the text underscores the need to keep the two forces in constant play—leader and base. Such an openness of methodology not only allows for James to archive but provides the impetus that allows for him to seek them out. The formal construction of *The Black Jacobins* in its chapter division, its prefatory framing, and its willingness to mediate art with analysis, leadership, and mass base formally demonstrate the sort of gap that requires such mediation. It does not shy away from pointing out the perils when tarrying with such gaps.

The Actuality of Revolutionary Violence

> In order to drive home the significance of this dismissal I have gone to great lengths of saying to public audiences that an unscrupulous head of government might find it necessary to shoot his Chief Justice while trying to escape, arrange for him to be run over by an errant motor lorry, have a bunch of doctors declare him to be medically unfit and, Kremlin-fashion, put him out of the way in an asylum, send him on a long holiday and beg the British government to make him a life peer on resignation, even invite him to dinner and poison him. But what a head of state does not do is to dismiss his Chief Justice after he has given a major decision on a matter in which the whole country is interested. *The very structure, juridical, political and moral, of the state is at one stroke destroyed, and there is automatically placed on the agenda a violent restoration of some sort of legal connection between government and population.*
>
> C.L.R. James, *Nkrumah and the Ghana Revolution*

Fifty ways to purge your political opposition: James's itemization faults Nkrumah not on his application of force but on his limiting of the democratic participation of the masses by undermining Ghana's judiciary. This is extraordinary if you consider *Nkrumah and the Ghana Revolution* as part of a sequence initiated by *The Black Jacobins*—a sequence that is both textual-historiographic and actual. I conclude this chapter by considering questions of political violence and restraint initiated in *The Black Jacobins* and continued in Cedric Robinson's *Black Marxism,* an auspicious note to end on considering the trajectory of Robinson's own voluminous scholarship. As Robin D. G. Kelley notes, "Eventually, Robinson came to the conclusion that it is not enough to reshape or reformulate Marxism to fit the needs of Third World revolution; instead, he believed all universalist theories of political and social order had to be rejected. In fact, Robinson's first book, *The Terms of Order: Political Science and the Myth of Leadership,* critiques the Western presumption—rooted as much in Marxism as in liberal democratic theory—that mass movements reflect social order and are maintained and rationalized by the authority of leadership."[111] Clearly, in light of my study's focus, I'm not prepared to abandon the problematic of radical leadership.[112] Rather, I want to reflect a bit on the question of restraint as formulated by Robinson in his discussion "The Nature of the Black Radical Tradition":

> Again and again, in the reports, casual memoirs, official accounts, eye-witness observations, and histories of each of the tradition's episodes, from the sixteenth century to the events recounted in last week's or last month's journals, one note has occurred and recurred: the absence of mass violence. Western observers, often candid in their amazement, have repeatedly remarked that in the vast series of encounters between Blacks and their oppressors, only some of which has been recounted above, Blacks have seldom employed the level of violence that they (the Westerners) understood the situation required. When we recall that in the New World of the nineteenth century the approximately 60 whites killed in the Nat Turner insurrection was one of the largest totals for that century; when we recall that in the massive uprisings of slaves in 1831 in Jamaica—where 300,000 slaves lived under the domination of 30,000 whites—only 14 white casualties were reported, when in revolt after revolt we compare the massive and indiscriminate reprisals of the civilized master class (the employment of terror) to the scale of violence of the slaves (and at present their descendants), at least one impression is that a very different and shared order of things existed among these brutally violated people. Why did Nat Turner, admittedly a violent man, spare poor whites? Why did Toussaint escort his absent "master's" family to safety before joining the slave

revolution? . . . And in that tradition [C.L.R.] James ambivalently found
Dessalines wanting for his transgressions of the tradition.[113]

Robinson is extending a line of thought from James—that the slaves'
response to their brutalization was "surprisingly moderate."[114] James
resorts to a strategic brevity, a matter-of-fact tone in a footnote, where
he holds his ground: "This statement has been criticized. I stand by it.
C.L.R.J."[115] His itemization of sadistic punishments meted out against
slaves as well as the militant reprisals for such torture is abstracted in
the form of a concise maxim: "The cruelties of property and privilege are
always more ferocious than the revenges of poverty and oppression."[116]

I am not questioning the integrity of Robinson's or James's respective
archive selection or their overlapping conclusions. Indeed it seems to me
that James's maxim is both sound and precise. James's formulation and
Cedric Robinson's extension prefigure and add onto a long tradition of
radical thought on the nature of political violence. This includes, just to
signal a few: Lewis R. Gordon's theorization of Fanon's "Tragic Revolutionary Violence," Merleau-Ponty's temporal wager of revolutionary violence as cessation of more acute violence tomorrow, and Fredric Jameson's
discussion of political violence and radical regimes: "It should be stressed
that the violence and physical repression to be observed in actually existing socialisms was always the response to genuine threats from the outside, to right-wing hostility and violence, and to internal and external
kinds of subversion (of which the US blockade of Cuba still offers a vivid
illustration)."[117] An example of proliferation as a strategy of restraint is
Sophie Wahnich's *In Defense of the Terror*, which argues that the Jacobin "Reign of Terror" was an expedient management strategy to quell the
violence of popular outrage directed against representatives of the *ancien
régime*.[118] Someone needs to do for theories of violence what Vassilis Lambropoulos did with great flair for *The Tragic Idea*.[119] I only want to suggest
that a properly tragic reading strategy can accept without glorifying or
sanitizing the blood for blood, violation for violation James registers in
The Black Jacobins. Robinson demonstrates that a tradition of restraint is
a consistent thread in the *actuality* of the Black Radical Tradition. James
generalizes this point with the concision of a maxim. Yet it does not have
to be this way to be claimed as in the tradition. Claiming is not the same
as romanticizing or eclipsing the fact that ultimately any kind of violence
against people should be opposed. An archive of restraint might provoke
the response—Yes. Of course. But why necessarily so? Should not one be

able to claim violent redress *in excess* as part of a radical political tradition without such excess attaining the status of aspiration? To claim the actuality of restraint but to not flinch in the face of excess—this is what I think accounts for the tone of James's footnote. Brecht's "On Violence" poses the riddle: "The headlong stream is termed violent / But the river bed hemming it in is / Termed violent by no one."[120] Obviously the river bed is a stand in for the ultimate violence—structural. I will end on that note.

James's "From Toussaint L'Ouverture to Fidel Castro" plays historical catchup and theorizes the ontological equality of Caribbean nation building, the actuality of both Haitian and Cuban struggles: "Toussaint L'Ouverture is not here linked to Fidel Castro because both led revolutions in the West Indies. Nor is the link a convenient or journalistic demarcation of historical time. What took place in French San Domingo in 1792–1804 reappeared in Cuba in 1958 . . . Castro's revolution is of the twentieth century as much as Toussaint's was of the eighteenth."[121] For E. San Juan Jr., James "pursues the antinomy between concrete universality and its geopolitical mediations in the specific region of the Caribbean."[122] James sketches the development of the modern Caribbean through three stages: (1) "The 19th Century," (2) "Between the Wars" and (3) "After World War II." The substrata, the engine propelling movement here, is the modernizing effects of the sugar plantation: "The sugar plantation has been the most civilising as well as the most demoralising influence in West Indian development."[123] Similar to the overall narrative logic of *The Black Jacobins*, James switches registers after providing a detailed analytic historical accounting of Caribbean history. He examines literature and intellectual history and posits a cultural field that links Fernando Ortiz's work, Césaire's *Cahier d'un retour au pays natal*, and the work of Trinidadian writer V. S. Naipaul. James argues for necessity as the structuring force of West Indian political leadership:

> There was therefore in West Indian Society an inherent antagonism between the consciousness of the black masses and the reality of their lives, inherent in that it was constantly reproduced not by agitators but by the very conditions of the society itself.[124]

> No West Indian but will have among its most resplendent stars the names of Jose Marti the political leader and Maceo the soldier. They were men in the full tradition of Jefferson, Washington, and Bolivar. That was their strength and that was their weakness.[125]

The tragic orientation here is apparent in the above juxtaposition. The main rift producing revolutionary Black mass-consciousness is structural—"the very conditions of the society itself," not spawned from outside. At the same time, leaders exist and are liability and virtue. To think these two contradictory scenarios, one needs to adopt a mediation device, with all its accompanying traps and virtues.

The actuality of revolutionary violence demands it is evaluated case per case. Toussaint's letter to the Directory declares that *"to re-establish slavery in San Domingo, this was done, then I declare to you it would be to attempt the impossible: we have known how to face dangers to obtain our liberty, we shall know how to brave death to maintain it."*[126] This pronouncement's matter-of-fact tone coupled with its radical resolve toggles between historical overdetermination and an almost natural development. Its coolness of pronouncement disables the ability to assess its worth a priori without engaging in the actuality of the phenomenon in question.

Speaking on the specific tragic use of violence Toussaint employs against his nephew General Moïse, San Juan Jr. notes a "strange duality"[127] in Toussaint's remarks, an assertion of autonomy from Bonaparte's France combined with his fidelity to the country. Note the contrast between Moïse and Toussaint's words:

> Whatever my old uncle may do, I cannot bring myself to be the executioner of my color. It is always in the interest of the metropolis that he scolds me; but these interests are those of the whites, and I shall only love them when they have given me back the eye that I lost in battle.[128]

> I took up arms for the freedom of my colour, which France alone proclaimed, but which she has no right to nullify. Our liberty is no longer in her hands. It is in our own. We will defend it or perish.[129]

Toussaint's order to execute his nephew crystallizes a Black Radical Tragic dispensation. In the act of execution, there is a failure to properly explain his actions to his base as well as a hasty rush to deed. It is important to recognize both Moïse and Toussaint are correct in their respective assertions. Moïse's fidelity to the masses of Haitian people is without question. He is the individual figure in James's study that most consistently represents the most radical and the most disenfranchised of Toussaint's multiple political bases. Toussaint's competing allegiance, in all its tragic consequence, is equally cogent. His fidelity to France as the strategic proclamation of liberty for the Africans of San Domingo coupled with his belief that Africans must protect that freedom by any means necessary is not a contradictory position. Toussaint's France is not France's France and it is most certainly not the France trying to reinstate slavery on the island. Haitian revolutionary use generates a variety of oppositions in leadership styles so that contemporary audiences can think through these problems. Both Dessalines and Toussaint in their differing styles participated in the constitutive mass/leader interdependence to different degrees of success and failure. Such varying degrees do not encourage one to abandon the problematic in its entirety. How you evaluate their respective contributions depends on what archive you access and what thought-problem you want to dramatize.

Peter Sloterdijk names his most recent study—*You Must Change Your Life*—after what he calls the "command from the stone," the forceful end of Rilke's poem "Archaic Torso of Apollo." "Rilke, under the influence of Auguste Rodin, whom he had assisted between 1905 and 1906 in Meudon as a private secretary, turned away from the art nouveau–like, sensitized-atmospheric poetic approach of his early years to pursue a view of art determined more strongly by the 'priority of the object.'"[130] Sloterdijk mines Rilke's sonnet for what it advocates about severance and perfection, what he calls the "perfection of the fragment." This sonnet is Rilke's "expression of thanks to Rodin, his mater in his Paris days, for the concept of the autonomous torso, which he had encountered in his workshop."[131] Persistent fascination with Rilke's "Apollo" is warranted because housed in its fourteen lines is a "conjured perfection . . . independently of its material carrier's mutilation—the authorization to form a message that appeals from within itself."[132] The lesson of "Apollo" is one of immanence. "The command from the stone" complicates a philosophical and aesthetic understanding of the whole as priority. In its fragmentary severed state, the careful reader (or, in Rodin's case, the careful viewer) finds what Sloterdijk calls "an entire principle of being."[133]

Two fragments that foreground problems of mediation. The first from Hazel Carby's previously discussed work on Paul Robeson, her use of a semicolon: "The Negro, as a creation of the modernist aesthetic, could never become a political comrade; and when Robeson himself determined to embody an alliance between art and activism for social change, his body was forever severed from the modernist aesthetic."[134] The next, one of Brecht's last poems, "And I Always Thought," the colon that follows the title in the first line:

And I always thought: the very simplest words
Must be enough. When I say what things are like
Everyone's heart must be torn to shreds.
That you'll go down if you don't stand up for yourself
Surely you see that.[135]

This juxtaposition illustrates the different work done by punctuation marks—Carby's semicolon and Brecht's colon. For Brecht, the colon functions as a kind of punctuational alienation/distancing effect. It casts a hue of suspicion on the words that follow. It suggests that you might want to reevaluate what you always thought. "The very simplest words" mediate understanding of a world, whereas such mediational understanding is a precondition for changing a world. It is a history that is outside the text but never accessible independent of the text, whether the words are simple or complex. In his last poetic offering, Brecht radically undermines a massive impetus of his entire work—part, because at least his song-cycles and performances contain an element of performance in excess of the textual. Brecht the poet, who employs simple words to achieve a desired revolutionary effect in a moment of acute self-criticism, punctures the rationale of his life praxis.

What does it mean to never be able "to become a political comrade"? The left side of the semicolon in Carby has a binding function, the right side the liberatory becoming of escape that then reinscribes part of the left side. The static, atavistic, and representationally vexed product of the modernist imagination—the so-called Negro—does not in the binding that is modernist fantasy have what it takes to *become* political comrade, to craft a space of becoming through revolution. In the first half of Carby's sentence, "The Negro" doesn't exist outside of a modernist representation. He is strictly a product of this representational calculus and as such cannot make the jump to a space of political comradeship, the space of revolutionary flux and contingency. Yet Robeson escapes again and again. Severing himself from the modernist aesthetic, Robeson reenters a space of contingent radical possibility—reenters because he was always there in defiance of modernist design. Carby continues to insist correctly on the imperative to think on the level of bodies. Robeson's escape reintroduces possibility and radical becoming. The semicolon in Carby's sentence denotes negation and dialectical reinscription, severing Robeson's body to claim his space of always already radical possibility. "Surely you see that" in Brecht is a literal and figurative last-ditch plea that words engender political commitment, and fidelity to ideas and the women and men who think them. Brecht writes words that facilitate radical transformation alongside a simultaneous acknowledgment that words are never enough. In both examples, the problem of mediation endures.

Peter Sloterdijk's "command from the stone" is actually multiple. Command issues forth commands. Within this speculative orbit, Brecht supplements Rilke's prescription and augments Rilke's defiant individualist fragment in all its brilliant epigrammatic verve. "You'll go down if you don't stand up for yourself. Surely you see that."

4

Tshembe's Choice

Lorraine Hansberry's Pan-Africanist Drama and Haitian Revolution Opera

(for Wesley Brown)

Negroes must concern themselves with every single means of struggle: legal, illegal, passive, active, violent and nonviolent . . . they must harass, debate, petition, give money to court struggles, sit-in, lie-down, strike, boycott, sing hymns, pray on steps,—and shoot from their windows when the racists come cruising through their communities.

Lorraine Hansberry

You can swagger like you rule this; Josey Wales. Unorganized revolt almost always mostly fails.

Gang Starr, "From JFK to LAX"

Rallying Against the Abstraction of Jean Genet

Lorraine Hansberry's late works[1] break from a U.S.-centric focus and reach toward Africa and Haiti to enact a global Black revolutionary politics on stage. Both Africa and the Caribbean function for Lorraine Hansberry as sites of expansion: a widening of the frame constituting her Black radical vision. This global reach also offers an opportunity to examine how the formal embodiment of a leader and mass problematic, what this project is calling the Black Radical Tragic, gets worked through in Hansberry's drama. Hansberry foregrounds a Black radical internationalist scale into American theater. She casts her explorative net wide, which contributes to her being unfairly criticized for her alleged reformist politics.

The relationship between scale and alleged reformism will be explored in this chapter. "The Marketplace of Empire," a term borrowed from Hansberry's *Les Blancs*, is an all-expansive, all-inclusive system, overdetermining much of where her characters live. Hansberry's drama is radical precisely in its acknowledgment of this all-inclusive economic and political domination that impacts individual leaders and masses, oppressors, and the oppressed. It is in a sense a long nineteenth-century framing. Like Marx's *Eighteenth Brumaire*, Hansberry frames necessity as a structuring field for improvisation, mining the politics of representation for tools to choreograph a freedom/necessity dance. By taking the premise seriously that people's actions are framed and limited by political economy and circumstances not chosen by themselves, "but rather circumstances encountered, given and transmitted from the past," her work thematizes the Black Radical Tragic. The marketplace is a totality that impacts everyone [albeit unevenly] in a society structured in dominance. It is tempting to recall Aijaz Ahmad's polemical corrective to Fredric Jameson's concept of "National Allegory." Ahmad questions the analytical use and coherency of "the three worlds theory":

> But one could start with a radically different premise: namely, the proposition that we live not in three worlds but in one; that this world includes the experience of colonialism and imperialism on both sides of Jameson's global divide (the "experience" of imperialism is a central fact of all aspects of life inside the USA, from ideological formation to the utilization of the social surplus in military-industrial complexes); that societies in formations of backward capitalism are as much constituted by the division of classes as are societies in the advanced capitalist countries; that socialism is not restricted to something called "the Second World" but is simply the name of a resistance that saturates the globe today, as capitalism itself does; that the different parts of the capitalist system are to be known not in terms of a binary opposition but as a contradictory unity—with differences, yes, but also with profound overlaps.[2]

Hansberry's "Third World" plays reflect and mediate her concerns about developments taking place in the burgeoning civil rights and Black Power movements. There is an explicit international and intertextual dynamic to these works: Hansberry's *Les Blancs*[3] chides the use of abstraction in Genet's *The Blacks*, much along the same line as this project's engagement with Eugene O'Neill.[4] The artist-activist milieu, in which Hansberry thrived, included such figures as Paul Robeson and W.E.B. DuBois. She was surely familiar with C.L.R. James's labors to stage and think the Haitian Revolution. Her play *Les Blancs* responds to French playwright Jean Genet's *Les Negres* (1958), which through the use of masks illustrates what Genet perceives as the arbitrariness of racism and the corrupting effects of power.

Like Eugene O'Neill's *The Emperor Jones*, Genet's play is an exercise in abstraction. It is a general meditation on power (the capital P "Power" attacked by Romantic poets). Oppressive structural relationships between specific actors are problematically generalized in Genet's play as a symptom of the "human condition." It utilizes a black versus white North American racialist context to indict, among other things, French imperial policy in Algeria. This slippage of contexts, associations, and subject matter constitutes the play's fundamental use of abstraction. Like O'Neill's *The Emperor Jones*, Genet's *The Blacks* exists in the "theatrical cauldron" of Black radical performance. It offered numerous opportunities for Black actors, committed to the liberation of African people in the diaspora. Genet purposely uses the struggle against racism and Black national oppression in the United States as a medium to explore French imperial policy in North Africa and, in doing so, crafts a theatrical work with an American audience in mind. Genet prefigures a "Culture Wars" tendency to itemize his own identity and structural positioning. From the introduction of his play's text: "This play, written, I repeat by a white man, is intended for a white audience, but if, which is unlikely, it is ever performed before a black audience, then a white person, male or female, should be invited every evening. . . . A spotlight should be focused upon the symbolic white throughout the performance. But what if no white person accepted? Then let white masks be distributed to the black spectators as they enter the theater."[5]

Hansberry could not tolerate Genet's abstraction. She referred to Genet's play as "a conversation between white men about themselves" and vowed to correct its flaws by positing a drama in which dialogue serves as "neither procrastination nor ego fulfillment but clarity, and whose culminating point is action."[6] Like O'Neill, Genet looks toward the African diaspora for inspiration injecting new life into his aesthetic. But unlike his modernist predecessor, Genet practiced uncompromising political solidarity with the Black Panthers as well as Palestinian revolutionaries[7] captured in his 1986 memoir about his time spent with both (*Prisoner of Love*, first published as *Un captif amoreux*). Genet is authentically and brilliantly radical, and this fact needs to be foregrounded in any critical engagement with his work. I have been examining the Black Radical Tragic as an aesthetic form in a sampling of Black radical drama and prose that thinks and stages Black radical collectivity. For Genet, Black radical collectivity is itself an aesthetic. What he regards as the Maoist politics of the Black Panther Party of Self-Defense[8] constitutes nothing less than a form of poetics:

> I think reflection is integral to poetic comprehension and vice-versa . . . I wonder if President Mao Tse-Tung would have successfully completed his Long March, the revolution, and the cultural revolution if he hadn't been a great poet. I wonder if it isn't because the black people are a Poet that they have been able to work so well toward finding a road to liberation in almost the same way that President Mao found that road.[9]

In the same article, Genet affirms that "the discoveries blacks have made about how to struggle politically lean curiously on a poetic sentiment about the world."[10] Genet's solidarity is profound and unwavering. Yet he constitutes his writing on both Black radical and Palestinian revolutionary strivings as aestheticized romance. Hansberry's corrective to Genet's abstractions posits one world unevenly occupied by oppressors and oppressed. She responds to Genet's abstractions with a radical specificity and a different sense of dramatic scale. I will examine three moments in *Les Blancs* as a way of introducing *Toussaint*, Hansberry's Haitian Revolution work. First, however, a brief digression on Genet's aesthetic as it relates to Black radical struggle, by way of his friend George Jackson. I gloss Genet's relationship to imprisoned radical intellectual George Jackson with specific attention to the question of method and study in Jackson, his insistence to directly contend with the problematic of the bourgeois family.

Books as "Murderous Acts": George Jackson's Praxis-Imperative to Study

> George Jackson's book is a murderous act, beyond all measure, but never demented, even if Jackson's sufferings and fevers drove him to the door of madness, a doctor never entered; it is a radical murder, undertaken in the solitude of a cell and the certainty of belonging to a people still living under slavery, and this murder, which is ongoing, is perpetrated not only against white America, against the American will to power, against what is called the entrepreneurial spirit; it is the systematic and concerted murder of the whole white world greedy to drape itself in the hides of nonwhite peoples; it is the—hopefully definitive—murder of stupidity in action.
>
> Jean Genet

"How is that, even more than ten years ago, he is our contemporary?"[11] asks Alain Badiou about his colleague Gilles Deleuze. We can ask the same about George Jackson, one of the twentieth century's most profound revolutionary theoreticians and astute formalists. In his introduction to *Soledad Brother: The Prison Letters of George Jackson*, Genet credits Jackson for revising the epistolary form utilized (implied but not named by Genet) in such works as Samuel Richardson's *Pamela: Or, Virtue Rewarded* (1740), *Clarissa: Or the History of a Young Lady* (1748), and *Sir Charles Grandison* (1753): "Many people would be amazed to hear that the epistolary narrative was still capable of affording us a resolutely modern mode of expression; yet if we merely juxtapose (one after another) a certain number of George Jackson's letters, we obtain a striking poem of love and combat."[12]

There is a generative and instructive temporal dynamic of Genet's politics of solidarity. Nostalgia as a structuring paradigm (a desiring machine if you will) functions for Genet as dialectic of present and past. In this regard, Genet is quite at home in a Black Radical Tragic vein. Like the Haitian revolutionary drama explored in this study, past serves as a useful template, comparable to Walter Benjamin's sense of sartorial splendor that gets reactivated every time it is rehearsed. Genet's reflections on Palestinian combatants (the *fedayeen*) offer up a model of transmission that resists perceiving inheritance as quantifiable, in other words, through the hegemonic apparatus of the financial quant or the highly compensated bean counter. It offers up a usable past that is a tragic yet fecund site of interpretive possibilities:

The present is always grim, and the future is supposed to be worse. The past and that which is absent are wonderful. But we live in the present, and into the world lived in the present the Palestinian revolution brought a sweetness that seemed to belong to the past, to that which is far and perhaps to that which is absent. For the adjectives that describe it are these: quixotic, fragile, brave, heroic, romantic, serious, wily, and smart. In Europe people talk only in figures. In *Le Monde* on 31 October 1985 there are three pages of financial news. The *fedayeen* didn't even count their dead.[13]

I will limit this brief framing discussion of Jackson to three relevant overlapping themes: (1) the centrality of method, (2) the imperative to maintain a studied engagement with revolutionary pasts, and (3) the willingness to concede the milieu of the family as a site of radical contestation.

Proper Name and Method in George Jackson

The main narrative arc of *Soledad Brother* not only marks the politicization and revolutionary transformation of its author, but it also traces a willingness to struggle with immediate family members (Mother, Father, Brother), as a site of pedagogic and dialogic engagement. This is not Andre Gide's "Families, I hate you!" but rather "Families, I hate you some of the time but I will engage in struggle with you always and unrelenting!" George Jackson's insights anticipate Žižek's spot-on plug for the family as a site of political struggle and the corresponding benefits of immanent critique: "The lesson of these impasses is not that one should bypass the family myth and turn directly to social reality; what one should do is something much more difficult: to undermine the family myth from within."[14] Akin to Paulo Freire's work on radical pedagogy in opposition to liberalism's emphasis on plurality and consensus, Jackson's understanding of dialogic is a conversation space among partisans. It is marking a line in the sand; yet, prior to demarcation, you engage in discussion. Writing to his attorney, Fay Stender, Jackson affirms:

> I had decided to reach for my father, to force him with my revolutionary dialectic to question some of the mental barricades he'd throw up to protect his body from what to him was an omnipresent enemy . . . I felt that if I could superimpose the explosive doctrine of self-determination through people's government and revolutionary culture upon what remained of his mind, draw him out into the real world, isolate and identify his real enemies, if I

could hurl him through Fanon's revolutionary catharsis, I would be serving
him, the people, the historical obligation.[15]

Historical obligation here implies history and tragic catharsis, wrestled away
from Aristotle's *Poetics*, inaugurating a fight-back. George Jackson is willing
to struggle with what Gide, Freud, Deleuze, and Guattari might identify as
the main confining milieu: the family. Family for Jackson is a site of studied engagement, the circulation of revolutionary texts, benchmark historical
events, and proper names. In one of many letters to his father pertaining to
the education of his brother, Jackson signals the importance of method:

> February 19, 1968
>
> Dear Robert,
>
> Too bad about Jon; I suggested upon your last visit that he may be getting
> too much TV. Anyway, you are absolutely correct in that these are his crisis
> years. You had better give him something good in the way of purpose, iden-
> tity, and method. It should be taken for granted that he is getting nothing
> along this line in school; if anything, these things are being trained out . . . so
> that he will be a good Negro, an individual, a nonperson, an intellectual
> dependent. If you do not know the definition of "purpose," "identity," and
> "method," it is already too late for Jon.
>
> I do not want to be addressed as George any longer. You will respect my
> wishes enough to use my middle name from this day on. I won't respond to
> any other.
>
> My work goes well here I am in health. I hope you are well.
>
> Take care of yourself,
>
> Lester[16]

In the context of the work as a whole, method is the component of this triad
that maintains some sort of coherency. It lacks the instability of Liberté
in C.L.R. James's play. Within the context of this particular letter, proper
names shift based on preferences of self-definition. A footnote early on in
the text indicates: "The author's father's name is Robert Lester Jackson.
The author addresses him as Robert or Lester depending on mood or circumstances."[17] Identity, bound up in the proper name, is a process marking an ongoing politicization for author, brother, mother, and father—what
Deleuze and Guattari might refer to as "becoming Black Panther." Or,
perhaps, "becoming George Jackson." Even the proper name of one of the
primary political formations to claim Jackson, the Black Panther Party for

Self-Defense, is a site and organizational milieu of contestation. Jackson's masterful *Blood in My Eye*, finished just days prior to his murder by San Quentin prison guards, presents a rich example of this: "All of this, of course means that we are moving, and on a mass level: Not all in our separate directions—but firmly under the disciplined and principled leadership of the Vanguard Black Panther Communist Party."[18] The Black Panther Party for Self-Defense (like Marcus Garvey's United Negro Improvement Association) claimed membership from various, often overlapping ideological tendencies—Marxist, Pan-Africanist, Revolutionary Black Nationalist, and the cacophony of nuanced interpretations housed under such umbrellas. The party did at a certain point in its development drop the "For Self- Defense" part of its name. By literally changing the proper name of the party, Jackson signals a methodological commitment to engage in a milieu and imprint it with his own preferred interpretation—I'll call it what I want and you all catch up. Positing what constitutes a revolutionary vanguard in Jackson's writings is a space of rehearsed negotiation rather than a priori conclusion.

For George Jackson, "People's War is improvisation and more improvisation."[19] This improvisatory spirit of negotiation is on display in *Soledad Brother's* struggle to define a revolutionary vanguard. Speaking of his grandfather, Jackson writes: "He was an extremely aggressive man, and since aggression on the part of the slave means crime, he was in jail now and then. I loved him."[20] In the same autobiographical sketch:

> I met Marx, Lenin, Trotsky, Engels, and Mao when I entered prison and they redeemed me. For the first four years I studied nothing but economics and military ideas. I met black guerillas, George "Big Jake" Lewis, and James Carr, W. L. Nolen, Bill Christmas, Tony Gibson, and many, many others. We attempted to transform the black criminal mentality into a black revolutionary mentality.[21]

The contrary nature of these two assertions requires dialectical mediation. "Aggression on the part of the slave means crime" signifies a position of radical inclusivity. Here, crime is not a neutral occurrence but an oppressive social relation defined by the oppressors to curtail the rebellion of the oppressed (in this instance the enslaved). At the same time, engagement with social milieus, proper names, and revolutionary antecedents, place-markers of old, ignite a process that desires the transformation of criminal mentalities into revolutionary ones. The first statement pierces the oppressors' ideological designation of crime, while the latter names that designation as something to be surpassed. Presenting this contradiction early on in the text has the effect of formally priming the reader of *Soledad Brother* to be attuned to the nuances of the book's dialectical leaps in both form and content. For George Jackson and Lorraine Hansberry, praxis of regimented collective study reveals instead of stifles future developments. Developments that persist, endure, and resist amnesia despite the fact that their chroniclers' lives are tragically cut short by either a state's bullet or an aggressive cancer. It is an example, if you will, of the dialectic of *"Le Partisan,"* Montreal bard Leonard Cohen's anti-fascist hymn, in which the chorus refrains *"J'ai repris mon arme"* (I have retaken my weapon). Retaken implies a prior taking, a prior rehearsal. Such revolutionary priors do not stifle present action or freeze action in a static mold of nostalgia but rather enrich the clarity of execution.

Negotiating *"The Market Place of Empire"*

> Black people and people of color and women will always be a threat to the system whenever they organize to empower themselves because the system is partly based on their disempowerment.
>
> Dhoruba Bin Wahad

Tshembe, Hansberry's protagonist in her anti-imperialist play *Les Blancs*, rails against "the marketplace of Empire."[22] For Tshembe, this phrase constitutes the way in which identity can be bought, sold, and bartered, a byproduct of an expansive capitalism, draping the globe. He uses the phrase to chastise his brother for replacing his family African proper name with the title "Father Paul Augustus." Hansberry had her own version of such a marketplace to negotiate. She consistently struggled to secure a space for her work in what Adrienne Rich identifies as "a theater apparatus commercial and capitalist in the extreme."[23] Hansberry's subtle negotiation of a highly commercialized landscape, coupled with the latent and manifest sexism of her critics, opened her up to attacks for what is misperceived as liberalism and faltering commitment to Black liberation. As Rich explains, Hansberry was "charged by critics, on the one hand, with having created a reactionary Black 'mammy' in Lena Younger and, on the other, with advocating the genocide of whites."[24] This refers to the incommensurate, critical judgments when you couple together reception of *A Raisin in the Sun* and *Les Blancs*. Amiri Baraka writing in the preface of the twenty-fifth-anniversary addition of *A Raisin in the Sun* and *The Sign in Sidney Brustein's Window* modifies his earlier critical view of *A Raisin in the Sun*. The play stages the tensions arising when a Black working-class family in Chicago has to decide how to spend insurance money after their father's death. Baraka revises his earlier interpretation that hastily dismissed Hansberry's work as liberal betrayal. Note Baraka's stubborn insistence to not reify symbolic registers of actual residential segregation:

> The concerns I once dismissed as "middle class"—buying a house and mov-
> ing into "white folks' neighborhoods"—are actually reflective of the essence
> of black people's striving and the will to defeat segregation, discrimination,
> and national oppression. There is no such thing as a "white folks' neighbor-
> hood" except to racists *and to those submitting to racism*. The Younger family
> is the incarnation—*before* they burst from the bloody Southern backroads
> and the burning streets of Watts and Newark onto TV screens and the world
> stage—of our common ghetto-variety Fanny Lou Hammers, Malcolm X's
> and Angela Davises. And their burden surely will be lifted or one day it cer-
> tainly will "explode."[25]

Les Blancs' African context echoes Hansberry's most famous work: her character Asagai from *Raisin in the Sun*, an African revolutionary intellectual who
inspires militant reflection in the character Walter Lee Younger Jr. *Les Blancs*,
a meditation on the return of Tshembe to his fictional homeland Zatembe to
bury his father, stages the question of African independence by any means
necessary. A scene was staged in 1963 for the Actors Studio Writers Workshop, featuring Arthur Penn, with Roscoe Lee Browne as Tshembe, Arthur
Hill as the American white liberal Charlie, and Pearl Primus as the dancer
who haunts Tshembe into action on behalf of the anticolonial revolutionaries. Hansberry appropriates a scene from Jomo Kenyatta's *Facing Mt. Kenya*
(1962) to reflect on the Hamlet-esque decision her protagonist is faced with
in terms of reconciling his competing allegiances to the two places he calls
home. Tshembe is presented with the dilemma of participating in the revolution to secure independence for Zatembe or returning to his wife and children
in London. In a discussion with Madame Nielsen (the knowing, sympathetic
wife of the racist missionary who runs Zatembe and who eventually sides
with the revolutionists and is killed), Tshembe articulates his dilemma:

> What will I do? Madame, I know what I'd like to do. I'd like to become an
> expert at diapering my son . . . to sit in Hyde Park with a faded volume of

Shakespeare and come home to a dinner of fried bananas with kidney pie and—(*He is fighting the tears now as a terrible anguish rises within him*)— turn the phonograph up loud, loud until the congo drums throb with unbearable sweetness—and then hold my wife in my arms and bury my face in her hair and hear no more cries in the night except those of my boy because he is cold and hungry or terribly wet. (*He hesitates*) I'd like—I'd like my brothers with me. Eric—and Abioseh. Do you remember when we were boys, Abioseh and I? How many times we . . . (*He cannot go on*) I want to go *home*. It seems your mountains have become mine, Madame.[26]

Earlier in the play, Tshembe designates his choice whether or not to join in the revolt as Shakespearean, alluding to *Hamlet*: "It's an old problem, really. . . . Orestes . . . Hamlet . . . the rest of them. . . . We've really got so many things we'd rather be doing."[27] This is a problem internal to action: "So many things we'd rather be doing." Tshembe has one of a series of arguments with the white liberal character Charlie on revolutionary tactics:

Oh, dear God, why? . . . Why do you all *need* it so?! This absolute *lo-o-ong-ing* for my hatred! I shall be honest with you, Mr. Morris. I do not "hate" all white men—but I desperately wish that I did. It would make everything infinitely easier! But I am afraid that, among other things, I have *seen* the slums of Liverpool and Dublin and the caves above Naples. I have *seen* Dachau and Anne Frank's attic in Amsterdam. I have seen too many raw-knuckled Frenchmen coming out of the Metro at dawn and too many hungry Italian children to believe that those who raided Africa for three centuries ever "loved" the white race either. I would like to be simple-minded for you, but— (*Turning these eyes that have "seen" up to the other with a smile*)—I cannot. I have . . . *seen*.[28]

Effiong argues that "Tshembe is ultimately ideologically unrestrained by his linkage to Europe signifies that entering into another culture does not presuppose self-rejection and neglect of one's cardinal cultural demands. Tshembe succeeds in finding a middle way: His attention is primarily redirected to his homeland, but he does not dismiss his pertinent European affiliations. In a sense, he is the conceptual equivalent of the play's form, an intricate synthesizing of European and African-centered creative and cultural values and paragons."[29] Hansberry talks about someplace and somewhere else to elaborate on the complexities of the present and collective future. The two dramatic works examined in this chapter take on the challenge of creating a staged representation comparable in its scale and expanse to the world it stages and interrogates. Everyone is indicted in a Hansberry landscape. A drama populated by heroes and victims gets transformed into a drama populated by classed, racialized, and gendered individuals, all set with the task of negotiating a hostile landscape. It is her ecumenical presentation of oppressive structures and their impact that led her work to be so hastily dismissed as liberal compromise. In the above passages, Hansberry via Tshembe challenges the very trope of a deliberate, Hamlet-esque tragic weighing of options as a hindrance to action. Effiong is shrewd in his judgment but perhaps his assessment needs to be slightly modified. In the complicated world of Hansberry's drama, Tshembe's homelands are both London and Africa. Tshembe's complex seeing links his struggle in Zatembe to the struggle of the European poor without collapsing such struggles under the auspice of the same. In a drama that privileges the way in which the world structures all its inhabitants in dominance, Tshembe is to evoke a self-designated label used by Assata Shakur (in some of her communication from exile in Cuba): a "reluctant warrior." Necessity and environment are the catalysts for radical struggle, but such an understanding can accommodate an understanding and allowance of voluntarism, personal resolve entering into the equation of what constitutes radical commitment—a warrior, but a reluctant one. I pursue this logic further by what I am calling the Epicurean (C.L.R.) James.

"British razor blades for Molotov": A Digression on the Epicurean James

"British razor blades for Molotov" is an entry from George Padmore's transatlantic shopping list. It comes from James R. Hooker's 1967 biography of James's comrade and childhood friend.[30] Its significance is manifold. It is literally how Padmore referred to the tasks he performed for Soviet luminaries. Part of what is at stake here is a provocation to think the errand and the gift, the delivery of fancy shiny things to radical dignitaries. A question is implied whether or not full-time revolutionaries should covet such fancy shiny things. In the spirit of Tshembe, I take seriously the transatlantic exchange of luxury goods and the revolutionary use of a good, smooth shave. British razor blades passed from a Trinidadian militant into the hands of a Soviet apparatchik. To think such an exchange is to reject an ethos of revolutionary morality in favor of an ethos of revolutionary *use*.

I juxtapose this shopping list item alongside a famous passage cited in the autobiography of C.L.R. James's associate Grace Lee Boggs. Snatched from a book by James's publisher, Frederic Warbugh, according to Boggs, a passage James "loved . . . and enjoyed reading it aloud to friends." How can we think about this performed reading by James outside the vanity in the recital of such a flattering (albeit vexed) portrait? James is modeling pedagogy of contradiction here to his friends alongside an Epicurean insistence that sensual pleasure and luxury matter:

> Despite the atmosphere of hate and arid dispute in his writings James himself was one of the most delightful and easy-going personalities I have known, colourful in more senses than one. A dark-skinned West Indian negro [*sic*] from Trinidad, he stood six feet three in his socks and was noticeably good-looking. His memory was extraordinary. He could quote, not only passages from the Marxist classics but long extracts from Shakespeare, in a soft lilting English which was a delight to hear. Immensely amiable, he loved the flesh-pots of capitalism, fine cooking, fine clothes, fine furniture and beautiful women, without a trace of the guilty remorse to be expected from a seasoned warrior of the class war. He was brave. Night after night he would address the crimes of the blood-thirsty Stalin, until he was hoarse and his wonderful voice a merely croaking in the throat. The communists who heckled him would have torn him limb from limb, had it not been for the ubiquity of the police and their insensitivity to propaganda of whatever hue. . . .
>
> If politics was his religion and Marx his god, if literature was his passion and Shakespeare his prince among writers, cricket was his beloved activity. He wrote splendid articles on county matches for the *Manchester Guardian* during the summer. Indeed it was only between April and October that he was in funds. Sometimes he came for the weekend to our cottage near West Hoathly in Sussex and turned out for the local team. He was a demon bowler and a powerful if erratic batsman. The village loved him, referring to him affectionately as "the black bastard." In Sussex politics were forgotten. Instead, I can hear today the opening words of *Twelfth Night*, delivered beautifully from his full sensitive lips. "If music be the food of love, play on, give me excess of it." Excess, perhaps, was James' crime, an excess of words whose relevance to the contemporary tragedy was less than he supposed.[31]

There is much going on here despite its problematic turns that include: the traffic of women implied in listing "beautiful women" as an entry in the list of the "fleshpots of capitalism," and Warburgh's obsessive insistence on commenting on James's complexion, the casual recuperation of "black bastard" as a term of endearment all merit relentless critique. James reminds his audience that an Epicurean pursuit of pleasure is not antithetical to a revolutionary ethos—it is only that the pursuit of pleasure (or rather the access to pleasure) needs to be democratized. James's insistence on repeat performances of Warburgh's fleshpot inventory assumes a standpoint of abundance as revolutionary defiance against an assumed position of chaste scarcity (six feet and three inches of socked abundance, actually). Today we are saturated with scarcity rhetoric in the current landscape of make-believe fiscal cliffs and so-called austerity. When the bourgeois hegemonic class employs such rhetoric it is to discipline and control; when an anti-hegemonic Left employs such rhetoric, it is a misguided strategy of self-important radical posturing. It substitutes morality for what we will soon show, by way of Brecht, as an understanding of the dialectical interdependence between individuals and structure. Constructing some sort of flimsy revolutionary ethos that would chastise Hansberry's Tshembe for desiring the creature comforts, the luxuries of his London homestead risks capture by rhetoric of control. It dresses up a faulty rhetoric of scarcity as revolutionary conviction. Such capture ultimately hinders a praxis that demands the socialization of abundance and the working toward the ultimate goal of revolution: majority control of the surplus as a precondition of radically changing the relations of production. Analysis of Padmore's shopping list teaches a comparable lesson as Hansberry's *Les Blancs*: British razor blades for all![32]

Lorraine Hansberry and Mother Courage: *Structure over Revolutionary Morality*

> The amiability or otherwise of Christophe has nothing to do with either the play or the history. All men do all things under certain circumstances, a lesson which your critic has not yet learnt, despite the steadily accumulating piles of evidence with which the post-war world has been furnishing him.
>
> C.L.R. James, response to *New Statesman* review, 28 March 1936

Hansberry theorizes her own version of Marx's thesis on causality, necessity, and freedom from *The Eighteenth Brumaire* in an episode of WNET's *Playwright at Work*.[33] She discusses a scene from her work-in-progress, the opera, *Toussaint*:

As I study history, that virtually all of us are what circumstances allow us to be and it really doesn't matter whether you are talking about the oppressed or the oppressor. An oppressive society will dehumanize and degenerate everyone involved—and in certain very poetic and very true ways at the same time it will tend to make if anything the oppressed have more stature—because at least they are arbitrarily placed in the situation of overwhelming that which is degenerate—in this instance the slave society so that—it doesn't become an abstraction. It has to do with what really happens to all of us in a certain context.[34]

The balance between individual and collective constitutive of what this study calls the Black Radical Tragic is staged in Hansberry's *Toussaint*. I want to situate "what really happens to all of us in a certain context," alongside Raymond Williams's analysis of what he calls the mature Brecht.[35] Brecht moves from a cynical rejection of a morally impoverished bourgeois world, to positing a way out through a path of revolutionary transformation, to showing the way in which the world acts on individuals, influencing the availability of their choices. This mature focus is best captured for Williams in Brecht's *The Good Woman of Sezuan*[36] and developed further in *Mother Courage* and *The Life of Galileo*:

> Brecht's mature drama works continually around this question. In *The Good Woman of Sezuan* goodness, under pressure, turns into its opposite, and then back again, and then both coexist. For the individual person, the dilemma is beyond solution. And this is conveyed with simplicity and power in Shen Te's transformation of herself into her tough male cousin, Shui Ta, who is first a disguise but then in effect takes on an independent existence. Thus the experience is generalized within an individual. It is not the good person against the bad, but goodness and badness as alternative expressions of a single being. This is complex seeing, and it is deeply integrated with the dramatic form: the character who lives this way and then that, enacting choice and requiring decision. No resolution is imposed. The tension is there to the end, and we are formally invited to consider it. . . .
>
> It is in *Mother Courage and her Children* that he finds a new kind of dramatic action which creates a substance comparable in intensity with the moral inquiry. . . . Criticism of the play has usually got off on the wrong track by starting with the question whether Mother Courage, as a person, is meant to be admired or despised. But the point is not what we feel about her hard lively opportunism: it is what we see, in the action, of its results. By

enacting a genuine consequence, Brecht raises his central question to a new level, both dramatically and intellectually.... The question then is no longer "are they good people?" (the decision taken before or after the play). Nor is it, really, "what should they have done?" It is, brilliantly, both "what are they doing?" and "what is this doing to them?"[37]

Focus on (usually exclusively male) heroes ceases and in Hansberry, stage-craft's challenge is to model a complex inquiry into environment and structure. Forms of social and economic organization[38] are both given priority on Hansberry's stage; individual and collective maintain constitutive tension. For example, the plantation economy in her *Toussaint* scene houses a combined articulation of slaves, absentee landowners, plantation managers who would rather be spending time in Paris, Creole wives of aforementioned plantation managers, and clerks sent to supervise the management of the managers. Such an expansive cast and shift in emphasis from individual action to structural determinants allow Hansberry's work to ask the two questions outlined in Williams's commentary on Brecht: both "What are they doing?" and "What is this doing to them?" This opens up space in the work to concentrate on historically neglected experiences in drama—for example, the role of women, however buttressed by the posthumous published end products that are offered up as her late work.[39] Expanding the field worries the line between individual and masses by shifting ground, so that serious dramatic work posits a sort of grand scheme of interconnectedness that in its materialist focus worries such a separation. Hansberry's ability to expand the field generously to dramatize the impact of oppressive structures on the oppressors as well as the oppressed contributed to the ad hominem critical reception of her plays—Harold Cruse's being the most egregious.[40] However, nowhere in her dramatic work or critical essays does this widening of focus equal class collaboration or submission to white supremacy. As Margaret B. Wilkerson argues, "few had recognized the strains of militance in the earlier voice of Lorraine Hansberry."[41] Her dramatic works' expansive vision, as it relates to the call for a widening of resistance strategies in the Black liberation struggle (detailed in this chapter's opening epigraph), connects with the broader political point animating my project.

I am proposing the Black Radical Tragic as a *form* that engages questions of radical leadership. An understanding of literary form comes from Lucien Goldmann's ideas pertaining to the interrelationship between worldview, expression, and form:

What we would like to emphasize now is the importance of a concept which Lukács utilized in 1905 and 1917, but which he seems to have abandoned today: the concept of "Form." If every feeling, every thought and, ultimately, every mode of human behaviour is *Expression*, it is necessary to distinguish within the totality of expressions the particular and preferred group of Forms which constitute the *coherent* and *adequate* expressions of a *world-view* on the planes of *behaviour, concept,* and *imagination*. Hence there are forms in life, in thought and in art, and their study constitutes one of the important tasks of the general historian of philosophy, literature and art and, above all, of the sociologist of knowledge.

World-views are social facts. Great philosophical and artistic works represent the *coherent* and adequate expressions of these world-views. As such, they are *at once individual* and *social* expressions, their content being determined by the *maximum of potential consciousness* of the group, of the social class in general, and their form being determined by the content for which the writer or thinker finds an adequate expression.[42]

Goldmann footnotes his passage:

Lukács once defined form "as the shortest way to the top."
However, the two meanings that the word "form" has in this section must be distinguished: the first, a *coherent* and *adequate* expression of a world-view, as opposed to eclecticisms; the second, a means of expression which is or is not adequate to the *content* that it expresses.[43]

Fittingly, Cruse begins his Hansberry discussion by criticizing her dismissive (and arguably reductive) account of Richard Wright's novel *The Outsider*, her inability—(literally, her lack of ability, according to Cruse) to engage with French existential thought in the novel form. This gives way to questioning Hansberry's leftist credentials—what is at stake here is Cruse's insistence that Hansberry's middle-class background makes her and her Harlem milieu unable to capture the worldview of Black workers in their performance-based literary forms: "their literary or 'cultural products' (Miss Hansberry's phrase) are, for the most part, second-rate because they reflect their creators' oversimplified and over-emotionalized views about their own ethnic group reality."[44] This group for Cruse includes Ossie Davis, Ruby Dee, John O. Killens, and Lloyd Brown, a person Cruse calls "the official Negro Communist-line man on Negro literature."[45] Reading Cruse, one gets a sense that there exists a static, impermeable thing called "the

Communist line" and that Hansberry and the like blindly submit to it without actually impacting, informing, and shaping that worldview (line) itself. He overextends Moscow's reach to science fiction worthy proportions and trivializes the capacities of independent Black radical thought. It is a Haitian Revolution historiography problem, really. James names his study *The Black Jacobins* not "The Blacks who are held sway over Jacobin militancy and Jacobin ideology." What is astonishing is that Cruse's critique of Hansberry cannot wage its critical force within a field on par with the expansive scale that Hansberry's dramas instantiate. Cruse combines discourses on the pathologies of Harlem and Harlemites in the same pages in which he highlights Hansberry and company's alienation from Harlem, as a marker of their middle-class inauthenticity. A failure to enact criticism of her work on par with the scale of her dramatic work contributes to misunderstanding such work. Indeed, class division and class struggle impact the field of African American cultural production. Still, Cruse wants to reductively parse communities into discrete classed and ideologically motivated entities—the very move Hansberry's dramatic works challenge.

Waging a War and Winning It: Lorraine Hansberry's Toussaint

> One does not negotiate with the state's use of terror, violent or premature death (actual physical death or disappearance through incarceration). One opposes it and in that opposition finds meaning in black suffering.
>
> Joy James

As Hansberry scholar Steven R. Carter notes, a manila folder labeled *Toussaint: A Musical Drama in 7 Scenes*, dated May 1958, rests among the author's files.[46] Included in her posthumously published autobiography is a note written in 1960, in which she lists future artistic projects:

> PROPOSED WORK—September, 1960:
> *The Sign in Jenny Reed's Window*, musical drama
> *A Revolt of Lemmings*, a novel
> *The Life of Mary Wollstonecraft*, full length drama
> (Thesis: Strong-minded woman of rationality; & a creature of history; nonetheless, a human being, destroyed many times over by "life as she is lived")
> *The Marrow of Tradition*, a full length drama
> *Les Blancs (The Holy Ones)*

> *The Drinking Gourd,* TV play—into stage play (?)
> some short stories
> The Musical
> *Toussaint,* an opera.[47]

Excerpts of the first scene and a series of Toussaint monologues are included in *To Be Young, Gifted, and Black* and Margaret B. Wilkerson includes the initial scene in her anthology *9 Plays by Black Women.*[48] Hansberry's interest in Toussaint commenced at an early age. In a list she composed as a child, Hansberry under the heading "MY FAVORITE" designates her heroes as Toussaint L'Ouverture and Hannibal.[49] Her work on the play commenced in May 1958 and continued until her death in 1965. Carter sketches how the work was always conceived as musical theater: "It is also clear that she thought of it in essentially musical terms at the beginning, somewhat later speaking of it as an 'opera,' and intended it to have the huge cast, elaborate sets, pageantry, and sweeping epic, larger-than-life confrontations generally associated with grand opera, though not all the dialogue would have been set to music."[50] Building on the musicality of James's play on Haiti, there is a way in which constituting her work as "opera" allows for more room on the stage to constitute the Haitian masses. Foregrounding musicality in the label "musical drama" and opera shows a Hansberry struggling with dramatic forms in order to cast the widest net in staging such a struggle of social transformation. Expansive scale in Hansberry reflects both actuality and aspiration. Speaking on the scenes unprinted and uncollected from Hansberry's archive, Carter describes: "a group of 'blacks and mulattoes,' including Prince Gaouguinou and his wife Pauline (soon to be parents of Toussaint), exit singing from a church where they encounter Pelagia, 'wise woman of the Bambara,' who prophesies that Pauline will soon bear 'a male child' who 'Will be a great chief, like the father of Gaouguinou!'"[51] He outlines other scenes, including the public execution of the liberator Mackandal, who preceded Toussaint, a "view of the rebel camp," battles between Toussaint's men and the Napoleonic officers, and the final treachery and death of Toussaint in a French jail. In 1961, she presents a work-in-progress scene for the National Education Television Broadcasting System. Wilkerson's text includes "A Note to Readers" by Hansberry dated December 1958:

> I was obsessed with the idea of writing a play (or at that time even a novel) about the Haitian liberator Toussaint L'Ouverture when I was still an adolescent and had first come across his adventure with freedom. I thought then,

with that magical sense of perception that sometimes lights up our younger years, that this was surely one of the most extraordinary personalities to pass through history. I think so now.

Since then I have discovered that it was a wide-spread obsession. Neither the Haitian Revolution nor the figures of Toussaint L'Ouverture or Christophe or Dessalines has gone wanting in dramatic or other fictional materials. Those I have troubled to read have offended my early dream. The exotic, the voodoo mysticism, the over rich sensuality which springs to mind traditionally with regard to Caribbean peoples has outlandishly been allowed to outweigh and, to my mind, distort the entire significance and genuine romance of the incredibly magnificent essence of the Haitian Revolution and its heroes.

The people of Haiti waged a war and won it. They created a nation out of a savagely dazzling colonial jewel in the mighty French empire. The fact of their achievement—of the wrestling of national freedom from one of the most powerful nations on the face of the earth by lowly, illiterate and cruelly divided black slaves—has, aside from almost immeasurable historical importance, its own core of monumental drama. One need not bow to the impulse to embellish it with romantic racism.

What the Haitian slaves accomplished under the leadership of the Steward of Breda is testimony to purpose and struggle in life. They who were slaves made themselves free. That is not, to argue with current vogues, a tired cliché of romanticism. It is a marvelous recognition of the only possible manner of life on this planet. L'Ouverture was not a God; he was a man. And by the will of one man in union with a multitude, Santo Domingo was transformed; aye—the French empire, the western hemisphere, the history of the United States—therefore: the world. Such then is the will and the power of man. Perhaps that is the secret of the greatness of humankind.[52]

There is an insistent, repetitive need to distance her project from the "tired cliché of romanticism." Hansberry is committed to the kernel of "genuine romance" exemplified in the Haitian Revolution. Teasing these two romances out is a generative task. She reproaches Romanticism as the kind of racialist dehumanizing scholarly lens—the "romantic racism" that C.L.R. James provided a corrective for in his study of the revolution. Past efforts to represent Haiti and the larger Caribbean in art are overdetermined by their focus on the exotic, mysticism, and a stereotypical hypersensuality that for Hansberry all eclipse the most important facet of that struggle: the seizure of power by "one man in union with a multitude"—in other words, the actuality of the revolution. Hansberry's *Toussaint* scene portrays a world in which the systemic frames and limits all its actors in key differentiated fashions, producing different levels of awareness in all parties involved. No one is exempt in her schematization.

Thanks to Margaret B. Wilkerson's anthology, we have Act I, Scene I to think about. The scene takes place prior to the revolution in the dressing room of Bayon De Bergier, a plantation manager in his mid-fifties. A discussion ensues between Bayon De Bergier and his wife pertaining to their miserable marriage and whether or not the African slaves of San Domingo will successfully revolt. Toussaint, for the action's duration, is offstage and only enters the action by proxy via the sound of his overseer lash. A moment of intimacy between Bayon's wife, Lucie, and her slave Destine is interrupted by Bayon's intrusion into Lucie's dressing room. In Hansberry's framing of the scene we revisit the sterile minuet examined in the James play. In Hansberry, such a minuet "tinkles":

> *The Great House of a sugar plantation on Santo Domingo in the 1780s—immediately before the outbreak of the Haitian Revolution.*
> *The massed voices of field slaves can be heard, welling up in the distance in a song of fatigue. Their music is an organ-toned plaint yet awaits a Haitian Moussorgsky. It is, of course, punctuated by the now distinctive rhythms of the island.*
> Oh, when will the sun go down!
> Oh, when will the shadows come?
> Shadows of night!
> Shadows of rest!
> Oh, when will the night hide the cane?
> Oh, when will the dark hide the sun?
> Night, the friend!
> Friend, the night!
> *As this strong music fades it is promptly replaced by the fragile tinkle of an 18th-century French minuet being played somewhere in the house on a delicate harpsichord. Exposed to us is the double boudoir of the plantation manager, BAYON DE BERGIER, and his wife. The décor suggests the lush, even vulgar overstatement of too luxurious appointment: thick floor coverings; excessive statuary; extravagant color; cushions and ornate furnishings chosen indiscriminately from prior and contemporary French periods.*[53]

The competing musical idioms not only mediate two opposing forces locked in struggle but also house two separate philosophical idioms on what constitutes "freedom." The "fragile tinkle" of the minuet is appropriate background music setting up Bayon's pecuniary tastes as overcompensation for the fact that he would much rather be in Paris. As Hansberry makes clear, Bayon is stuck in his managerial position; however, his dependence on and alignment to the plantation economy is not the same as the positioning of the slaves, the free man Toussaint, or Lucie, his Creole wife. Hence the contrast with the music of the field slaves. The anticipation of a Haitian Moussorgsky refers to the Russian piano composer Modest Petrovich Mussorgsky (1839–1881), important for Hansberry because he is considered one of the first composers to promote a distinctive Russian national style of composition and performance. This challenge relates to her first experience of the possibilities of dramatic theater, when as a young college student at the University of Wisconsin she stumbled into a rehearsal of Sean O'Casey's *Juno and the Paycock* and became overwhelmed with O'Casey's combination of Irish particularity and universal concerns for freedom: "One of the most sound ideas in dramatic writing . . . is that in order to create the universal, you must pay very great attention to the specific. Universality, I think, emerges from truthful identity of what is. . . . In other words, I think people, to the extent we accept them and believe them as who they're supposed to be, to that extent they can become everybody."[54] The overstatement of luxury characteristic of Bayon's dressing chambers is an attempt to cover up his shaky footing in the social stratosphere that is Haitian plantation society. The main action of the scene involves the preparation for a dinner party in which he and Lucie will entertain Marcel Petion, the courier of Noe—Bayon's employer/absentee owner of the plantation. Bayon pleads to Lucie, "many years her husband's junior, in her late twenties or early thirties,"[55] protesting the fact that she has to entertain his guests: "He has come to survey the plantation, return to France and give his personal estimation to Noe. That is all that matters and need matter. Except that he is to be well entertained. (*Almost pleading.*) I am placing a great deal of hope in his report. If I am to continue for another year I must have a good report. (*Through his teeth, to himself.*) Just one more year."[56] The complexities of power and rank in the context of a Santo Domingo plantation are staged as a domestic squabble. In Hansberry's sketch, there is enough misery to go around. Lucie, whose Creole status renders Bayon's assessment of his marriage to her as "settling," in the act of complaining about the burden to entertain unwanted guests performs a biting critique of the gendered and racialized division separating the couple while she simultaneously oppresses her own attendant house slave and resists her oppressive husband, "as is the fashion of the wives of Santo Domingo."[57]

> *Lucie. (With dismissive laughter from the depths of the cushions where she absently fingers her long dark hair.)* Oh, Bayon, Bayon, Bayon. The point remains that I am in no mood to hear your dull, tiresome talk of acreage and harvest or an equally dull, discussion of the present political state of affairs of France. The current palpitations of the Directory don't interest me. Napoleon himself doesn't interest me. . . . I am not interested in one single word your guests will have to say and I won't wish to hear one single word that they have said when they are gone.[58]

Bayon casually dismisses his wife's "considerable theatrical talents" and insists that she participate in the buttering up of the man who will give his managerial duties the official stamp of approval. The successful continuation of such duties, literally off the back of the indentured and enslaved plantation laborers, will help secure his flight to Paris. For Lucie, both her marriage and her life have morphed into "one long sigh"[59]—repeating the above lament against stifling boredom. Bayon responds to her jibe with an accompanying lament—"if I could only tell you about my agonies." Bayon's self-indulgent cry provokes and enrages Lucie, who reminds her husband of the fact that he in the past referred to her Creole status as "buccaneer flesh"[60] and described her ancestors as "the baggage of the Paris gutters" and "prostitutes and refuse of the prisons of France dumped in that Bay out there." Hansberry captures the class, race, and gender divisions permeating the mixed economy of slave and free labor in the complexities of her dramatic language and staging of the emotional warfare between her characters. In response to her husband's request for forgiveness, she replies: "Oh, but tell me, how *does* one forgive hearing how one's own grandmother was—'spawned'? And my father—'the whelp of the discharge of an incoherent panting buccaneer!'"[61] Immediately following Bayon's complaint of agony, Lucie reminds him of his prior infidelity with one of the female slaves:

> Oh, Bayon, don't! It's too dreadful when you are feeling—"agonized." . . . It is the measure of our marriage, Bayon, that you wear the clay from her grave right into our bedroom now. Remember when you still cared enough to at least have the mud meticulously cleaned before you came home to me after your visits up there? As late as last year we still had such a fine pretense about it all. I had, I think, a shred of love left for you because of that. For the effort. *(She is holding the boots facing his back; he has bowed his head again.)* Do you still take wild orange blossoms? I have often wondered about the specialness of orange blossoms. Did she used to wear them in her hair?

And when you put them on her grave, does she cry out to you in the haunting patois? *"Oh, mon petit, my strong one! My ivory God! How good that you come to visit me! Do you still love me, my love, my master!—"*

(*He wheels and comes across her with fierce violence and tears the boots from her hand and hurls them the length of the room. She watches, unmoved, and then saunters to the balcony herself and looks up to the mountains, continuing her taunting.*)

What made you bury her up there, Bayon? It's so far for your visits. Was it some special romantic plea on the deathbed perhaps? Ah yes. (*Bitterly affecting the mannerisms of an imaginary dying woman, eyes half closed and suffering.*) Did she look at you with those great dark eyes and say as she lay in your arms— (*She points.*) *"Up there, my master! Up there on the leeward side of Mont Croix! I would like to be buried up there, facing out to the sea which brought you to me and near where your God is said to live—"* Was it something like that, Bayon?[62]

Hansberry foregrounds both the gendered violence and sexual brutality integral to a world made up of both free and enslaved labor. The main rhythm of the scene consists of a sequence of such eruptions coupled with Bayon's temporarily successful attempt to quell such conflict, as well as Lucie's conflicted resignation to her lot. The entire scene proceeds along a repeating arc of eruption, pacification, eruption, and appeasement. Bayon's first attempt to put out the fire is in his query why his wife inflicts such self-torture. He presumptuously claims, "We will forget all of it—when we are home—in France," to which Lucie replies, "I AM home, Bayon . . . I am Creole. This is my home."[63] This points to an ongoing preoccupation with home and belongingness in Hansberry. Bayon, the main beneficiary of the plantation structure, is still dependent upon a stellar report from M. Petion. Lucie claims a contradictory belongingness to Santo Domingo society while asserting her separateness from its Black inhabitants. She decries her husband as a "poor little petit bourgeois who likes to sit astride his horse out there in the fields play-acting at being master not merely manager of a great plantation, while his so highly esteemed employer esteems nothing at all except the favors of the currently fashionable courtesans of Paris!" In a mock ventriloquism of her husband's dismissive voice, she berates herself as a "poor little Creole pig who lacks all sense of refinements of style which should accompany the playing of a minuet."[64] Systemic antagonism is accompanied by a crisis in perception. This is captured in a debate on Toussaint's leadership qualities and in the concluding scene in which the servant Destine helps Lucie dress for her guests.

In response to Bayon's claim that his wife's self-hatred tops that of her slaves, Lucie declares, "A creature purchased is a creature purchased."[65] This flattening

out of the difference between enslaved labor and domestic servitude is interrupted by the sound of Toussaint offstage brutalizing a slave with the crack of
his whip. Lorraine Hansberry's offstage scene of subjection prefigures Saidiya
V. Hartman's ethical insistence (by way of Frederick Douglass's witnessing of
the whipping of his Aunt Hester) to not reproduce scenes of brutality against
enslaved Africans ("the ease at which such scenes are usually reiterated") at
risk of desensitizing the dread of such acts: "Rather than inciting indignation,
too often they immure us to pain by virtue of their familiarity."[66] Bayon is convinced that Toussaint is a loyal worker who would never run away. He misreads
Toussaint's performance of disinterest in the talk of rebellion and revolt among
the slaves. Conversation between husband and wife on whether or not Toussaint
is a "brute" and whether he enjoys his task of punishing the slaves morphs into
a complicated discussion on the slippery nature of the designation "free man":

> *Lucie.* Yes, I think so. How strange the two of you are together in the
> fields. You, in your wide-brimmed hat astride your horse, *seeming to
> command.* And he, the slave, beside you, barefoot in that yellow hand-
> kerchief and hideous face—commanding.
> *Bayon.* I have tried to explain to you again and again that he is not a
> slave.
> *Lucie.* Well, is he free?
> *Bayon.* No, he is not free either.
> *Lucie.* Then he must be a slave. IF you are not one then you must be the
> other.
> *Bayon.* It is a special situation. You are a woman, you cannot understand
> it.
> *Lucie. (With deliberate wide-eyed innocence.)* Oh, but explain it to me,
> Bayon. I will try very hard to understand it. And explain about your-
> self. Are you a free man, Bayon?
> *Bayon.* Of course I am a free man.
> *Lucie.* Then why haven't you left Santo Domingo long ago? That is what
> you have wanted more than anything else for a long time—to be run-
> ning about Paris. What is it that keeps a *free* man where he does not
> wish to be? Tell me, what is freedom, Bayon de Bergier?
> *Bayon.* As an abstraction that is something that no one can answer. Least
> of all, these days, a Frenchman.[67]

This penultimate action consolidates the main philosophical work of
Hansberry's drama. Bayon is tripped up by the slippage between free and

unfree and responds to Lucie's interrogation of the language he employs by declaring his confidence in Toussaint as "a steward who knows how to drive men." The distinction between man and slave is what is at stake here. He responds to her corrective and modifies his statement from "a steward who knows how to drive men" to "steward who knows how to drive slaves." To this Lucie replies, "Could it be possible, Bayon, that if Toussaint knows how to command men, not merely slaves—since you use the words the same—that he may command even you?"[68] In Hansberry's scene, an out is never realized but always on the horizon. In a society that continuously calibrates its hierarchical organization in order to hide how its subjects are both oppressed and oppressors, the maintaining of the cultural coherence of its categories is an impossible task. This is clear in the appendix of "Key Speeches" Wilkerson includes in her anthology. Napoleon's recognition of the force of the men he attempts to subjugate back into slavery is a force for both inspiration and trepidation for Toussaint:

> *Toussaint.* We have something in our favor, Biassou. The Europeans will always *underestimate* us. They will believe again and again that they have come to fight *slaves. (He smiles at Biassou.)* They will be fighting free men thinking they are fighting slaves, and again and again—that will be their undoing. . . .
>
> *Toussaint.* (To Christophe) You see, Henri, I am a very wise man and we wise men, ha!—we don't make the same mistakes that ordinary men make. Take this, this Napoleon Bonaparte, for instance, this Napoleon Bonaparte and myself; we recognize one another. He is different from the others. He is the first of the Europeans to know who I am; and who the blacks of Santo Domingo are. He is that wise; he is therefore the first enemy of scale I will have matched wits with. This Bonaparte, Henri, he deserves his reputation.
>
> *Toussaint.* Destine, I am frightened. For the first time. I am frightened. I saw them in the harbor today. He has sent all of France for us and we are doomed. For the first time we have been measured for our worth and he has sent all of France. All the guns of France; all the soldiers, all the generals, surely. We are doomed, Destine. They have come to make war on *men*, not slaves, and we are doomed.[69]

A calculus, determining enemies of scale, is a tricky operation. In these speeches, Hansberry builds on James's concerns and offers us competing viewpoints on the complexity and flexibility of recognition. Again, so much of the scene and these proposed key speeches have to do with a crisis of perception afflicting all those who share the same landscape. The calculus is so slippery because as we see in *Toussaint*, the categorical boundaries separating free from unfree are subject to change. Oppressive structures can be smashed as well as their accompanying cultural categories. After this discussion, Lucie is attended to by Destine in a dressing room. She expresses her attraction to Destine and voices the fact that Destine actually despises her. Lucie responds to Destine's effort to appease her mistress by again claiming insider knowledge based on a sense of place and belongingness:

> You do not think I am either kind or beautiful. You fool the others with your grins and silences, but I am not Monsieur Bergier, Destine! I can look into those little black eyes of yours and know all there is to know. You hate me. You hate my flesh and the scent and it repels you to touch me—you would like to put those strong fingers around my neck and choke me until there is no more life left! You despise me, you despise my children . . . all of us.
>
> Be still, or I shall have you whipped! You do not think I am beautiful at all. Above all you do not think I am as beautiful as you are with your chiseled cheekbones and panther eyes! (*She strikes the slave across the face. The woman sits perfectly still with her eyes lowered.*) You savage! Don't you know that I am not some ignorant Frenchwoman—I am a Creole and I know the blacks! I know you! You dream of murdering me in my bed. I was born knowing. It is the curse of the Creole that we *all* know. . . . I cannot bear your sullen impertinence day after day! Why, dear God, have I been so good to you . . . knowing that you are only waiting—waiting . . . that you are only waiting.[70]

This eruption is quelled when Destine commences her massaging of Lucie. This erotically charged display is arrested by Bayon's interruption. Lucie shouts back to her husband's disapproving gaze: "My pleasures are my own—monster! Monster!"[71] Even the act of tenderness and sensual expression is overdetermined by the oppressive social structuring of the plantation economy. In such a place, nobody's pleasures are truly their own. The world of the Bayons, aptly described by Lucie as "suffocating,"[72] houses actors that can as quickly flip the scripts of their designated hierarchical roles.

Hansberry's Haiti play is named for an individual hero-leader relatively absent in the course of the action of the anthologized scene. Solely Toussaint's gesture, the cracking of the whip, invades the action of the scene.

James, on the other hand, renames his drama from *Toussaint Louverture* to the collectivist *The Black Jacobins*, yet the individual hero Toussaint figures in most of the play's action. Glissant names his work after the individual leader, yet such a leader occupies a world where temporality itself is blurred as well as the line separating the living and the dead and discrete geographic locales. Both James and Hansberry include the plantation's Madame on their stage; yet Hansberry does more to develop the complexity of the precarious position she occupies in the Haitian plantation and slave economy. Hansberry dramatically represents the Madame's precarity while simultaneously refusing to gloss over her oppressive actions and positionality. Complexity in a Hansberry landscape never means class collaboration. Her scene's momentum is propelled more by its tense, masterfully woven dialogue, in contrast to James's play, which turns so much on its use of stage direction.

As Lucie is quick to point out in her meditation on freedom, her constantly evoked language of possibility corresponds to the rickety foundation of concepts and language used to describe social organization. In his framing notes for *Les Blancs*, Nemiroff describes Hansberry's wish to craft a dramatic aesthetic "multileveled in structure" yet "taut enough to contain and focus the complexity of personalities, social forces and ideas in the world she had created."[73] Her dramatic work successfully meets this challenge and further develops the tragic opposition between leader and masses. Her short-lived career produced a work that contains both with equal weight of focus. The potential for revolt, rebellion, and revolution is crystallized in the language of her stagecraft. Such precarious footing demands a strategic openness that can accommodate sitting, lying down, praying, singing, and shooting from windows when the racists come cruising.

Conclusion

Malcolm X's Enlistment of Hamlet *and Spinoza*

Whether 'tis nobler in the mind to suffer
The slings and arrows of outrageous fortune,
Or to take arms against a sea of troubles,
        And by opposing end them?

Hamlet, 3.1

We must not be led by the urgency of our situation to destroy the
means we want to make use of.

Bertolt Brecht, The Messingkauf Dialogues

"Backpedaling into May-flower Time"

I conclude with some observations on Malcolm X's use of lines from William
Shakespeare's *Hamlet*, starting with an engagement with Guyanese novelist,
critic, and political activist Jan Carew's reflections of his time with Malcolm
in England.[1] I end with Malcolm's commentary on seventeenth-century philosopher-theologian Baruch Spinoza. Recall a discussion between Carew and
Malcolm X on the question of Haitian revolutionary leadership:

> I reminded him that during the Haitian revolution, the only person that Tous-
> saint L'Ouverture could trust implicitly was Agé, a white Jacobin who was his
> chief of staff. Agé hated the bigoted French almost as much as Dessalines did,
> I told him. Don't worry, he said, with a broad smile, I might not have a white
> chief of staff. But I'll work with everyone who believes in my cause.... Really?
> I said, looking up at him with mock disbelief, but his rejoinder was a serious
> one. Yes. But I've got to go about building a movement carefully. The last thing
> an Egyptian friend said to me when we were parting is that I should never get
> too far ahead of my followers, because if I'm so far ahead that I'm out of sight,
> they might turn back. I don't want that to happen.[2]

Malcolm X participated in the Oxford Union Presentation Debate on 3 December 1964, shortly after he returned from making pilgrimage to Mecca.[3] The Presentation Debate signals the last event of the term in which the president of the Oxford Union invites the person she respects the most to take on Oxford's rival, Cambridge, in the spirited contestation of a motion. Cricket, rugby, and debate all are key theaters of warfare between the two rivals. The occasion's motion was a July 1964 remark by Barry Goldwater upon his acceptance of the nomination for U.S. president at the Republican National Convention in San Francisco: "Extremism in defense of liberty is no vice, moderation in the pursuit of justice is no virtue." Goldwater's remark was initially a defense of the right-wing John Birch Society.

Malcolm, the fifth of six speakers, followed Conservative Party Parliament member Humphrey Berkeley (who opposed the motion along with Lord Stoneham, Labour Party Member of the House of Lords, and Christie Davies, Cambridge Student Union president). On Malcolm's side in support of a radical reinterpretation of Goldwater's statement were Scottish Communist Party member, revolutionary nationalist, and poet Hugh MacDiarmid, and Anthony Abrahams, a Jamaican student and president of the Oxford Union. Tariq Ali, Oxford student chair of the debate, discusses the debate in his memoir *Street Fighting Years*.[4] MacDiarmid's homage to his various friendships entitled *The Company I've Kept* refers to Malcolm as "a brilliant speaker" and "an extremely able and attractive personality."[5] Speaking on how the "sacrosanct image of Oxford [was] shattered by . . . the fist of revolutionary logic," Lebert Bethune writes:

> The irony of his being at Oxford in a debate against, of all people, the Earl of Lonford, Privy Councillor to the Queen (whatever that might mean), wasn't lost on Malcolm. But while smiling at that, he pointed out to me that the office of presidency of the Oxford Union was held then by a black Jamaican, who was proposing the motion for the debate. He also pointed out that the incoming president for the following term was a Pakistani. I didn't believe then, nor on reflection, that Malcolm was rejoicing in the symbolic "domination" of Oxford by men of color, but it was a matter of more than simple irony for him.[6]

In a videotaped interview, Abrahams stated: "I have never been as sorry for a man as I was for Humphrey Berkeley [a Left-leaning Conservative parliamentarian] that night, because Malcolm took his speech and, I mean, he just tore him up."[7] Berkeley sparked Malcolm's rage (as well as his sense of humor) when he unfairly referred to him as "North America's leading exponent of apartheid,"[8] comparing Malcolm to South Africa's Verwoerd, and stated that for Malcolm "Liberty . . . means racial segregation."[9] In light of the ill-conceived comparison between Malcolm and a key ideologue of South African apartheid, it is interesting to note that during Malcolm's visit Abrahams was "gated" in his chambers after 6:00 P.M. because of his participation in a protest in response to the jailing of Nelson Mandela. Malcolm in solidarity with his host's confinement refused to attend the evening functions planned by the university. Instead, Abrahams's flat was transformed into an all-night meeting spot, where Malcolm and the Oxford radical student body exchanged ideas.

In a televised interview, the former Oxford Union president painted a picture of Malcolm as an organic intellectual dedicated to Black internationalism. He highlighted Malcolm's "gift of analogy," the fact that he never repeated himself during his stay, his poignant differences with Dr. King yet his respect for strategic flexibility, and the expression of his thoughts "at a totally cerebral level." Antonio Gramsci's concept of the "organic intellectual" captures well Malcolm's position as theoretician of the Black liberation movement:

> Every social group, coming into existence on the original terrain of an essential function in the world of economic production, creates together with itself, organically, one or more strata of intellectuals which give it homogeneity and an awareness of its won function not only in the economic but in the social and political fields. . . .
>
> The mode of being of the new intellectual can no longer consist in eloquence, which is an exterior and momentary mover of feelings and passions, but in active participation in practical life, as constructor, organizer, permanent persuader and not just a simple orator (but superior at the same time to the abstract mathematical spirit); from technique-as-work one proceeds to technique-as-science and to the humanistic conception of history, without which one remains "specialized" and does not become "directive" (specialized and political).[10]

Malcolm X's capacity as an individual leader is insufficient without "social contestation," and "active participation in practical life," as spokesperson for his political base. I use "base" here not in a stilted, static, or mechanistic sense but rather in the sense of what community one organizes and what interests one represents in one's presentation and advocacy. Malcolm's success as a Black radical intellectual and organizer (his "won function") can be accredited to the fact that in his rhetorical strategies and models of organization he simultaneously appeals to and mobilizes his broad social base (the Black proletariat) as well as his ever-expanding, always already international political base (revolutionary Black nationalists and their allies), without vacillating on principles.

Malcolm addressed the Oxford audience with characteristic humor, candor, and commitment. In the first half of his speech he denounced bombardment campaigns against villages in the Congo. His remarks capture a dialectical fidelity and utter faithlessness in the American legislative, congressional, and judicial branches to secure justice and protection for the majority of Black people. He oscillates between specific attention to the particularity of the American Black Freedom struggle to more Pan-Africanist pronouncements, in fellowship with international allies. By way of enacting such an oscillation, Malcolm shows how these two locales (domestic and international) are always already linked and interdependent. In his remarks, he substitutes the more narrow identity marker of "position" with the more systemic-oriented keyword "condition." Malcolm's remarks enact a further clarification of a mass-line radical Black internationalism that he would mark the duration of his life. He transforms Goldwater's formulation beyond its original meaning:

> I read once, passingly, about a man named Shakespeare. I only read about him passingly, but I remember one thing he wrote that kind of moved me. He put it in the mouth of Hamlet, I think it was, who said, "To be or not to be"—he was in doubt of something. [*Laughter.*] "Whether it was nobler in the mind of man to suffer the slings and arrows of outrageous fortune"— moderation—"or to take up arms against a sea of troubles and by opposing end them."
>
> And I go for that. If you take up arms, you'll end it. But if you sit around and wait for the one who's in power to make up his mind that he should end it, you'll be waiting a long time.
>
> And in my opinion the young generation of whites, blacks, browns, whatever else there is—you're living at a time of extremism, a time of revolution, a time when there's got to be a change. People in power have misused it, and now there has to be a change and a better world has to be built, and the only way it's *going to be built is with* extreme methods. And I for

one will join in with anyone, I don't care what color you are, as long as you want to change this miserable condition that exists on this earth.[11]

Malcolm's Oxford podium remarks, coupled with his conversations with Jan Carew, offer up a concluding cross-section of the political concerns underlying my project. Malcolm mediates between the particular and the universal and articulates a different understanding of how the tragic functions in Shakespeare's *Hamlet*, how to engage with the past, and, most important, the relationship between leader and base in the context of revolutionary struggle. Reflecting on his Oxford visit, Malcolm recounts to Carew:

> I honestly didn't know what to expect when Tony Abrahams phoned to invite me to Oxford. . . . I remember clearly that the minute I stepped off the train, I felt I'd suddenly backpedaled into Mayflower-time. Everything was smaller than I expected, and slower and older. Age was just seeping out of the pores of every stone. The students were wearing caps and gowns as if they graduated the first day they arrived and were then handed diplomas years later, and they were riding bicycles that should've been dumped long ago. I couldn't help wondering if I'd made a mistake accepting the invitation to take part in the debate. But Tony Abrahams had met me at the train station and, somehow, his Jamaican ease banished some of my doubts. . . . Looking back, I must admit that I liked Oxford. It was old and cold, but the students had open, inquiring minds. It was a place where a ruling class reserved a special space for the best of minds to be thrown into a brain-pool where they could learn to think their way out of any situation, no matter how difficult. That's something Black folks need to look into, but we would have to shape ours differently; *we'd have to carve out our space to think in the middle of a struggle in the inner cities, and from there we would have to see the whole world. Still, at the end of every one of those four days, when I was alone in my guest apartment, the hustle and bustle of Harlem never failed to break into the silence and remind me that there at Oxford, I was near the top of a pyramid while below were the oppressed carrying it on their backs.*[12] [emphasis added]

Oxford, that strange Mayflower-like "old and cold" place, provides for Malcolm a further strategy, a further institutional paradigm, and a further methodological example to relate to the specific contours of his praxis as part of the Black Radical Tradition. Oxford for Malcolm offers up a template. The conduct of the students provides another example for negotiating "societies structured in dominance,"[13] hence expanding his ken of vision. There was an international makeup internal to the Oxford student body. However, for Malcolm specifically, and the Black Radical Tradition in general, it is not a one-sided case of strict appropriation and application of a different theoretical or institutional example to local environs. Malcolm's intervention at Oxford changed the caliber of that institution. He worked on Oxford as much as Oxford worked on his own clarification of vision. The theory and praxis nexus essential for moving the struggle forward connects the "in the middle" of the inner city to an international community. The moment that the individual leader settles in the serene isolation of the English quiet, his one of multiple bases, the "hustle and bustle of Harlem" seeps in, disrupting the illusion of serenity. Malcolm is not hostile to the pressure-cooker or think-tank aspect of Oxford; rather, he is troubled by the specific precondition of withdrawal from society for training by the students. He works in solidarity with two publics in the above passage: both the Harlem public and the mass of Oxford students he builds with during late-night sessions. The "hustle and bustle" of Harlem invades the chimera of stillness at Oxford much like in C.L.R. James's *preface* to *The Black Jacobins: Toussaint L'Ouverture and the San Domingo Revolution*: "it was in the stillness of a seaside suburb that could be heard most clearly and insistently the booming of Franco's heavy artillery, the rattle of Stalin's firing squads and the fierce shrill turmoil of the revolutionary movement striving for clarity and influence."[14] Malcolm's negotiation with multiple masses in his political organizing, teaching, and speaking reminds that the problematic of leader versus base in the Black radical imagination never means that such a base is either singular or static. It is in flux and subject to change at different points of a struggle, highlighting the precariousness of negotiating communication between parties, the room for error, and the expansive frame necessary to narrate, describe, or perform its complexities. The base is also not a still mass waiting to be activated by the leader. There is a constitutive interdependence to such an exchange.

I want to think about the concluding stammer of Malcolm's oration. His characteristic eloquence of speech is momentarily arrested at the point of highlighting a strategic alliance across the "races" that has yet to be achieved in North America but might be on the horizon, part of his violently cut-down strategic agenda to "join with anyone to change the miserable conditions that exist on this earth." He briefly stumbles on the declaration of a strategy to build a better world stating: "and the only way it's going to be built with it it it with with it [*sic*] is with extreme methods."[15] On par with C.L.R. James's Haiti writings, the strategic vision necessary to achieve the sort of organizational "interracial" political unity to pursue "extreme methods" cannot be predicted in advance of such strategies' actualization. Perhaps resonating here is one of Lenin's mantras (attributed to Napoleon): engage and then look. *"On s'engage et puis . . . on voit"* translated as: "First engage in a serious battle and then see what happens."[16] Political strategy is tethered to what Georg Lukács theorizes as "the actuality of the revolution":

> For Lenin, on the other hand, *compromise is a direct and logical consequence of the actuality of the revolution.* If this actuality defines the basic character of the whole era, if the revolution can break out at any moment—either in a single country or on a world scale—without this moment ever being determinable; if the revolutionary character of the whole epoch is revealed in the ever-increasing decay of bourgeois society, which results in the most varied tendencies continuously interchanging and criss-crossing, then the proletariat cannot begin and complete its revolution under "favourable" conditions of its own choosing, and must always exploit all those tendencies which—however temporarily—further the revolution or which can at least weaken its enemies.[17]

Lukács proceeds to unpack the "Leninist theory and tactic of compromise" by reiterating the *Eighteenth Brumaire*'s point that "men" make history but not under their chosen circumstances. It "follows from the knowledge that history always creates new conditions; that therefore moments in history when different tendencies intersect never recur in the same form; that tendencies can be judged favourable to the revolution today which are a mortal danger to it tomorrow, and vice versa."[18] Conditions change, contingencies wreak both havoc and reward; yet templates of past revolutions exist. They exist to be studied and reactivated within present actualizations of performance. They exist as improvised fields of study, ripe with new insights. Performance, as it turns out, never occurs in the same form. What if, in the last instance, the revolutionary vanguard is not the monopoly repository of an elect political savvy (in other words, experts) but rather simply those who put in the most *rehearsal* time?

Malcolm's *Hamlet* reclaims doubt as a hallmark of radical inquiry and revolutionary praxis. Effective radical political praxis cannot be

idealistically pursued without transforming a material base whose organizational matrix remains bourgeois rule and white supremacy. In other
words, *Hamlet's* doubt from the perspective of Black radicalism has a
materialist base. Hamlet's doubt implies and centers the indeterminate and unknown of revolutionary embarking. This reclamation of the
past, this encounter that happens by way of reading, occurs for Malcolm
only "passingly." Once activated in the contemporary conjuncture of the
Oxford Union Presentation Debate, *Hamlet's* doubt serves its function,
hence the leap to something else, to an as yet undetermined somewhere
else. The second-life (and third and fourth and fifth) of *Hamlet's* revolutionary doubt renders that revolution permanent. It is a lesson learned by
a careful consideration of Haitian revolutionary performance. It is a constant engagement that yields a proliferation of "wait and see."

Malcolm's brief stammer constitutes a bulwark against future claiming
of his legacy in a way that dilutes its force. It is a bulwark against co-opta-
tion. Malcolm's stammer is prophetic in light of how his own legacy will
be contested by various Left ideological tendencies, often at the expense of
his own self-identified positioning within traditions of Revolutionary Black
Nationalism. Arnold Rampersad expertly captures the relationship between
Malcolm's textual afterlives and the needs of others: "Malcolm has become
his admirers. In the process, the truth of his life, insofar as we can gauge the
truth about an individual or recover it from history, is more or less immate-
rial. Malcolm has become the desires of his admirers, who have reshaped
memory, historical record and the autobiography, according to their wishes,
which is to say, according to their needs as they perceive them."[19] Everyone
wants to annex Malcolm in the service of different political agendas. In a
spirited critique of Manning Marable's *Malcolm X: A Life or Reinvention*,
activist-attorney-scholar Kamau Franklin writes: "Depending on the writers' personal interests with respect to controlling the public discourse and
on their status as allies, professed friends, or detractors of Malcolm's, every
conversation on Malcolm X since his death has been aimed at telling Black
people what we should believe in about him and the movement he personi-
fied. Laying claim to having insight into the mantle of the fiery leader of
Black self-determination cannot be undervalued."[20] Franklin's essay performs a brilliant balancing act: through a critique of Marable's text he both
repositions Malcolm in a field of Revolutionary Black Nationalism while
simultaneously forcing a break, a slowing down of the tendency to annex
Malcolm's legacy to past, present, and future developments. Malcolm's legacy, like the Haitian Revolution, gets constantly reactivated within an acute

contestation of *use*. In this spirit, I want to shift directions. Instead of claiming Malcolm, let us examine Malcolm claiming another. Let us consider an example of Malcolm X claiming an ally (or at least a site of interest). His declaration at Oxford that he will "join with anyone" takes an interesting turn in his autobiography. Malcolm joins in fraternity of thinking alongside seventeenth-century philosopher-theologian Baruch Spinoza. He annexes him to the Black Radical Tradition by way of the designation "Spinoza, a black Spanish Jew."[21]

Malcolm X's "Spinoza, a Black Spanish Jew": On the Proper Name

> He died at eventide, when the sun lay like a brooding sorrow above the western hills, veiling its face; when the winds spoke not, and the trees, the great green trees he loved, stood motionless. I saw his breath beat quicker and quicker, pause, and then his little soul leapt like a star that travels in the night and left a world of darkness in its train
>
> W.E.B. DuBois, "Of the Passing of the First-Born"

> The chiefs of the council do you to wit, that having known the evil opinions and works of Baruch de Spinoza, . . . that the said Espinoza should be excommunicated and cut off from the nation of Israel; and now he is hereby excommunicated with the following anathema: With the judgment of angels and of the saints we excommunicate, cut off, curse and anathematize Baruch de Spinoza, . . . : by the 613 precepts which are written therein, with the anathema wherewith Joshua cursed Jericho, . . . and with all the curses which are written in the law. Cursed be he by day and cursed be he by night. Cursed be he in sleeping and cursed be he in walking. . . . The Lord shall not pardon him, the wrath and fury of the Lord shall henceforth be kindled against this man, . . . The Lord shall destroy his name under the sun, and cut him off for his undoing from all the tribes of Israel, . . . And we warn you, that none may speak with him by word of mouth, nor by writing, nor show any favor to him, nor be under one roof with him, nor come within four cubits of him, nor read any paper composed or written by him.
>
> Excommunication decree of Baruch de Spinoza
> as read by Rabbi Aboab

From the chapter "Saved" in *The Autobiography of Malcolm X*:

Spinoza impressed me for a while when I found out that he was black. A black Spanish Jew. The Jews excommunicated him because he advocated a pantheistic doctrine, something like the "allness of God," or "God in everything." The Jews read their burial services for Spinoza, meaning that he was dead as far as they were concerned; his family was run out of Spain, they ended up in Holland, I think.

I'll tell you something. The whole stream of Western philosophy has now wound up in a cul-de-sac. The white man has perpetrated upon himself, as well as upon the black man, so gigantic a fraud that he has put himself into a crack. He did it through his elaborate, neurotic necessity to hide the black man's true role in history.[22]

Neurosis, vindication, and, most important, theoretical richness—something Malcolm's commentary delivers in abundance. Yet it only delivers when we *use* it; when readers activate Malcolm's theoretical richness as "representations we can use" through a labor of reading. What should we make of Malcolm's curious designation of Spinoza? Is this a version of the psychoanalytic argument Freud posits and Edward Said revisits that reads Moses the Egyptian (African) as repressed patriarch and return-of-the-repressed trauma vis-à-vis European Jewry?[23] Is this a conflation of Spinoza's past and Malcolm's present: an allusion to how racial formation works both in reference to Spinoza's own Spanish Sephardic background in the context of his family's migration to Holland and his own excommunication from his Amsterdam synagogue? Is this a reference to the complexity of racial formations of twentieth-century American Jewry? What theoretical lesson is housed in Malcolm *preserving* the status identification Jewish coupled with the proper name Baruch Spinoza, given the fact that Spinoza himself was excommunicated? What Black Radical Tragic lesson is underscored here in Malcolm's insistence to not decouple Spinoza from his religious affiliation from birth? What sort of Haitian revolutionary lesson is housed here? A detour by way of the philosophical density of Spinoza's dream-work and Brazilian slave rebellions helps clarify.

Some chronological grounding is helpful. In 1600 the Espinosa family emigrates from Portugal to Nantes, then to Amsterdam. Thirty-two years later Baruch D'Espinosa is born in Amsterdam (four years after Descartes moves to Holland). In 1638 the Great Portuguese Synagogue is founded in Amsterdam and Spinoza studies at its rabbinic school. In 1656 Spinoza is banished from the Jewish community of Amsterdam. He goes on to study

Latin humanities, science, and philosophy at Van den Enden's school and in 1660 leaves Amsterdam to live with the Collegians of Rijinsburg and works on his *Treatise on the Emendation of the Intellect.*[24] As Lewis S. Feuer's archival dream-work on Spinoza argues:

> Shortly after his excommunication from the Amsterdam Jewish synagogue in 1656, Spinoza went to live among the Collegiant-Mennonite community at Rhynsburg. The Mennonites were a pacifist mystical group, with a vaguely communistic heritage derived from their anabaptist forerunners. The community at Rhynsburg in their theology was much akin to the English Quakers, though they expressed their mysticism in the language of Descartes. Pieter Balling was a noble representative of the group. . . . He was devoted to Spinoza, and prepared the Dutch translation of his first published work, *The Principles of Descartes' Philosophy.* . . . Now in 1664, Balling's child had sickened and died. He turned, grief-stricken, to Spinoza, and wrote how he had heard omens of his child's death even when the child was well,—"Sobs like those it uttered when it was ill and just before it died."[25]

Feuer goes on to detail the complicated development of ideas about race and Africa in Amsterdam and the linkages between Spinoza's Amsterdam Synagogue and the trade of African flesh in Brazil. He analyzes the financials of the Dutch West India Company as they relate to slavery in Brazil and itemizes stock holdings and profit margins for members of Spinoza's Synagogue in Amsterdam. The company guaranteed religious freedom for Jews, then under continuous persecution, making Brazil an attractive space for migration. The slave rebellion in Pernambuco, Brazil, offers a precedent for the military strategic positioning of James's *Black Jacobins* in late eighteenth- and early nineteenth-century Haiti. The 1630 Dutch West India Company's conquering of Pernambuco was thwarted in 1654 by the joint campaign ventures of the Portuguese and a slave rebellion led by Henrique Diaz, who "fought beside the Portuguese in what was for them a war of liberation" and "became the colony's governor and was further rewarded by the Portuguese commander in 1656 with a deed to the lot of the Jewish cemetery."[26] Contingent imperial alliance works to pursue *liberté* (*liberdade*) for enslaved Africans in Brazil by any means necessary. Rabbi Isaac de Fonseca Aboab, reader of Spinoza's excommunication decree, according to Feuer's archival research, "stood with the besieged Jews in the siege of Pernambuco. A Portuguese expedition, inspired by priestly words, had in 1646 launched an attack with the hope of exterminating the Jews."[27] Implied here is the tragic irony of a Dutch Brazilian Jewish community's implication in the institution of African slavery while simultaneously always already under anti-Jewish assault by the Portuguese. *Antigone's* tragic logic of competing right becomes in this historical conjuncture a logic of competing genocides. It is a tragic logic that would benefit by way of thinking alongside C.L.R. James's dialectically rigorous protocol captured in his early twentieth-century Haiti writings: "The race question is subsidiary to the class question in politics, and to think of imperialism in terms of race is disastrous. But to neglect the racial factor as merely incidental is an error only less grave than to make it fundamental."[28] Malcolm's calculus of Spinoza as black Spanish Jew works as a brilliant, almost utopian, nominal historical revisionism. Theological excommunication is linked with the tragic complicity in African slavery and persecution of Jewish communities in Brazil. Malcolm's preservation of Spinoza's religious affiliation, despite excommunication, his identification with him as Black implies an alternative scenario. In the utopian imaginative framework of Malcolm's naming, in other words by the prefix and suffix Malcolm adds onto the proper name Spinoza and metonymic sleight of hand, the Jewish community of Brazil sides both against Portuguese colonialism with their accompanying murderous anti-Jewish racism and opportunistic and fleeting antislavery praxis *and* in solidarity with Black Brazilians' righteous war of liberation and armed struggle against slavery. Wouldn't it be nice? In this speculative staging, Malcolm claims Spinoza as political comrade, however briefly. He refuses to relinquish Spinoza's Jewish identification, in defiance of Spinoza's excommunicators. Like the refusal to abandon the problematic of Haitian revolutionary (Black radical) leadership, both Malcolm and the writers examined in this book heed Brecht's warning "to not be led by the urgency of our situation to destroy the means we want to make use of."[29]

Premature Death and the Death of a Child

> Be on my side. I'll be on your side. There is no reason for you to hide.
> Neil Young, "Down by the River"

Linkage between Spinoza's excommunication and Henrique Diaz's slave rebellion works itself out in a dream. Spinoza mines his night visions for philosophical and representational *use* and *refusal*. He employs dream-work to confront a friend mourning the tragic death of his young child. Here is an excerpt from Spinoza's Letter 17 to Pieter Balling (20 July 1664):

As for the omens which you mention, namely, that while your child was still well and strong you heard groans such as he uttered when he was ill and just before he died, I am inclined to think that these were not real groans but only your imagination; for you say that when you sat up and listened intently you did not hear them as clearly as before, or as later on when you had gone back to sleep. Surely this shows that these groans were no more than mere imagination which, when it was free and unfettered, could imagine definite groans more effectively and vividly than when you sat up to listen in a particular direction.

I can confirm, and at the same time explain, what I am here saying by something that happened to me in Rijinsburg last winter. When one morning just at dawn I awoke from a very deep dream, the images which had come to me in the dream were present before my eyes as vividly as if they had been real things, in particular the image of a black, scabby Brazilian whom I had never seen before. This image disappeared for the most part when, to make a diversion, I fixed my gaze on a book or some other object; but as soon as I again turned my eyes away from such an object while gazing at nothing in particular, the same image of the same Ethiopian kept appearing with the same vividness again and again until it gradually disappeared from sight.

I say that what happened to me in respect of my internal sense of sight happened to you in respect of hearing. But since the cause was quite different, your case was an omen, while mine was not. What I am now going to tell you will make the matter clearly intelligible.

The effects of the imagination arise from the constitution either of body or of mind. To avoid all prolixity, for the present I shall prove this simply from what we experience. We find by experience that fevers and other corporeal changes are the cause of delirium, and that those whose blood is thick imagine nothing but quarrels, troubles, murders and things of that sort. We also see that the imagination can be determined simply by the constitution of the soul, since, as we find, it follows in the wake of the intellect in all things, linking together and interconnecting its images and words just as the intellect does its demonstrations, so that there is almost nothing we can understand without the imagination instantly forming an image.

This being so, I say that none of the effects of the imagination which are due to corporeal causes can ever be omens of things to come, because their causes do not involve any future things. But the effects of imagination, or images, which have their origin in the constitution of the mind can be omens of some future event because the mind can have a confused awareness beforehand of something that is to come. So it can imagine it as firmly and vividly as if such a thing were present to it.

For instance (to take an example like your case), a father so loves his son that he and his beloved son are, as it were, one and the same. And since (as I have demonstrated on another occasion) there must necessarily exist in Thought an idea of the affections of the essence of the son and what follows there from, and the father by reason of his union with his son is a part of the said son, and in its affections likewise participate in the ideal essence of his son, and in its affections and in what follows there from, as I have elsewhere demonstrated at some length.[30]

For Feuer, the epistolary dream schema serves a repressive function for Spinoza. The image of "a black, scabby Brazilian" is Diaz himself. Rabbi Aboab's performative speech act (the reading of the excommunication decree) is in fact a repetition with a difference—an amplified echoing of his condemnation of Diaz. Spinoza's logic separating soul from bodily causes contradicts his own categories, in which the body/soul divide is in fact not a divide at all but rather an interdependent relationship.[31] Feuer argues that "Spinoza's assertion that nonominous dreams are purely physically caused can therefore be regarded as a symptom of his own resistance to an analysis of his unconscious."[32] For Antonio Negri, Spinoza's Letter 17 is an iteration of "the Caliban problem—that is, the problem of the liberatory force of the natural imagination." It is "located within the highest abstraction of philosophical mediation."[33] For our purposes, coupling the history of Black radical resistance against slavery in Brazil as a narrative frame to think (and console) the loss of an infant offers a distillation of the rhetorical and political-aesthetic work of the Black Radical Tragic.

Indeed *Body & Soul* (Spinoza and Oscar Micheaux).

But also "Blood and Judgment" (*Hamlet* and Georg Lukács):

And blest are those,
    Whose blood and judgment are so well commingled,
    That they are not a pipe of Fortune's finger
    To Sound what stops she pleases [*Hamlet* 3.2, 63–66]

Blood and judgment: both their opposition and their unity only derive from the biological sphere as the immediate and general basis of human existence. Concretely, both express a man's social being in his harmony or dissonance with the historical moment, in practice and in theory.³⁴

In Malcolm X's two employments of proper names, we see the theoretical richness of his thought process. One of Malcolm's employments insists on the actuality of the revolutionary predicament as a question of thoughtful deliberation on the limits of moderation (Hamlet's question "Is it better to . . . "). The other defies clerical authority by reinstating Spinoza's religious membership by way of description and the proper name—"Spinoza, a Black Spanish Jew." Malcolm's *Hamlet* insists reckoning with radical actuality as a matter of deliberation and choice, whereas his Spinoza insists on radical openings generated by way of speculative possibility.

A Black Radical Tragic framework demands thinking the acute subjective pain of Dr. W.E.B. DuBois's and Pieter Balling's deaths of their infant children alongside premature death as structural policy, precisely because such overlap corresponds with the actuality of how people experience loss. Black Radical Tragic form constitutes the expansive suppleness necessary to contain such a coupling. The form itself is expansive because the material conditions that place Black life under duress are so. Subjective experience of loss cannot transform political economies, but they are often the building blocks and impetus to work toward such a goal. Ruth Wilson Gilmore's exacting definition of racism helps to clarify: "The state-sanctioned and/or exploitation of group differentiated vulnerabilities to pre-mature death, in distinct yet densely interconnected political geographies."³⁵ Performance can bridge the expanse of such interconnected political geographies and construct a field wide enough to co-join subjective and systemic *vulnerabilities*.

The individual-mass tension constitutive of the Black Radical Tragic maintains its urgency in a post-independence, post–Black Arts era as both aesthetic strategy and political problematic. C.L.R. James's observation for the Caribbean in his *appendix* to *The Black Jacobins* that "within a West Indian island the old colonial system and democracy are incompatible"³⁶ rings true for the so-called postcolonial present. Repressive police apparatuses, the war machine, the structural reality of both super-exploitation and premature death as policy function as obscene reminders that democracy, even in the limited sense of how democracy is lauded and narrated from above, does not exist for the majority of the African diaspora. This is one reason to encourage, constantly reimagine, and actualize an always already international Black united front radical politic.

An aesthetic strategy that stages such a revolutionary process and keeps the individual and the mass in constant dialectical tension admits the following truth: From a phenomenological standpoint, oppressed nationalities feel structural losses on an individual level. The state represses individuals through legal and extralegal means (including murder), actively underdeveloped infrastructures take the lives of individual family members, individual leaders are marked for death as potential "rising messiahs" by various counterintelligence initiatives, and even if capital logic does not individually and intentionally scope and create collateral damages, we feel such losses on an individual plane. Individual family members are mourned not as part of some sort of mass construct, waiting for revolutionary activation, or as characters in an emplotted narrative. In a Black Radical Tragic framework, individual representation acts as a launching pad, a heuristic to mediate international and local mass-based concerns through the theme of tragic loss. "One Step Ahead of Heartbreak" is still one step ahead. Effective radical struggle must be waged collectively; yet the setbacks and losses along the way register themselves as acute subjective trauma.

Indeed, "there is no reason to hide." Yet the operative hegemonic logic where we live invests daily in creating more hiding spaces and weaving its Thermidorian camouflage. A resistance optic that can defy this tendency, a radical framework that can traverse such interconnected space has to muster the seeing power of Lorraine Hansberry's Tshembe. It must wrestle with the problems of organizational actualization, totality, and the question of the use of physical force. The Black Radical Tragic provides an aesthetic framework that insists thinking how to build the organizational structures to actualize such a highly mediated as well as immediate *complex seeing*. It is a model of proliferating use honed by the discipline of multiple rehearsals.

A reason to be optimistic: We have yet to reach intermission.

Coda

Black Radical Tragic Propositions

You know Gil, you shouldn't be afraid of what is *actual*.

Amiri Baraka on Gil Noble's *Like It Is*, 2002

Actuality and thought—more precisely the Idea—are usually
opposed to one another in a trivial way, and hence we often hear it
said therefore that, although there is certainly nothing to be said
against the correctness and truth of a certain thought, still nothing like it is to be found or can actually be put into effect. Those
who talk like this, however, only demonstrate that they have not
adequately interpreted the nature either of thought or actuality. For,
on the one hand, in all talk of this kind, thought is assumed to be
synonymous with subjective representation, planning, and intention, and so on; and, on the other hand, actuality is assumed to be
synonymous with external, sensible existence.

G.W.F. Hegel, *The Encyclopaedia Logic*

I. Simone de Beauvoir's *Force of Circumstance* famously describes her
failed efforts to stave off *exhaustion*:

> In the car, he talked feverishly: in forty-eight hours' time, the
> French Army would be invading Tunisia, blood would be flow-
> ing in torrents. We joined Sartre for lunch; the conversation
> lasted until two in the morning; I finally broke it off as politely
> as possible by explaining that Sartre needed sleep. Fanon was
> outraged, "I don't like people who hoard their resources," he
> commented to Lanzmann, whom he kept up till eight the next
> morning. Like the Cubans, the Algerian revolutionaries never
> slept more than four hours a night.[1]

Fanon's attitude here has been called many things. I understand it as an ideal of radical generosity.

II. *Missing a friend*: The last time I saw Chen, proprietor of *Recto/Verso Books* in New Brunswick, New Jersey, he responded, smiling, to my customary greeting: "I'm exhausted. It's capitalism, it leaves us all *exhausted*." Following his tragic death, I had a recurring dream of us delivering (in a *Datsun*) parcels of books "in service of the revolution." My last visit, he set aside a six-hundred-page tome, which applies Marxist-Leninist theories of self-determination to Tibet. I imagine he thought I was in want for some clarity.

III. The Swans' "Bring the Sun/Toussaint L'Ouverture" is a generative thirty-four-minute exercise in sonic *exhaustion*: battering guitar riffs, long durations of ambient noise and hiss, percussive fits, spoken incantations, sawing noises (perhaps the tree of liberty or the sadism of the French ruling class), frantic horse galloping (recordings of actual horses, prohibited entry into the studio). With twelve minutes remaining, following sounds of Jura Mountain sleigh bells, whistling, and complex instrumentation, a chant commences. It begins with an elongated pronunciation of Toussaint L'Ouverture, sounding like the *Terminator* version of Chief Inspector Jacques Clouseau—such a display of artifice contains a challenge: a track of such length encourages parsing its different movements. Thinking such movements as stages. It foregrounds its constructiveness as a reminder that the constitution of such stages is always a retroactive procedure.

Band front man Michael Gira sees the Haitian Revolution as "the fulcrum of Western civilization":

> He was a master horseman, and that's one of the things that helped him win the battles against France, because he could go from one side of the island to the other in an impossible amount of time and completely surprise the other troops. It was a very bloody and cruel revolution, just unbelievably, psychedelically vicious, on both sides. I don't want to describe the saw [sound] on that song, but someone will read the biography and see why it's there.
>
> The Haitian Revolution is a subject that's compelling to me, it's the fulcrum of Western civilization: slavery, the idea of freedom and democracy, and liberation all come together in this big violent moment, and then Haiti becomes the tragedy that it is now. It's an epic tale.[2]

Tragedy and epic; slavery, freedom, democracy, and liberation—the Haitian Revolution becomes a field in which genre and political epistemology get parsed. An interviewer notes, "The group has sounded this massive live, but never on record."³ *Archival strivings* toward the scale of performance—the *archive* pushes toward the *actual* when in fact their relationship is one of interdependence. *Abstraction* as both separate and converging procedure serves an expository function—it tells a story.

IV. An interrogation of the logic of firsts: "II B.S. (RZA's Mingus Bounce Mix)" is a variation on Charles Mingus's "II B.S.," itself a variation on Mingus's 1957 "Haitian Fight Song." The longish finger-solo in "Haitian Fight Song" is a repetitive preamble: a position of retreat-in-study initiating a multi-instrumental frontal assault. Both study-retreat and assault belong to realm of thought. Both retreat and assault belong to the realm of action: Lenin reading Hegel in the interwar period; Mingus reading Freud in the period of permanent war. RZA's remix holds out the bait only to explode preconceptions of how the loop functions. He fabrics a loop palimpsest that constitutes a totality, preserving and building upon a complexity that in the Mingus track was already there. He slows down Mingus's bass solos, incorporates a select number of sounds (cymbals, explosions, galloping, a lasso whirl?), and interrogates the logic of the sample chop. RZA alters and abstracts the arrangement of Mingus's "II B.S.," bookending it with Mingus's fingering and a horn squawking of Henry Dumas proportions. His palimpsest re-arrangement preserves the coherency of Mingus's work by truncating and adding onto something that was already there. Perhaps this is a sonic analogue of the unfinished character of the Haitian Revolution, announcing and instantiating its own proliferation. It complicates a sense of its own origins. By way of the RZA and Mingus's mastery, the aesthetic contains such lessons. Listen.

V. Repetition as technology and method: "C.L.R. James was the only person I knew in those days who had a copying machine in his apartment, and they were big in those days. That machine was crucial to his working methods then."⁴—Aldon Nielsen

VI. Michael McKeon's *The Secret History of Domesticity* makes an exacting argument for the virtues of abstraction characteristic of Marxian method: "Abstraction is not a dogmatic shutting down but an experimental opening up of discovery, a way of generating concrete particularity by tentatively constituting a whole susceptible to analysis into parts. Abstraction entails not the occlusion but the explication of concretion, just as system may work not to exclude, but to ensure the acknowledgment of, contradiction."⁵ Consider a market woman's retort to the accusation of selling rotten eggs:

> "What? She replies, my eggs rotten! You say that about my eggs? You? Did not lice eat your father on the highways? Didn't your mother run away with the French, and didn't your grandmother die in a public hospital? Let her get a whole shirt instead of that flimsy scarf; we know well where she got that scarf and her hats: if it were not for those officers, many wouldn't be decked out like that these days, and if their ladyships paid more attention to their households, many would be in jail right now. Let her mend the holes in her stockings!"⁶

Fittingly, Hegel demonstrates the mass-line character of *abstract* thinking's subsuming logic by way of snapping and signifying.⁷

VII. *The United States, that likes to call itself the United Nations. . . .* Selective employment of proper names has dire political consequences—consider Haiti and Congo as two test cases. Haitian director Raoul Peck's film *Lumumba: La mort d'un prophète* is structured by Peck's narrations of his mother's account of Patrice Lumumba's assassination.

> "My mother told me: 'Lumumba managed to stay in power for only two months. But what kind of power? America interfered once again, instead of the Belgians. America under the guise of the UN, the United Nations. The others followed suit, as usual.'"⁸

Peck's narrative through line reflects the *actuality* of his family history. As an *abstraction* or narrative strategy it grounds the political in a framework of generations, the familial, and weaves a Pan-Africanist continuity linking a Caribbean island with an African country through reminiscence. The cinematic narrative conjures the individual locus of "my mother" to do its collective work. Lumumba's murder, for Fanon, initiates a challenge in the form of a question from his essay in *Pour la Revolution Africaine*: "Lumumba's Death: Could We Do Otherwise?" In the English translation of this book, *for*—a partisan—declaration becomes *toward*—a temporal, directional aspiration. Lumumba's death for Fanon is a personal loss (he was indeed Lumumba's colleague and contemporary) as well as a political defeat. This converging of the personal and political takes the form of a query—"Can We Do Otherwise?" A question in a Black Radical Tragic vein claims ownership—"we"—of an individual loss, a criminal defeat that it cannot be held accountable but and at the same it must. Tragic embrace of this loss, a head-on self-critical accounting generates other possibilities. In positing the question it clears a space for the "otherwise." Fanon condenses his insights on defeat in the form of a maxim on continuity: "Hesitation in murder has never characterized imperialism."[9]

Lumumba traveled his country's provinces as beer salesman—the condition of possibility for his radical unification project. This is a Haitian revolutionary protocol—an imperative that Toussaint, on horseback, knew very well but forgot.

VIII. A thoughtful friend asks for a recommendation for a "good old-fashioned economic determinist history of New World slavery." With serious reservations, this request is answered with Eugene D. Genovese's *From Rebellion to Revolution: Afro-American Slave Revolts in the Making of the Modern World*. Sibylle Fischer puts forth an uncompromisingly brilliant critique of Genovese's analysis of problems of political alliance, land reform, and labor in Haitian revolutionary history:[10]

> In a plot that bears alarming similarities to the Stalinist rhetoric of modernization and economic necessity, Pétion and Boyer are taken to task *not* for their role in the consolidation of minoritarian Mulatto power, or for their failure to put in place institutions that would guarantee political participation of the largely illiterate rural population, but for "political relaxation" and "land reform." There is something almost gleeful in this account that assigns a severely curtailed space to liberty and equality: the revolutionary movement is reduced to a kind of switch, when in the name of liberty and equality a more modern but equally oppressive, economic regime is ushered into being. Genovese's admiration for the modern, albeit "iron," rule of Christophe, and his failure to distinguish between Christophe and Dessalines, can be understood in the context of a historical perspective that sees progress as convergence toward "the mainstream of world history'" and modernity, not deprived of any cultural, political, or moral meaning, as inseparably linked to modernization.[11]

Fischer defies the tendency to utilize the prefix "Stalinist" as a grisly foreclosure of thought. Instead, in her deft formulation "Stalinist" does comparative work, bringing to the fore Genovese's productivism bias. The key here is "similarities." It is a rehearsal of C.L.R. James's triangulated narrative scheme.

Derek Walcott's "What the Twilight Says: An Ouverture" painfully acknowledges ambivalence in the face of the architectural monument to a Haitian revolutionary productivism, Christophe's citadel:

> There was only one noble ruin in the archipelago: Christophe's massive citadel at La Ferrière. It was a monument to egomania, more than a strategic castle: an effort to reach God's height. It was the summit of the slave's emergence from bondage. Even if the slave had surrendered one Egyptian darkness for another, that darkness was his will, that structure an image of the inaccessible achieved. To put it plainer, it was something we could look up to. It was all we had.[12]

Christophe's citadel was many things, but certainly not "all we had." The Black Radical Tragic marshals the expanse to think together Fischer's and Walcott's formulations, their difference in continuity.

IX. In the same year C.L.R. James stages *Toussaint Louverture*, Georg Lukács distinguishes between "Narrate" and "Describe" whereas:

> Description contemporizes everything. Narration recounts the past. One describes what one sees, and the spatial "present" confers a temporal "present" on men and objects. But it is an illusory present, not the immediate action of the drama. The best modern narrative has been able to infuse the dramatic element into the novel by transferring events into the past. But the contemporaneity of the observer making a description is the antithesis of the contemporaneity of the drama. Static situations are described, states or attitudes of mind of human beings or conditions of things—still lives.[13]

Description lacks the dynamism of Narration; it renders reader and narrator as passive observers (*Zuschauer*). Both Description and Narration constitute a temporal dynamic, a toggling between past and present—just by different degrees. Both (as Lukács was well aware) are always in play despite his analytical separation. James lauds W.E.B. DuBois's *Black Reconstruction in America* for going "further in regard to the demonstration of the essential verities of Marxism than anybody except perhaps Lenin and Marx himself."[14] In light of this, I want to offer up a contrast of two "wait and see" accounts pertaining to radical alignment. The first illustrates "To Describe": from Joseph Stalin's *Dialectical and Historical Materialism*: "The proletariat was developing as a class, whereas the peasantry as a class was disintegrating. And just because the proletariat was developing as a class the Marxists based their orientation on the proletariat. And they were not mistaken, for, as we know, the proletariat, subsequently grew from an insignificant force into a first-rate historical and political force."[15] The second, "To Narrate" from DuBois's *Black Reconstruction* on "The General Strike":

> What the Negro did was to wait, look and listen and try to see where his interest lay. There was no use in seeking refuge in any army which was not an army of freedom; and there was no sense in revolting against armed masters who were conquering the world. As soon, however, as it became clear that the Union armies would not or could not return fugitive slaves, and that the masters with all their fume and fury were uncertain of victory, the slave entered upon a general strike against slavery by the same methods that he had used during the period of the fugitive slave. He ran away to the first place of safety and offered his services to the Federal Army. So that in this way it was really true that he served his former master and served the emancipating army; and it was also true that this withdrawal and bestowal of his labor decided the war.[16]

Description's attention to minutiae is an expository smokescreen for the very same minutiae's lack of relationship to an analytical totality. My appropriation of Lukács to contrast DuBois and Stalin is concerned solely with this aspect of Lukács's argument. Stalin's description (which is certainly not detailed) is insufficient because he evacuates contingency from his historical dialectic. He evacuates contingency from the totality that is the process of revolutionary becoming. Stalin's assertion that Marxists bid on the proletariat because it was a developing class undermines dialectical understandings of motion to their core. Instead of taking flight at dusk, *The Owl of Minerva* takes off only during preferable air and light conditions.[17] In Stalin's describing, there is willful ignoring of the fact that one cannot incorporate the final results in an act because entering the act changes the very thing itself. Necessity is always retroactive necessity and it is a failure of description that presumes you can include into the act its own result. Contrary to this, DuBois's "wait, look and listen" *narration* resonates with a *Hamlet-esque* deliberation, an intellectual weighing of options characteristic of the act, whether political or ideational. The slaves' deliberation and decision change the coordinates of the world stage by repeating what they already in fact did—the "withdrawal and bestowal of labor" that "decides the war."

X. The Black Radical Tragic takes its temporal cues from Dr. DuBois. By way of the imperative *to perform*, the plays smash the pretense of an "illusory present." The performance repetitions of the Haitian Revolution engage a Black radical past and transubstantiate it into Lukács's "immediate action." Drama is particularly suited to capture dialectical thought in action because one can literally see the moves. *To Narrate* as works of drama it refuses to relinquish attention to the individual in recognition of the fact that where we live denies protection and prestige to racialized, gendered, and classed individuals by design.

The Black Radical Tragic is an expansive formal configuration, philosophical orientation, and stage-framework that understands that what Raymond Williams calls "the death of liberal tragedy" assumes an extension of democratic rights that the Black Radical Tradition knows is false. It is wide enough to balance a general preoccupation with Black transformative struggle, suffering, and insurgent sociality that connects Toussaint with Lumumba in a world system without playing down the particularity announced in DuBois's *Black Reconstruction*: "No matter how degraded the factory hand, he is not real estate."[18]

Victor Bulmer-Thomas frames a trajectory from his massive *Economic History of the Caribbean Since the Napoleonic Wars* as "From Scarce to Surplus Labour in the Caribbean."[19] The cluster of dramatic repetitions of the Haitian Revolution has their own ideas on what to do with the surplus. It stages Toussaint's "attempting the impossible"[20] alongside Michel-Rolph Trouillot's understanding of the Haitian Revolution as "An Unthinkable History."[21] The Black Radical Tragic in performance socializes the surplus of the Haitian Revolution, reactivating its intelligence and force each opening of a book or partition of a curtain.

Notes

The epigraphs come from Hortense Spillers, Saidiya Hartman, Farah Jasmine Griffin, Shelly Eversley, and Jennifer L. Morgan, "'Whatcha Gonna Do?': Revisiting 'Mama's Baby, Papa's Maybe: An American Grammar Book': A Conversation with Hortense Spillers, Saidiya Hartman, Farah Jasmine Griffin, Shelly Eversley, & Jennifer L. Morgan," *Women's Studies Quarterly: The Sexual Body* 35(Spring–Summer 2007): 306, and *The Polymath: Or, The Life and Opinions of Samuel R. Delany, Gentleman*, dir. Fred Barney Taylor (Maestro Media Productions, 2009).

1. David Scott, *Conscripts of Modernity: The Tragedy of Colonial Enlightenment* (Durham, NC: Duke University Press, 2004); Michel-Rolph Trouillot, *Silencing the Past: Power and the Production of History* (Boston: Beacon Press, 1995); Michel-Rolph Trouillot, *Haiti: State Against Nation: Origins & Legacy of Duvalierism* (New York: Monthly Review Press, 1990); Carolyn E. Fick, *The Making of Haiti: The Saint Domingue Revolution from Below* (Knoxville: University of Tennessee Press, 2004); Nick Nesbitt, *Universal Emancipation: The Haitian Revolution and the Radical Enlightenment* (Charlottesville: University of Virginia Press, 2008); Joan Dayan, *Haiti, History, and the Gods* (Berkeley: University of California Press, 1995); Sibylle Fischer, *Modernity Disavowed: Haiti and the Cultures of Slavery in the Age of Revolution* (Durham, NC: Duke University Press, 2004); David Patrick Geggus, *Haitian Revolutionary Studies* (Bloomington: Indiana University Press, 2002); Laurent Dubois, *Avengers of the New World: The Story of the Haitian Revolution* (Cambridge, MA: Belknap Press of Harvard University Press, 2004); Wim Klooster, *Revolutions in the Atlantic World: A Comparative History* (New York: New York University Press, 2009); Amy Wilentz, *The Rainy Season: Haiti—Then and Now* (1989; reprint, New York: Simon and Schuster, 2010); Susan Buck-Morss, *Hegel, Haiti, and Universal History* (Pittsburgh: University of Pittsburgh Press, 2009); Nicholas Mirzoeff, *The Right to Look: A Counterhistory of Visuality* (Durham, NC: Duke University Press, 2011); Ralph Korngold, *Citizen Toussaint* (London: Victor Gollancz Ltd., 1945); Aimé Césaire, *Toussaint Louverture: La Révikytuib française et le problème colonial* (Paris: Présence Africaine, 1981); Madison Smart Bell, *Toussaint Louverture: A Biography* (New York: Pantheon Books, 2007); *Toussaint L'Ouverture: The Haitian Revolution*, ed. Nick Nesbitt, introduction by Dr. Jean-Bertrand Aristide (New York: Verso, 2008); *African Americans and the Haitian*

Revolution: Selected Essays and Historical Documents, ed. Maurice Jackson and Jacqueline Bacon (New York: Routledge, 2010).

2. Michael McKeon, "A Defense of Dialectical Method in Literary History," *Diacritics* 19.1 (Spring 1989): 85.

3. I would like to thank Richard Dienst for kindly offering this formulation.

4. For an early twentieth-century application of the concept of self-determination to Haiti, see James Weldon Johnson, "Self-Determining Haiti: The American Occupation," *The Nation*, no. 111, 28 August 1920.

5. For further reading on how self-determination is framed within the theoretical orbit of Black radicalism and a larger anticolonial context, see James Forman, *Self-Determination: An Examination of the Question and Its Application to the African-American People*, rev. ed. (Washington, DC: Open Hand Publishing, 1984). Amiri Baraka and the Afro-American Commission of the Revolutionary Communist League (MLM), *The Black Nation: The Afro American National Question* (1979; reprint, Newark, NJ: Unity & Struggle Publications, 1992); C.L.R. James, *C.L.R. James on the "Negro Question,"* ed. Scott McLemee (Jackson: University Press of Mississippi, 1996); Harry Haywood, *Black Bolshevik: Autobiography of an Afro-American Communist* (Chicago: Liberator Press, 1978); E. Franklin Frazier, *Race and Culture Contacts in the Modern World* (Boston: Beacon Press, 1957), 219–23; Erez Manela, *The Wilsonian Moment: Self-Determination and the International Origins of Anticolonial Nationalism* (New York: Oxford University Press, 2007).

6. Yanis Varoufakis, "How I Became an Erratic Marxist," *The Guardian*, 18 February 2015, http://www.theguardian.com/news/2015/feb/18/yanis-varoufakis-how-i-became-an-erratic-marxist (accessed 10 June 2015).

7. "I consider Marxism the one philosophy of our time which we cannot go beyond and because I hold the ideology of existence and its 'comprehensive' method to be an enclave inside Marxism, which simultaneously engenders it and rejects it." Jean-Paul Sartre, *Search for a Method*, trans. Hazel E. Barnes (New York: Vintage Books, 1963), xxxiv. The encounters staged in this book argue for modifying Sartre's formulae through the logic of substitution and addition. This project asserts by a series of juxtapositions and readings that both Marxism and Black radicalism are the horizon thus far that "we cannot go beyond." Both Marxism and Black radicalism exist within a relationship of complementary engendering and rejection.

8. C.L.R. James, *Marxism for Our Times: C.L.R. James on Revolutionary Organization*, ed. Martin Glaberman (Jackson: University Press of Mississippi, 1999), 23.

9. Bertolt Brecht, *The Messingkauf Dialogues* (1964, originally titled *Dialogue aus dem Messingkauf*), trans. and ed. John Willett (London: Methuen, 2002), 6.

10. *Ibid.*

11. Alain Badiou, *Metapolitics*, trans. Jason Barker (London: Verso, 2006), 23.

12. Baraka, *The Black Nation*, 61. The epigraphs at the beginning of this section come from Joe Cleary, "The Antinomies of Self-Determination," in *Literature, Partition and the Nation State: Culture and Conflict in Ireland, Israel, and Palestine* (Cambridge: Cambridge

University Press, 2002), 35, and Emily Dickinson, *Final Harvest: Emily Dickinson's Poems*, ed. Thomas H. Johnson (New York: Back Bay Books, 1976), 24.

13. V. I. Lenin, "Draft Theses on National and Colonial Questions for the Second Congress of the Communist International" (1920), in *Collected Works, 2nd ed., vol. 31, trans.* Julius Katzer (Moscow: Progress Publishers, 1965), 144–51.

14. Raymond Williams, *Keywords: A Vocabulary of Culture and Society, rev. ed.* (1976; New York: Oxford University Press, 1983), 98.

15. Omar Dahbour, *Illusion of the Peoples: A Critique of National Self-Determination* (Lanham, MD: Lexington Books, 2003), 9.

16. Nikhil Pal Singh, Alys Eve Weinbaum, David Kazanjian, Brent Edwards, and Josefina Saldana, "Exacting Solidarities," in "Letters," *London Review of Books* 21.12 (10 June 1999), http://www.lrb.co.uk/v21/n12/letters (accessed 10 August 2014).

17. In a practical sense, self-determination here could be understood as an aspiring rung in what Lenin theorized as dual power.

18. C.L.R. James, "Preliminary Notes on the Negro Question" (1939), in *C.L.R. James on the "Negro Question," ed.* Scott McLemee (Jackson: University Press of Mississippi, 1996), 11.

19. For a brilliant theoretical elaboration on the *concrete*, see Karel Kosik, *Dialectics of the Concrete: A Study of Man and World* (1976), trans. Karel Kovanda and James Schmidt (Hingham, MA: D. Reidel Publishing Company, 2012).

20. C.L.R. James, "The Revolutionary Answer to the Negro Problem in the United States" (1948), in *C.L.R. James on the "Negro Question," ed.* Scott McLemee (Jackson: University Press of Mississippi, 1996), 139, 141–42.

21. Ibid., 146–47.

22. C.L.R. James, "Black Power" (1967), https://www.marxists.org/archive/james-clr/works/1967/black-power.htm (accessed 8 August 2014).

23. Ibid.

24. Jacques Derrida, quoted in Jonathan Culler, *Literary Theory: A Very Short Introduction* (1997; reprint, Oxford: Oxford University Press, 2000), 12.

25. G.W.F. Hegel, *Philosophy of Right* (1821), trans. S. W. Dyde (Mineola, NY: Dover, 2005), 43, 44.

26. Frank Kirkland, "Susan Buck-Morss, *Hegel, Haiti, and Universal History*," *Logos: A Journal of Modern Society & Culture* 11.2–3 (Spring–Summer 2012), http://logosjournal.com/2012/spring-summer_kirkland/ (accessed 27 November 2012).

27. *Respecting the naming protocols of Kirkland's essay, I purposely utilize this appellation over the Haitian Revolution.*

28. Kirkland, "Susan Buck-Morss, *Hegel, Haiti and Universal History.*"

29. Ibid.

30. Ibid.

31. Ibid.

32. Gary Wilder, *Negritude, Decolonization, and the Future of the World* (Durham, NC: Duke University Press, 2015), 20.

33. Sergei Eisenstein, *Selected Works: Writings, 1922–34, vol. 1, ed. and trans.* Richard Taylor (London: BFI Publishing, 1988), 154.

34. Patrick Griffith, "C.L.R. James and Pan Africanism: An Interview," *Black World* 21.1 (November 1971): 4–13.

35. Gordon K. Lewis, *Main Currents in Caribbean Thought: The Historical Evolution of Caribbean Society in Its Ideological Aspects, 1492–1900* (Lincoln: University of Nebraska Press, 2004), 259.

36. Walter Benjamin, "Thesis on the Concept of History," Thesis XII, quoted in Michael Löwy, *Fire Alarm: Reading Walter Benjamin's "On the Concept of History,"* trans. Chris Turner (London: Verso, 2005), 78.

37. Ibid., 82.

NOTES TO THE OVERTURE

"'Thermidorian' is the name for that which, whenever a truth procedure terminates, renders that procedure unthinkable." Badiou, *Metapolitics*, 138. The epigraphs come from Lisa Robertson, *Occasional Work and Seven Walks from the Office for Soft Architecture*, 3rd ed. (Toronto: Coach House Books, 2011), 138, and Michael McKeon, "Theory and Practice in Historical Method," in *Rethinking Historicism from Shakespeare to Milton*, ed. Ann Baynes Coiro and Thomas Fulton (Cambridge: Cambridge University Press, 2012), 42.

1. Laurent Dubois, *Haiti: The Aftershocks of History* (New York: Metropolitan Books, 2012), 135.

2. For historical works that chart the connections between John Brown and Toussaint L'Ouverture, see W. E. Burghardt DuBois, *John Brown* (1909; reprint, New York: International Publishers, 1996); and Matthew J. Clavin, *Toussaint Louverture and the American Civil War: The Promise and Peril of a Second Haitian Revolution* (Philadelphia: University of Pennsylvania Press, 2010).

3. The concept "poetry of the past" and "The Great Man Theory" come from Karl Marx's *Eighteenth Brumaire of Louis Bonaparte* (1852), a work that will be discussed in later chapters.

4. This formulation is from Kaja Silverman's talk "Unfinished Business" at the "Panorama: New Perspectives on Richter" symposium at Tate Modern, London, 21 October 2011. For Silverman's perceptive reading of Richter's paintings inspired by Germany's Red Army Faction, see Kaja Silverman, *Flesh of My Flesh* (Stanford, CA: Stanford University Press, 2009).

5. Robin D. G. Kelley, *Freedom Dreams: The Black Radical Imagination* (Boston: Beacon Press, 2002).

6. A formulation often recited by Amiri Baraka in the context of political organization.

7. Richard Dienst contributed this understanding. I am thankful for his razor-sharp insights and willingness to share.

8. Georg Lukács, *History and Class Consciousness: Studies in Marxist Dialectics*, trans. Rodney Livingston (Cambridge, MA: MIT Press, 1971).

9. Edward W. Said, *Culture and Imperialism* (New York: Vintage, 1994), 270.

10. Frantz Fanon, *The Wretched of the Earth*, trans. Richard Philcox (New York: Grove, 2004), 237.

11. Immanuel Wallerstein, "Fanon and the Revolutionary Class," in *The Capitalist World- Economy* (1979; reprint, Cambridge: Cambridge University Press, 1997), 251.

12. Walter Benjamin, "Mexican Embassy," in *One-Way Street and Other Writing*, trans. J. A. Underwood (London: Penguin Classics, 2009), 53.

13. V. I. Lenin, *The Teachings of Karl Marx* (1915; reprint, New York: International Publishers, 1964), 18.

14. Glenn Magee, *Hegel Dictionary* (London: Continuum Publishing, 2011), 248.

15. Fredric Jameson, *The Hegel Variations: On the Phenomenology of Spirit* (London: Verso, 2010), 18.

16. The critical literature on Raymond Williams is immense. For the purpose of this book, I found the following contributions invaluable: *Cultural Marxism in Postwar Britain: History, the New Left, and the Origins of Cultural Studies*, ed. Dennis Dworkin (Durham, NC: Duke University Press, 1997); Terry Eagleton, "Criticism and Politics: The Work of Raymond Williams," *New Left Review* 1.99 (1976): 3–23; Anthony Barnett, "Raymond Williams and Marxism: A Rejoinder to Terry Eagleton," *New Left Review* 1.99 (1976): 47–64; Terry Eagleton, "Resources for a Journey of Hope: The Significance of Raymond Williams," *New Left Review* 1.13–14 (1962): 22–35; Raymond Williams, *Drama from Ibsen to Eliot* (London: Chatto and Windus, 1952); Raymond Williams, *Drama from Ibsen to Brecht* (Oxford: Oxford University Press, 1969); Raymond Williams, *Drama in Performance* (1954; reprint, Middlesex: Penguin Books, 1968).

17. "The metaphysics of Christianity and Marxism are anti-tragic. That, in essence is the dilemma of Modern tragedy." George Steiner, *The Death of Tragedy* (1961; reprint, New Haven, CT: Yale University Press, 1980), 324.

18. For a sense of the diversity of rigorous thought done under the rubric of Eurocentrism, consult Samir Amin, *Eurocentrism*, trans. Russell Moore (New York: Monthly Review Press, 1989); Martin Bernal, *Black Athena: The Afroasiatic Roots of Classical Civilization*, vol. 1, *The Fabrication of Ancient Greece, 1785–1985* (New Brunswick, NJ: Rutgers University Press, 1989); and Vassilis Lambropoulos, *The Rise of Eurocentrism: Anatomy of Interpretation* (Princeton, NJ: Princeton University Press, 1993).

19. George Thomson, *Aeschylus and Athens: A Study in the Social Origins of Drama* (1940; reprint, New York: Grosset and Dunlap, 1968).

20. Kenneth Surin, "Raymond Williams on Tragedy and Revolution," in *Cultural Materialism: On Raymond Williams*, ed. Christopher Prendergast (Minneapolis: University of Minnesota Press, 1995).

21. Raymond Williams, *Modern Tragedy* (1966), ed. Pamela McCallum (Canada: Broadview Press, 2006), 33–34. Another edition of this work published in London by Verso in 1979 contains an afterword, a dramatic consideration on Milton.

22. Williams, *Modern Tragedy*, 55.

23. Ibid., 57.

24. Raymond Williams, "From Hero to Victim: Notes on the Development of Liberal Tragedy," *New Left Review* 1.20 (1963): 2.

25. Williams, *Modern Tragedy*, 60.

26. Ibid., 62.

27. Ibid., 67.

28. Ibid.

29. Gloria T. Hull, "Notes on a Marxist Interpretation of Black American Literature," *Black American Literature Forum* 12.4 (1978): 151.

30. Williams, *Modern Tragedy*, 89.

31. For an elaboration on this problem, see Jacques Racière, *The Names of History: On the Poetics of Knowledge*, trans. Hassan Melehy (Minneapolis: University of Minnesota Press, 1994).

32. Stuart Hall, "Cultural Studies and Its Theoretical Legacies," in *Stuart Hall: Critical Dialogues in Cultural Studies*, ed. Kuan-Hsing Chen and David Morley (London: Routledge, 1996), 263.

33. "Cultural Studies and the Politics of Internationalization: An Interview with Stuart Hall by Kuan-Hsing Chen," in *Stuart Hall*, ed. Chen and Morley, 394.

34. Raymond Williams, *Culture and Society, 1780–1950* (New York: Columbia University Press, 1983); Raymond Williams, *The Long Revolution* (Westport, CT: Greenwood Press, 1975).

35. C.L.R. James, "Marxism and the Intellectuals" (1961), in *Spheres of Existence: Selected Writings* (London: Allison and Busby Limited, 1980), 113–14.

36. Ibid., 113.

37. Ibid., 114.

38. Ibid., 115.

39. Ibid., 117.

40. Ibid., 118.

41. On this point of James's consistent faith in the masses, see E. San Juan Jr., "Beyond Postcolonial Theory: The Mass Line in C.L.R. James's Works," in *Beyond Postcolonial Theory* (New York: St. Martin's Press, 1999), 227–50; and Paget Henry, "C.L.R. James, African, and Afro-Caribbean Philosophy," in *Caliban's Reason: Introducing Afro-Caribbean Philosophy* (New York: Routledge, 2000), 47–67.

42. The epigraphs come from Devendra Banhart, "The Body Breaks," *Rejoicing in the Hands* (Young God Records, 2004), and Frantz Fanon, *Black Skin, White Masks*, trans. Richard Philcox (1952; reprint, New York: Grove Press, 2008), xi.

43. Frantz Fanon, *Troubles mentaux et Syndromes psychiatriques dans l'hérédo-dégénerescence spinocérébelleuse: Un cas de malade de Friedreich avec de possession* (Lyon, 1951).

44. For an insightful analysis of phylogeny, ontogeny, and sociogeny in Fanon's work, see Sylvia Wynter, "Towards the Sociogenic Principle: Fanon, Identity, the Puzzle of Conscious Experience, and What It Is Like to Be 'Black,'" in *National Identities and Sociopolitical Changes in Latin America*, ed. Durán-Cogan and Mercedes F. Gómez-Moriana

Antonio (New York: Routledge, 2001), 30–65. For a comparative study of C.L.R. James's and Frantz Fanon's respective intellectual projects, see Nelson Maldonado-Torres, "Frantz Fanon and C.L.R. James on Intellectualism and Enlightened Rationality," *Caribbean Studies* 33.2 (July–December 2005): 149–94.

45. Alice Chekri, *Frantz Fanon: A Portrait*, trans. Nadia Benabid (Ithaca, NY: Cornell University Press, 2006), 16.

46. Bertolt Brecht, *The Messingkauf Dialogues* (1965), trans. John Willett (London: Methuen, 1978), 40.

47. Frantz Fanon, *Peau noire, masques blancs* (Paris: Éditions du Seuil, 1952), 183.

48. Frantz Fanon, *Black Skin, White Masks* (1952), trans. Charles Lam Markmann (1986; reprint, Sidmouth: Pluto Press, 2008), 176.

49. Fanon, *Black Skin, White Masks*, Philcox translation, 201.

50. Walter Benjamin, "Theses on the Philosophy of History" (1940), in *Illuminations*, ed. Hannah Arendt, trans. Harry Zohn (New York: Schocken Books, 1968), 260.

51. Surely this resonates with Slavoj Žižek's reading of Lenin's maxim "to begin from the beginning" in his reading of Lenin's 1922 "Notes of a Publicist." Slavoj Žižek, "How to Begin from the Beginning," *New Left Review* 57 (May–June 2009): 43–55.

52. "I sit with Shakespeare and he winces not. Across the color line I move arm in arm with Balzac and Dumas, where smiling men and welcoming women glide in gilded halls. From out the caves of evening that swing between the strong limbed earth and the tracery of the stars, I summon Aristotle and Aurelius and what soul I will, and they come all graciously with no scorn nor condescension." W.E.B. DuBois, "On the Training of Black Men," in *The Souls of Black Folk* (1903) (New York: Bantam Books, 1989), 76.

53. Fanon, *Black Skin, White Masks*, Philcox translation, 201–2.

54. Walter Benjamin, *Selected Writings, Volume I: 1913–1926*, ed. *Marcus Bullock and Michael W. Jennings (Cambridge, MA: Belknap Press of Harvard University Press, 2004),* 293.

55. Herbert Aptheker, *One Continual Cry: David Walker's Appeal to the Colored Citizens of the World, 1829–1830* (New York: Humanities Press, 1965).

56. Fanon, *Black Skin, White Masks*, Philcox translation, 198.

57. Martin Puchner, "Marxian Speech Acts," in *Poetry of the Revolution: Marx, Manifestos, and the Avant-Gardes* (Princeton, NJ: Princeton University Press, 2006), 23–32.

58. Paul Robeson, "Ho Chi Minh Is the Toussaint L'Ouverture of Indo-China," originally published as "Here's My Story," *Freedom*, March 1954. Reprinted in *Paul Robeson Speaks: Writings Speeches Interviews, 1918–1974*, ed. Philip S. Foner (New York: Brunner/Mazel Publishers), 377–78.

59. David Macey, *Frantz Fanon: A Biography* (New York: Picador, 2000), 38.

60. For an electrifying account of Vietnamese military strategy, see General Vo Nguyen Giap, *People's War People's Army: The Viet Công Insurrection Manual for Underdeveloped Countries* (New York: Frederick A. Praeger, 1962).

61. "Create two, three, many Vietnams (Message to the Tricontinental, April 1967)," in *Che Guevara Reader*, 2nd ed., ed. David Deutschmann (Melbourne: Ocean Press, 2003), 350–62.

62. Edouard Glissant, "Author's Note" (1978), in *Monsieur Toussaint: A Play* (London: Lynne Reinner Publishers, 2005), 14.

63. Fanon, *Black Skin, White Masks*, Philcox translation, 185.

64. I am borrowing here from Shu-Mei Shih's perceptive insights on the double-signification of *comparison* in Fanon. Shu-Mei Shi, "Comparative Racialization," in *A Dictionary of Cultural and Critical Theory*, ed. Michael Payne and Jessica Rae Barbera (Cambridge: Blackwell, 2010), 143.

65. Macey, *Frantz Fanon*, 134. Verso's posthumous expanded edition of Macey's Fanon biography preserves this formulation and its wording. David Macey, *Frantz Fanon: A Biography* (2000; reprint, London: Verso, 2012), 132.

66. C.L.R. James, "How I Would Rewrite *The Black Jacobins*" (1971), *Small Axe* 8 (2000): 99. For an insightful commentary on this part of James's lecture, see Anthony Bogues, *Black Heretics, Black Prophets: Radical Political Intellectuals* (New York: Routledge, 2003), 80–81.

67. Frantz Fanon, *A Dying Colonialism*, trans. Haakon Chevalier (New York: Grover Press, 1965), 35–98, 121–46.

68. Christian Filostrat, "Appendix Interview with Josie Fanon, Frantz Fanon's Widow," in *Negritude Agonistes: Assimilation Against Nationalism in the French-Speaking Caribbean and Guyane* (Cherry Hill: Africana Homestead Legacy Publishers, 2008), 160–61.

69. The epigraph source is Bertolt Brecht, *Über Lyrik*, ed. Elisabeth Hauptmann and Rosemarie Hill (Frankfurt am Main: Suhrkamp, 1968), 46.

70. Introduction to *Brecht's Poetry of Political Exile*, ed. Ronald Spiers (Cambridge: Cambridge University Press, 2000), 7. Consult also, in this extraordinary volume, David Constantine's "The Usefulness of Poetry."

71. "Letter, Walter Benjamin to Theodor Wisengrund-Adorno. Paris, 31.5.1935," in *The Complete Correspondence: 1928–1940*, ed. Henri Lonitz, trans. Nicholas Walker (Cambridge, MA: Harvard University Press, 1999), 89.

72. Walter Benjamin, "Conversations with Brecht," in *Understanding Brecht* (1966), trans. Anna Bonstock (London: Verso, 2003), 109–10.

73. Wolfgang Fritz Haug, "Philosophizing with Marx, Gramsci, and Brecht," *Boundary 2* 34.3 (Fall 2007): 146. For more on Brecht's relationship to East Asia, see Anthony Tatlow, *Shakespeare, Brecht, and the Intercultural Sign* (Durham, NC: Duke University Press, 2001); and Anthony Tatlow, *The Mask of Evil: Brecht's Response to the Poetry, Theatre, and Thought of China and Japan, A Comparative and Critical Evaluation* (Bern: Peter Lang, 1977).

74. Walter Benjamin, "From the Brecht Commentary," in *Understanding Brecht*, 31.

75. Bertolt Brecht, *Bertolt Brecht: Journals*, trans. Hugh Rorrison, ed. John Willett (New York: Routledge, 1996), 3–4. The spelling and punctuation irregularities here conform to the original transcription.

76. Gayatri Chakravorty Spivak, "Scattered Speculations on the Question of Value," *Diacritics* 15.4 (Winter 1985): 73–93; Spivak, "What's Left of Theory?" in *An Aesthetic Education in the Era of Globalization* (Cambridge, MA: Harvard University Press, 2012), 191–217.

77. Benjamin, "Conversations with Brecht," 121.

78. James wanted Baraka to write a new foreword for a reprint edition of his *Notes on Dialectics* that never materialized.

79. Brecht, *Journals*, 234.

80. See Brent Hayes Edwards, "The 'Autonomy' of Black Radicalism," *Social Text* 67 (Summer 2001): 1–13.

81. Santiago Colás, "Silence and Dialectics: Speculations on C.L.R. James and Latin America," in *Rethinking C.L.R. James*, ed. Grant Farred (Cambridge: Blackwell, 1996), 136.

82. Jacques Roumain, "Sales Nègres"/"Filthy Negroes," *When the Tom-Tom Beats: Selected Prose & Poetry*, trans. Joanne Fungaroli and Ronald Sauer (Washington, DC: Azul Editions, 1995), 84–85.

83. Miguel Mellino, "The *Langue* of the Damned: Fanon and the Remnants of Europe," *South Atlantic Quarterly* 112.1 (Winter 2013): 79–80.

84. Ibid., 80.

NOTES TO CHAPTER 1

1. Gilles Deleuze and Félix Guattari, *A Thousand Plateaus: Capitalism and Schizophrenia*, trans. Brian Massumi (Minneapolis: University of Minnesota Press, 1987), 204.

2. Cheryl Wall, *Worrying the Line: Black Women Writers, Lineage, and Literary Tradition* (Chapel Hill: University of North Carolina Press, 2005).

3. Fredric Jameson, *The Political Unconscious: Narrative as a Socially Symbolic Act* (Ithaca, NY: Cornell University Press, 1981), 35.

4. Eugene O'Neill, *Anna Christie/The Emperor Jones/The Hairy Ape* (New York: Vintage International, 1995). The epigraphs come from Avery F. Gordon, *Ghostly Matters: Haunting and the Sociological Imagination* (Minneapolis: University of Minnesota Press, 1997), 17, and Common, *Nobody's Smiling* (Def Jam Recordings, 22 July 2014).

5. For more information on the imperial history of the United States in Haiti, consult Mary A. Renda, *Taking Haiti: Military Occupation and the Culture of U.S. Imperialism, 1915–1940* (Chapel Hill: University of North Carolina Press, 2001); Paul Farmer, *The Uses of Haiti*, 2nd ed. (Monroe, ME: Common Courage Press, 2003); and Randall Robinson, *An Unbroken Agony: Haiti, from Revolution to the Kidnapping of a President* (New York: Basic Books, 2007).

6. Cedric Robinson, *Black Marxism: The Making of the Black Radical Tradition* (1983; reprint, Chapel Hill: University of North Carolina Press, 2000), 72–73.

7. *The Emperor Jones* premiered at the Playwright's Theatre in 1920. It was revived by the Provincetown Players in 1924 and 1926. An operatic version premiered at the Metropolitan Opera House in 1933.

8. Egil Tornqvist, *A Drama of Souls: Studies in O'Neill's Super-naturalistic Technique* (New Haven, CT: Yale University Press, 1970).

9. Shannon Steen, "Melancholy Bodies: Racial Subjectivity and Whiteness in O'Neill's *The Emperor Jones*," *Theatre Journal* 52 (2000): 346.

10. Carme Manuel, "A Ghost in the Expressionist Jungle of O'Neill's *The Emperor Jones*," *African American Review* (Spring–Summer 2005): 7.

11. Tzvetan Todorov, *The Fantastic: A Structural Approach to a Literary Genre*, trans. Richard Howard (Ithaca, NY: Cornell University Press, 1975), 76–77.

12. Toni Morrison, *Beloved* (New York: Plume, 1988), 274.

13. Gordon, *Ghostly Demarcations*, 63–64.

14. Houston Baker Jr., *Modernism and the Harlem Renaissance* (Chicago: University of Chicago Press, 1987), 7.

15. Edward W. Said, *Freud and the Non-European* (London: Verso in Association with the Freud Museum, London, 2003), 25–27.

16. Ruby Cohn, "Black Power on Stage: *Emperor Jones* and *King Christophe*," *Yale French Studies*, no. 46 (1971): 41–47.

17. John Berger, *And Our Faces, My Heart, Brief as Photos* (1984; reprint, New York: Vintage International, 1991), 92.

18. Nikos Papastergiadis, *Modernity as Exile: The Stranger in John Berger's Writing* (Manchester: Manchester University Press, 1993), 18.

19. Raymond Williams, *Key Words: A Revised Vocabulary of Culture and Society* (New York: Oxford University Press, 1983), 126.

20. Nathan Irvin Huggins, *Harlem Renaissance* (New York: Oxford University Press, 1973), 296.

21. Louis Kantor, "O'Neill Defends His Play of Negro" (1924), in *Conversations with Eugene O'Neill*, ed. Mark W. Estrin (Jackson: University Press of Mississippi, 1990), 48.

22. O'Neill, *Anna Christie/The Emperor Jones/The Hairy Ape*, 7.

23. Ibid.

24. Ibid., 9.

25. Ibid., 23.

26. Ibid., 33.

27. Ibid., 32.

28. Ibid., 33.

29. Ibid., 34–35.

30. Alain Locke, *The New Negro* (1925; reprint, New York: Atheneum, 1983), 153.

31. Walter Benjamin, *Illuminations*, ed. Hannah Arendt, trans. Harry Zohn (New York: Schocken Books, 1968), 255.

32. Ibid., 257.

33. The epigraphs come from Vladimir Nizhny, *Lessons with Eisenstein*, trans. and ed. Jay Leyda and Ivor Montagu (New York: Hill and Wang, 1962), 83–84; Amiri Baraka, quoted in D. H. Melhem, *Heroism in the New Black Poetry: Introductions and Interviews* (Lexington: University Press of Kentucky, 1990), 257; and from a private conversation.

34. Mise-en-shot's precise meaning fluctuates in Nizhny's volume. It most often refers to the parsing of a shot into its component parts (thus implying the task of editing) while always approaching these components in dialectical relationship to a mise-en-scène. For Eisenstein, the dialectician who peppers his writings with insight from

Hegel, Marx, Engels, Lenin, and Stalin, cinematic *mise-en-scène* is an unapologetically higher progression, a higher development that subsumes all that is progressive in theatrical *mise-en-scène* while overcoming via technological innovation theater's limitations. One is struck by the breadth of literary references found in his theoretical writings: Kleist's marionettes, Engel's insight on the doctrine of Calvinistic predetermination, the chorus in Greek Attic tragedy, his nascent concept of the "inner film-monologue" patterned after narrative technique in Joyce's *Ulysses* all find a home in his prose. Eisenstein (like Brecht) defended Joyce from the ill reception he received from many Marxist critics. The two auteurs had a hearty intellectual friendship and Eisenstein planned (but never realized) a film adaptation of Marx's *Capital Volume 1*, in which Joyce's *Ulysses* provided the formal inspiration.

35. Nizhny, *Lessons with Eisenstein*, 24.

36. Elin Diamond, *Unmaking Mimesis: Essays on Feminism and Theater* (London: Routledge, 1997), xiv; Bertolt Brecht, "On Gestic Music" (1957), in *Brecht on Theatre: The Development of an Aesthetic* (1964), ed. and trans. John Willett (New York: Hill and Wang, 1992), 104–6.

37. Nizhny, *Lessons with Eisenstein*, 48–49.

38. Sergei Eisenstein, "A Course in Treatment," in *Film Form: Essays in Film Theory* (1949), ed. and trans. Jay Leyda (San Diego: Harcourt, 1997), 85.

39. Ibid., 86.

40. Nizhny, *Lessons with Eisenstein*, 3.

41. Ibid., 44.

42. Ibid., xiii.

43. Ibid., 92.

44. Amiri Baraka, "Understanding Readiness," in *Somebody Blew Up America and Other Poems* (Philipsburg, St. Martin: House of Nehesi Publishers, 2003), 21–23; Stokely Carmichael and Michael Ekwueme Thelwell, *Ready for Revolution: The Life and Struggles of Stokely Carmichael {Kwame Ture}* (New York: Scribner, 2003).

45. Fredric Jameson, "The Vanishing Mediator; or, Max Weber as Storyteller" (1973), in *The Ideologies of Theory: Essays, 1971–1986, vol. 2, The Syntax of History* (Minneapolis: University of Minnesota Press, 1989), 3–34.

46. On Césaire's text's relationship to the Nazi Holocaust, consult "'Un Choc en Retour': Aimé Césaire's Discourse on Colonialism and Genocide," in Michael Rothberg, *Multidirectional Memory: Remembering the Holocaust in the Age of Decolonization* (Stanford, CA: Stanford University Press, 2009), 66–107.

47. Thanks to Professor Sydney Finkelstein for recommending this radio program. *Hello Americans*, episode 3, "The Islands," 29 November 1942. The epigraph source is Orson Welles and Peter Bogdanovitch, *This Is Orson Welles* (1992; reprint, New York: Da Capo Press, 1998), 374.

48. Jameson, *The Political Unconscious*, 9.

49. Minkah Makalani, *In the Cause of Freedom: Radical Black Internationalism from Harlem to London, 1917–1939* (Chapel Hill: University of North Carolina Press, 2011).

50. "Letter from George Padmore to Dr. Alain Locke," 19 December 1936, in C.L.R. James, *Toussaint Louverture: The Story of the Only Successful Slave Revolt in History, A Play in Three Acts*, ed. Christian Høgsbjerg (Durham, NC: Duke University Press, 2013), 217.

51. C.L.R. James, "On the Origins," *Radical America* 2.4 (July–August 1968): 25.

52. Aimé Césaire, *Discourse on Colonialism* (1955), trans. Joan Pinkham (New York: Monthly Review Press, 2000), 36–37.

53. Eisenstein, "A Course in Treatment," 87. For more on Dumas, see Jean Lucas-Dubreton, *The Fourth Musketeer: The Life of Alexander Dumas*, trans. Maida Castelhun Darton (New York: Coward-McCann, 1928). For a detailed account of Eisenstein's "Haiti projects" as well as his friendship with Paul and Essie Robeson, see Ronald Bergan, *Sergei Eisenstein: A Life in Conflict* (Woodstock: The Overlook Press, 1999), 266.

54. S. J. Woolf, "O'Neill Plots a Course for the Drama" (1931), in *Conversations with Eugene O'Neill*, 116–17.

55. Namesake of the massive buried sea treasure that is the precious metaled condition of possibility for Edmond Dantès's transformation to the Count of Monte Cristo.

56. Eisenstein, "A Course in Treatment," 89–90.

57. Ibid., 90.

58. Tom Reiss, *Black Count: Glory, Revolution, Betrayal, and the Real Count of Monte Cristo* (New York: Crown, 2012).

59. On more current violations of Haiti's sovereignty, consult Paul Farmer, *The Uses of Haiti*, 3rd ed. (Monroe: Common Courage Press, 2006); Noam Chomsky, Paul Farmer, and Amy Goodman, *Getting Haiti Right This Time* (Monroe: Common Courage Press, 2004); Peter Hallward, *Damning the Flood: Haiti and the Politics of Containment* (London: Verso, 2007); and Robinson, *An Unbroken Agony*.

NOTES TO CHAPTER 2

1. Jacques Lacan, "The Splendor of Antigone," in *The Seminar of Jacques Lacan, Book VII: The Ethics of Psychoanalysis, 1959–1960*, ed. Jacques-Alain Miller, trans. Dennis Porter (New York: Norton, 1992), 245.

2. Ibid., 244.

3. C.L.R. James, *The Black Jacobins: Toussaint L'Ouverture and the San Domingo Revolution* (1938, 1963) (New York: Vintage, 1989), 291 (hereafter *The Black Jacobins-history*).

4. C.L.R. James, *The Black Jacobins*, in *The C.L.R. James Reader*, ed. Anna Grimshaw (Oxford: Blackwell, 1992), 67–111 (hereafter *The Black Jacobins-play*).

5. A typescript with annotations of the 1934 play-script is now held in the Jack Haston collection (a British Trotskyist and acquaintance of James) at the Hull History Center, Hull, U.K. Prior to that it was archived at the Brynmor Jones Library at the University of Hull. "Toussaint L'Ouverture: the story of the only successful slave revolt in history: a play in 3 acts" [by CLR James] (109 pp.), GB 050 U DJH/21/1, U DJH/21/1, c. 1936. I am grateful to James scholar Christian Høgsbjerg for discovering the 1934 play-script and

sending me the typescript from: C.L.R. James, *C.L.R. Toussaint Louverture: The Story of the Only Successful Slave Revolt in History; A Play in Three Acts* (C.L.R. James Archives), ed. Christian Høgsbjerg (Durham, NC: Duke University Press, 2012). A different version of the 1967 revision anthologized by Grimshaw can be found in the Playscript Collection of the Schomburg Center for Research in Black Culture, New York Public Library [Sc MG 53]. The Special Collections Library of Penn State University has two 1967 versions: [VF Lit 0581R]. I am grateful to Aldon Nielsen for sending me a copy of the 1967 version.

6. An outstanding collection of scholarship on James's play is steadily amassing, which includes Fionnghuala Sweeney, "The Haitian Play: C.L.R. James' *Toussaint Louverture* (1936)," *International Journal of Francophone Studies* 14.1–2 (2011): 143–63; Nicole King, "C.L.R. James, Genre and Cultural Politics," in *Beyond Boundaries: C.L.R. James and Postnational Studies*, ed. Christopher Gair (London: Pluto Press, 2006), 13–38; Reinhard Sander, "C.L.R. James and the Haitian Revolution," *World Literatures in English* 26.2 (1986): 277–90; Gordon Collier, "The 'Noble Ruins' of Art and the Haitian Revolution: Carpentier, Césaire, Glissant, James, O'Neill, Walcott and Others," in *Fusion of Cultures?* ed. Peter O. Stummer and Christopher Balme, Ansel Papers 2 (Atlanta: Rodopi, 1996), 269–328; Lindsey R. Swindall, *The Politics of Paul Robeson's Othello* (Jackson: University of Mississippi Press, 2011), 59–65; Paul Robeson Jr., *The Undiscovered Paul Robeson: An Artist's Journey, 1898–1939* (New York: John Wiley and Sons, 2001), 239; Frank Rosengarten, *Urbane Revolutionary: C.L.R. James and the Struggle for a New Society* (Jackson: University of Mississippi Press, 2008), 220–32; Kent Worcester, *C.L.R. James: A Political Biography* (Albany: State University of New Press, 1996), 35; Paul Buhle, *C.L.R. James: The Artist as Revolutionary* (1988; reprint, London: Verso, 1993), 56–57; Aldon Lynn Nielsen, *C.L.R James: A Critical Introduction* (Jackson: University Press of Mississippi, 1997); and Anthony Bogues, *Caliban's Freedom: The Early Political Thought of C.L.R. James* (London: Pluto Press, 1997).

7. For further reading, see Paul B. Miller, "Enlightened Hesitations: Black Masses and Tragic Heroes in C.L.R. James's *The Black Jacobins*," *MLN* 116.5 (2001): 1069–90; Nick Nesbitt, "Troping Toussaint, Reading Revolution," *Research in African Literatures* 35.2 (2004): 18–33; J. Michael Dash, "The Theater of the Haitian Revolution/The Haitian Revolution as Theatre," *Small Axe* 9.2 (2005): 16–23; and Louis-Phillippe Dalembert, J. Michael Dash, Edwidge Danticat, Danny Laferriere, and Evelyn Trouillot, "Roundtable: Writing, History, Revolution," *Small Axe* 9.2 (2005): 189–99.

8. Edward W. Said, *Beginnings: Intention and Method* (1975; reprint, New York: Columbia University Press, 1985), 71.

9. Fred Moten, "Not in Between: Lyric Painting, Visual History, and the Postcolonial Future," *Drama Review* 47.1 (Spring 2003): 127–48.

10. Peter Hallward, "Edouard Glissant Between the Singular and the Specific," *Yale Journal of Criticism* 11.2 (1998): 449–50; Edouard Glissant, *Le discours antillais* (Paris: Seuil, 1981); Edouard Glissant, *Poétique de la Relation* (Paris: Gallimard, 1993).

11. I found this undated telegram (quoted in the epigraph following the heading) from Nazim Hikmet to Paul Robeson during a July 2011 visit to the Marx Memorial Library,

Clerkenwell Green, London. Upon my arrival, they were processing recently received materials on Paul Robeson. The archivists were gracious enough to allow me to copy the material in return for helping them place certain proper names, Harlem-based markers, etc. I have not been able to locate an appropriate suggested citation format for this source or a date for the communiqué.

For a précis and roster of the first ten years of productions of the Incorporated Stage Society (London), see the following book facsimile from the collection of the University of Michigan Library: *The Incorporated Stage Society: Ten Years, 1899 to 1909* (London: Chatwick Press, 1909). The Stage Society commenced with a production of George Bernard Shaw's *You Can Never Tell* at the Royalty Theatre on the 26 November 1899. An auspicious start for the theater company—defiant of London's current censorship and profanity codes, this production was greeted with police raids. The original program of James's play is housed at the Victoria and Albert Theatre & Performance Archives, Incorporated Stage Society (1936), "Toussaint Louverture: A Play in Three Acts by C.L.R. James" [program], 15 and 16 March, London.

12. Reviews and announcements on James's play include "Toussaint Louverture," *Daily News Chronicle*, 11 March 1936; "Paul Robeson: Stage Society Does Not Give Him Great Part," *Evening News*, 17 March 1936; "Toussaint Louverture," *Glasgow Herald*, 19 March 1936; "Paul Robeson in Negro Play a Dignified Study," *Morning Post*, 17 March 1936; "Stage Society: 'Toussaint Louverture' by C.L.R. James," *The Times*, 17 March 1936; P.L.M., "Paul Robeson as Slave Leader," *Daily Herald*, 17 March 1936; Stephen Williams, "Robeson as Negro Leader," *Evening Standard*, 17 March 1936; Ivor Brown, "'Toussaint L'Ouverture' by C.LR. James," *The Observer*, 22 March 1936; G.W.B., "Toussaint L'Ouverture: A Play. By C.L.R. James," *Sunday Times*, 22 March 1936; Wilson M. Disher, "Mr. Robeson's Thrilling Part," *Daily Mail*, 17 March 1936; "Negro Play," *Sunday Times*, 1 March 1936; and W.A.D., "Paul Robeson as Toussaint: Drama of a Liberator," *Daily Telegraph*, 17 March 1936.

13. Excerpts from these two reviews are compiled in C.L.R. James, "Paul Robeson: Black Star" (1970), in *Spheres of Existence: Selected Writings* (Westport, CT: Lawrence Hill and Company, 1980), 258–59.

14. Scott, *Conscripts of Modernity*, 74.

15. Ibid., 130.

16. *The Black Jacobins*-play, 71.

17. *The Black Jacobins*-history, 24–25.

18. Ibid., x.

19. Raymond Williams, *Drama in Performance* (1954; reprint, London: Penguin, 1968), 12.

20. *The Black Jacobins*-play, 77.

21. Ibid., 73.

22. Ibid., 99.

23. Ibid., 73–74.

24. Ibid., 74.

25. Ibid., 75–76. Michelle Ann Stephens relates this moment in the play to her theorization of "Black Empire." Stephens, *Black Empire: The Masculine Global Imaginary of*

Caribbean Intellectuals in the United States, 1914–1962 (Durham, NC: Duke University Press, 2005), 213.

26. *The Black Jacobins-play*, 75.

27. Ibid.

28. Ibid., 77.

29. Ibid., 78.

30. *Don Giovanni: A Comic Opera in Two Acts*, music by Wolfgang Amadeus Mozart, words by Lorenzo Da Ponte, English version by Edward J. Dent (London: Oxford University Press, 1938). The epigraph source is Theodor Adorno, *"Monograms" Minima Moralia: Reflections from Damaged Life* (1951), trans. E.F.N. Jephcott (London: Verso, 1974), 203.

31. Liane Curtis, "The Sexual Politics of Teaching Mozart's Don Giovanni," *NWSA Journal* 12.1 (2001): 119–42.

32. Edward W. Said, *On Late Style: Music and Literature Against the Grain* (New York: Pantheon, 2006), 69.

33. *The Black Jacobins-play*, 71.

34. Ibid., 70–71.

35. Ibid., 103.

36. Ibid., 104.

37. Frantz Fanon, *The Wretched of the Earth* (New York: Grove Press, 1963), 311.

38. Wye Jamison Allanbrook, *Rhythmic Gesture in Mozart: "Le nozze di Fiagro" and "Don Giovanni"* (Chicago: University of Chicago Press, 1984), 80.

39. Mladen Dolar, "If Music Be the Food of Love," in *Opera's Second Death* by Slavoj Žižek and Mladen Dolar (New York: Routledge, 2002), 47–48.

40. Maynard Solomon, *Mozart: A Life* (New York: Harper Collins, 1995), 514.

41. Ibid., 519.

42. Ibid., 506.

43. *Don Giovanni*, 74 .

44. Dolar, "If Music Be the Food of Love," 49.

45. James, *Toussaint Louverture*, 81.

46. For a Deleuzian theory of "machines," see Gerald Raunig, *A Thousand Machines: A Concise Philosophy of the Machine as Social Movement*, trans. Aileen Derieg (Los Angeles: Semiotext[e], 2010). This slim volume houses a wonderful exposition on the political importance of the bicycle.

47. The title of the heading comes from Anthony Bogues, who presents an inspiring take on what he calls the "heretic stream of the Black Radical Tradition" in *Black Heretics*, 10, 16, 72.

48. *The Black Jacobins-history*, 279.

49. Slavoj Žižek, *On Belief* (London: Routledge, 2001), 7.

50. Ibid., 8.

51. Lacan, "The Splendor of Antigone," 245.

52. *The Black Jacobins-play*, 76.

53. Ibid., 97.

54. Ibid., 98.

55. *The Black Jacobins-history*, 284.

56. Ibid., 286.

57. Scott, *Conscripts of Modernity*, 162.

58. Fick, *The Making of Haiti*, 209.

59. Wolfgang Schivelbusch, "Optimistic Tragedies: The Plays of Heiner Müller," *New German Critique*, no. 2 (Spring 1974): 1004-13.

60. Heiner Müller, *Germania*, trans. and annot. Bernard and Caroline Schütze, ed. Sylvère Lotringer (New York: Semiotext[e], 1990), 13.

61. Bertolt Brecht, *The Measures Taken and Other Lehrstücke* (1955), **ed.** John Willet and Ralph Manheim, trans. Carl R. Mueller (New York: Arcade Publishing, 2001), 28.

62. Jonathan Kalb, *The Theater of Heiner Müller* (New York: Limelight Editions, 2001), 28.

63. Brecht, *The Measures Taken, introductory note*. This is an unnumbered excerpt from Brecht's article "The German Drama: Pre-Hitler," published in *Left Review*, London, July 1936. Brecht, *Brecht on Theatre*, 77–80.

64. Brecht, *The Measures Taken*, 25.

65. Ibid., 24.

66. Andreas Huyseen, "Producing Revolution: Heiner Müller's *Mauser* as Learning Play," in *After the Great Divide: Modernism, Mass Culture, Postmodernism* (Bloomington: Indiana University Press, 1986), 82.

67. Kalb, *The Theater of Heiner Müller*, 52.

68. Ibid., 55.

69. Heiner Müller, "Brecht vs. Brecht," in *Germania*, 133.

70. Huyseen, *After the Great Divide*, 87.

71. Heiner Müller, *Three Plays: Philoctetes the Horatian Mauser*, trans. Nathaniel McBride (London: Seagull Books, 2011), 93–94.

72. Alain Badiou, *Philosophy for Militants*, trans. Bruno Bosteels (New York: Verso, 2012), 33–34; Badiou discusses *The Measures Taken* and Brecht more broadly in Alain Badiou, *The Century*, trans. Alberto Toscano (Cambridge: Polity, 2005), 39–57, 111–30.

73. The epigraph source is Peter Hallward, "An Interview with Jean-Bertrand Aristide," *London Review of Books*, 22 February 2007, 9.

74. J. Michael Dash, *Edouard Glissant* (Cambridge: Cambridge University Press, 1995), 91–92.

75. William Shakespeare, *Coriolanus* (London: Methuen, 1987), 236.

76. Aimé Césaire, *Notebook of a Return to the Native Land*, trans. and ed. Clayton Eshelman and Annette Smith (Middletown, CT: Wesleyan University Press, 2001), 16.

77. Dash, *Edouard Glissant*, 16.

78. For further reading, consult Edouard Glissant, *Caribbean Discourse: Selected Essays [Le discours antillais]* (1981), trans. J. Michael Dash (Charlottesville: University Press of Virginia, 1989); Edouard Glissant, *L'Intention poétique* (Paris: Seuil, 1969); Glissant, *Poétique de la Relation*; Celia M. Britton, *Edouard Glissant and Postcolonial Theory:*

Strategies of Language and Resistance (Charlottesville: University Press of Virginia, 1999); and Nathaniel Mackey, *Discrepant Engagement: Dissonance, Cross-Culturality, and Experimental Writing* (Cambridge: Cambridge University Press, 1993).

79. Hallward, "Edouard Glissant Between the Singular and the Specific," 441–64; Peter Hallward, "Edouard Glissant: From Nation to Relation," in *Absolutely Postcolonial: Writing Between the Singular and the Specific* (Manchester: Manchester University Press, 2001), 66–125.

80. Glissant, *Monsieur Toussaint*, 21.

81. Moten, "Not in Between," 113.

82. Glissant, *Monsieur Toussaint*, 15–16.

83. Ibid., 11–12.

84. Ibid., 13.

85. Ibid., 16.

86. Glissant, *Caribbean Discourse*, 201.

87. Augusto Boal, *Theatre of the Oppressed* (1974) in *Teatro do Primido*, trans. Charles A. McBride and Maria-Odila Leal McBride (New York: Theatre Communications Group, 1985), 46.

88. Glissant, *Le discours antillais*, 800–801.

89. Dash translates this passage somewhat differently: "The central focus of this work is precisely that, just as Martinican reality can only be understood from the perspective of all possible implications, abortive or not, of this cultural relationship, and the ability to transcend them, so the proliferation of visions of the world is meant only for those who try to make sense of them in terms of similarities that *are not to be standardized*. That these poetics are inseparable from the growth of the people, from their time for belonging and imagining." Glissant, *Caribbean Discourse*, 254.

90. I am grateful to Brent Hayes Edwards for his help with questions of French translation. All errors are my own.

91. Hallward's awe-inspiring study on Deleuze is helpful to consult in this regard as it relates to Deleuze's notion of *becoming*. Peter Hallward, *Out of This World: Deleuze and the Philosophy of Creation* (London: Verso, 2006), 3, 61, 109, 140, 153.

92. To "take part" is Robert A. Hill's spot-on formulation encapsulating in two words the essence of C.L.R. James's commitment to radical participatory democracy. Robert A. Hill, preface to *You Don't Play with Revolution: The Montreal Lectures of C.L.R. James*, ed. David Austin (Edinburgh: AK Press, 2009), xii–xvi.

93. Aimé Césaire, *Return to My Native Land* (1956), trans. John Berger and Anna Bostock (Middlesex: Penguin, 1969).

94. John Berger, "Twelve Theses on the Economy of the Dead," in *Hold Everything Dear: Dispatches on Survival and Resistance* (New York: Pantheon Books, 2007), 5.

95. Glissant, *Monsieur Toussaint*, 115–16.

96. *The Black Jacobins-history*, 406.

97. Aimé Césaire, "Letter to Maurice Thorez," trans. Hassan Chike Jeffers, in M. Salah, *How to Liberate Marx from His Eurocentrism: Notes on African/Black Marxism*, http://

diversity.wustl.edu/wp-content/uploads/2012/08/Hassan_Documenta-Notebook_91.pdf (accessed 15 June 2015), 38.

98. Robert A. Hill, "In England, 1932–1938," in *C.L.R. James: His Life and Work*, ed. Paul Buhle (London: Allison and Busby Limited, 1986), 61–80.

99. George Lamming, *The Pleasures of Exile* (1960; reprint, Ann Arbor: University of Michigan Press, 1992), 36.

100. Hill, "In England, 1932–1938," 73.

101. C.L.R. (Cyril Lionel Robert) James Papers, Boxes 5 and 2, Rare Book and Manuscript Library, Columbia University Library.

102. Bertolt Brecht, *Stories of Mr. Keuner*, trans. Martin Chalmers (1966; reprint, San Francisco: City Lights, 2001).

103. C.L.R. James, *Special Delivery: The Letters of C.L.R. James to Constance Webb, 1939–1948*, ed. Anna Grimshaw (Oxford: Blackwell, 1996), 89–92.

104. James, *Spheres of Existence*, 256.

105. Ibid.

106. Ibid.

107. *The Black Jacobins*-history, 276.

108. C.L.R. James, "Black Power" (1967), in *Spheres of Existence: Selected Writings* (Westport, CT: Lawrence Hill and Company, 1980); C.L.R. James, *Nkrumah and the Ghana Revolution* (1962; reprint, London: Allison and Busby, 1982); C.L.R. James, "Walter Rodney and the Question of Power," in *Walter Rodney, Revolutionary and Scholar: A Tribute*, ed. Edward A. Alpers and Pierre-Michel Fontaine (Los Angeles: Center for Afro-American Studies, 1982), 133–46.

109. James, *Letters*, 89.

110. See Swindall, *The Politics of Paul Robeson's Othello*.

111. James, *Letters*, 90.

112. Bogues, *Caliban's Freedom*, 46.

113. The epigraphs come from Said, *Beginnings*, 3, and Franz Kafka, *The Zuraü Aphorisms* (1931), trans. Roberto Calasso (New York: Schocken Books, 2006), 20.

114. James A. Snead, "Repetition as a Figure of Black Culture," in *Black Literature & Literary Theory*, ed. Henry Louis Gates Jr. (1984; reprint, New York: Routledge, 1990), 67.

115. Said, *Beginnings*, 30.

116. C.L.R. James, *The Black Jacobins*, signed typescript and mimeograph, Pattee Library and Paterno Library, Pennsylvania State University, 50616992.

117. Michelle Cliff, *Abeng* (New York: Plume, 1995), 3.

NOTES TO CHAPTER 3

The epigraphs come from Kwame Nkrumah, *Ghana: The Autobiography of Kwame Nkrumah* (1957; reprint, New York: International Publishers, 1984), 44, and Georg Lukàcs, *Lenin: A Study in the Unity of His Thought* (1924), trans. Nicholas Jacobs (London: Verso, 1997), 80–81.

1. Robinson, *Black Marxism*, 171.

2. Belinda Edmondson, *Making Men: Gender, Literary Authority, and Women's Writing in Caribbean Narrative* (Durham, NC: Duke University Press, 1999); Christian Høgsbjerg, *C.L.R. James in Imperial Britain* (Durham, NC: Duke University Press, 2014); Stephen Howe, "C.L.R. James: Visions of History, Visions of Britain," in *West Indian Intellectuals in Britain*, ed. Bill Schwarz (Manchester: Manchester University Press), 153–74.

3. C.L.R. James, *Letters from London*, ed. Nicholas Laughlin (Maraval: Prospect Press, 2003), 14.

4. John Berger, "Auguste Rodin" (1967), in *Selected Essays*, ed. Geoff Dyer (New York: Vintage International), 164.

5. Hazel V. Carby, *Race Men* (Cambridge, MA: Harvard University Press, 1998).

6. I want to acknowledge the recent work of Michelle Ann Stephens on the impact of racialization on understandings of nakedness, flesh, and skin in the Robeson pictures and other sites. My book was too far along in production to incorporate it when I discovered her insightful work. This is true for the work of Jean-Luc Nancy and Federico Ferrari as well. Michelle Ann Stephens, *Skin Acts: Race, Psychoanalysis, and the Black Male Performer* (Durham, NC: Duke University Press, 2014); Jean-Luc Nancy and Federico Ferrari, *Being Nude: The Skin of Images* (2006), trans. Anne O'Byrne and Carlie Anglemire (New York: Fordham University Press, 2014).

7. Judith Cladel, *Rodin* (Paris: Éditions Aimery Somogy, 1948), plates 5 and 7, pages unnumbered.

8. http://www.rodin-web.org/works/1878_baptist.htm (accessed 7 January 2013).

9. C.L.R. James, *Notes on Dialectics: Hegel-Marx-Lenin* (1948; Westport, CT: Lawrence Hill and Company, 1980), 171–84.

10. Ibid.

11. Rainer Maria Rilke, *Auguste Rodin* (Mineola, NY: Dover, 2006), 4, 16.

12. Ibid., 33.

13. Ibid., 14–15.

14. James, *Letters from London*, 13–14.

15. Rosalind E. Krauss, *Passages in Modern Sculpture* (New York: Viking, 1977), 29.

16. Carby, *Race Men*, 54.

17. Frantz Fanon, *Peau noire, masques blancs* (Paris: Éditions du Seuil, 1952), 6.

18. Fanon, *Black Skin, White Masks*, Markmann translation, 2.

19. John Berger, *Ways of Seeing* (1972; reprint, London: Penguin Books, 1977), 54.

20. Carby, *Race Men*, 116.

21. *The Black Jacobins-history*, x.

22. Krauss, *Passages in Modern Sculpture*, 20–21.

23. Ibid., 26.

24. Ibid., 27.

25. "Mediation," in *A Dictionary of Marxist Thought*, 2nd ed., ed. Tom Bottomore, Laurence Harris, V. G. Kiernan, and Ralph Milibrand (Oxford: Blackwell, 1991), 373.

26. Michael Inwood, "Mediation," in *A Hegel Dictionary* (Oxford: Blackwell, 1999), 184.

27. Ibid., 184–85.

28. Georg Lukács, "Moses Hess and the Problems of Idealist Dialectics," in *Tactics and Ethics: Political Writings, 1919–1929*, trans. Michael McColgan (London: NLB, 1973), 189.

29. Anna Grimshaw, "C.L.R. James: A Revolutionary Vision," in *The C.L.R. James Reader*, ed. Anna Grimshaw (Oxford: Blackwell, 1992), 10.

30. C.L.R. James, "Dialectical Materialism and the Fate of Humanity" (1947), in *The C.L.R. James Reader*, ed. Grimshaw, 164.

31. Ibid., 167.

32. Ibid., 173.

33. San Juan, *Beyond Postcolonial Theory*, 231.

34. James, "Dialectical Materialism and the Fate of Humanity," 173–74.

35. Williams, *Keywords*, 22.

36. Ibid., 206–7.

37. David Scott's research demonstrates that James in 1963 added six new paragraphs to the thirteenth chapter of *The Black Jacobins*, entitled "The War of Independence." These chapters emphasize the "tragic" dimensions of James's argument and include the author's definition of hamartia. See *The Black Jacobins-history*, 289–92.

38. C.L.R. James, "Letters to Literary Critics," in *The C.L.R. James Reader*, ed. Grimshaw, 222.

39. Ibid.

40. Ibid., 227.

41. C.L.R. James, "Notes on *Hamlet*" (1953), in *The C.L.R. James Reader*, ed. Grimshaw, 243.

42. Fredric Jameson, George Forster Lecture 2012, https://www.youtube.com/watch?v=qh79_zwNI_s (accessed 1 July 2014).

43. James, *Special Delivery*, 5.

44. San Juan, *Beyond Postcolonial Theory*, 227–50.

45. Robinson, *Black Marxism*, 266.

46. C.L.R. James, *Beyond a Boundary* (1963; reprint, Durham, NC: Duke University Press, 1993), 151.

47. Scott, *Conscripts of Modernity*, 16.

48. Lacan, "A Commentary on Sophocles's *Antigone*," 251.

49. Scott, *Conscripts of Modernity*, 20.

50. Michael McKeon, *The Origins of the English Novel: 1600–1740* (1987; reprint, Baltimore: Johns Hopkins University Press, 2002), 8.

51. Scott, *Conscripts of Modernity*, 4.

52. Ibid., 7.

53. Ibid., 13.

54. Ibid., 59.

55. Ibid., 135.

56. Donald E. Pease, "The Crisis of Critique in Postcolonial Modernity," *Boundary 2* 37.3 (2010): 187.

57. Edward W. Said, "A Lingering Old Order," *in On Late Style*, 106.

58. Alex Dupuy, "Toussaint-Louverture and the Haitian Revolution: A Reassessment of C.L.R. James's Interpretation," in *C.L.R. James: His Intellectual Legacies*, ed. Selwyn R. Cudjoe and William E. Cain (Amherst: University of Massachusetts Press, 1995), 106. "To Make the Natives Buy Lancashire Goods" comes from C.L.R. James, "Abyssinia and the Imperialists" (1936), in *The C.L.R. James Reader*, ed. Grimshaw, 63.

59. See Winston James, *Holding Aloft the Banner of Ethiopia: Caribbean Radicalism in America, 1900–1932* (London: Verso, 1998). A delightful poetic treatment of the Pan-Africanist rage against Mussolini can be found in the 1935 Garvey poem "Mussolini—Scourge of God!" Marcus Garvey, *The Poetical Works of Marcus Garvey*, ed. Tony Martin (Dover: Majority Press, 1983), 82–83.

60. Hill, "In England, 1932–1938," 75.

61. *The Black Jacobins-history*, 383.

62. Ibid., 384.

63. "A gang of shady characters push their way forward to the court, into the ministries, to the head of the administration and the army, a crowd of the best of whom it must be said that no one knows whence he comes, a noisy, disreputable, rapacious bohème that crawls into braided coats with the same grotesque dignity as the high dignitaries of Soulouque." Karl Marx, *The Eighteenth Brumaire of Louis Bonaparte* (1852; reprint, Moscow: Progress Publishers, 1984), 118. The epigraph source is Walter Rodney, *Walter Rodney Speaks: The Making of an African Intellectual*, introduction by Robert Hill, foreword by Howard Dodson (Trenton, NJ: Africa Word Press, 1990), 28–29.

64. Again, analogy to Haiti and its revolutionary unfolding functions as use: "Soulouque's regime became a famous subject of satire in France, partly because making fun of the Haitian emperor was a way for the French to make fun of their own ruler, Louis Napoleon. Napoleon was no particular friend of Haiti, which he once called a 'land of barbarians.' But after he crowned himself Napoleon III in 1851, putting an end to three years of democratic renewal, his furious critics accused him of imitating the Haitian leader. Karl Marx, in his legendary account of Napoleon's rise to power, lampooned the court of Napoleon III as a 'noisy, disreputable, rapacious bohème' that had the 'same grotesque dignity as the high dignitaries of Soulouque.' The comparison deeply bothered the French ruler. When satirists in Paris described the creation of Versailles as soulouquerie, turning the Haitian emperor's fabled excesses into a derogatory tag, Napoleon issued an edict specifically prohibiting the use of that word." Dubois, *Haiti*, 146.

65. The scholarship on *The Eighteenth Brumaire* is immense. I found the following works helpful in these efforts to think about the text: Kojin Karatani, *History and Repetition* (2004), ed. Seiji M. Lippit (New York: Columbia University Press, 2012); Paul A. Bové, "The Metaphysics of Textuality: Marx's *Eighteenth Brumaire of Louis Bonaparte* and Nietzsche's *Use and Abuse of History*," in *Mastering Discourse: The Politics of Intellectual Culture* (Durham, NC: Duke University Press, 1992), 65–87; Martin Harries, "Homo Alludens: Marx's *Eighteenth Brumaire*," in *Scare Quotes from Shakespeare: Marx, Keynes, and the Language of Reenchantment* (Stanford, CA: Stanford University Press, 2000),

54–92; and Dominick LaCapra, "Reading Marx: The Case of *The Eighteenth Brumaire*," in *Rethinking Intellectual History: Texts Contexts Language* (Ithaca, NY: Cornell University Press, 1983), 268–90.

66. Brian Meeks, "Re-Reading *The Black Jacobins*: James, the Dialectic and the Revolutionary Conjuncture," *Social and Economic Studies* 43.3 (1994): 95.

67. Marx, *The Eighteenth Brumaire of Louis Bonaparte*, cited in *The Black Jacobin-history*, 44.

68. Ibid.

69. "Hegel remarks somewhere that all facts and personages of great importance in world history occur, as it were, twice. He forgot to add: the first time as tragedy, the second as farce. . . . Men make their own history, but they do not make it just as they please; they do not make it under circumstances chosen by themselves, but under circumstances directly encountered, given and transmitted from the past" (Marx, *The Eighteenth Brumaire of Louis Bonaparte*, 10). James as a studied expert on Hegel and Marx would not miss the tragic designation in the first wave of Marx's formulation. This further underscores my point that the tragic tone exists all along in his text.

70. *The Black Jacobins-history*, x.

71. Ibid.

72. James, *Nkrumah and the Ghana Revolution*; James, "Black Power," 221–36; C.L.R. James, "Walter Rodney and the Question of Power," in *Walter Rodney, Revolutionary and Scholar: A Tribute*, ed. Edward A. Alpers and Pierre-Michel Fontaine (Los Angeles: Center for Afro-American Studies, 1982),133–46.

73. *The Black Jacobins-history*, x.

74. Ibid., xi.

75. Ibid., 279.

76. Ibid., vii.

77. C.L.R. James, *You Don't Play with Revolution: The Montreal Lectures of C.L.R. James*, ed. David Austin (Edinburgh: AK Press, 2009), 139–40.

78. *The Black Jacobins-history*, 123.

79. Ibid., 127.

80. Ibid., 139.

81. James, *Nkrumah and the Ghana Revolution*, 18–22.

82. Jean-Paul Sartre, "Replies to Structuralism," trans. R. D'Amico, *Telos*, no. 9 (Fall 1971): 114, or *L'Arc*, no. 30 (1966): 94, quoted in Jameson, *The Political Unconscious*, 47.

83. The source of the title of the heading is: C.L.R. James, "Every Cook Can Govern: A Study of Democracy in Ancient Greece and Its Meaning for Today," *Correspondence* 2.12 (1956), https://www.marxists.org/archive/james-clr/works/1956/06/every-cook.htm (accessed 19 June 2005).

James focuses here on what he views as the radical key to Athenian democracy, the fact that the people rotate in and out of different civic and governmental positions, gaining experience and a sort of rotating expertise and incorporation.

84. Kara M. Rabbitt, "C.L.R. James's Figuring of Toussaint Louverture: *The Black Jacobins* and Literary History," in *C.L.R. James: His Intellectual Legacies*, ed. Selwyn R. Cudjoe and William E. Cain (Amherst: University of Massachusetts Press, 1995), 121.

85. Ibid., 120.

86. Aristotle, quoted in Rabbitt, "C.L.R. James's Figuring of Toussaint Louverture," 122.

87. Pabst M. Battin, "Aristotle's Definition of Tragedy in the Poetics," *Journal of Aesthetics and Art Criticism* 33.3 (1975): 293–302.

88. Santiago Colás, "Silence and Dialectics: Speculations on C.L.R. James and Latin America," in *Rethinking C.L.R. James*, ed. Grant Farred (Cambridge: Blackwell, 1996), 137.

89. Aristotle, quoted in Rabbitt, "C.L.R. James's Figuring of Toussaint Louverture," 121.

90. James, "Preface to Criticism" (1955), in *The C.L.R. James Reader*, ed. Grimshaw, 255.

91. *The Black Jacobins-history*, 240.

92. Ibid., 283.

93. Ibid., 262.

94. C.L.R. James, "How I Would Rewrite *The Black Jacobins*," *Small Axe* 8 (2000): 99.

95. Ibid., 106–7.

96. Ibid., 106.

97. Ibid., 111.

98. Colás, "Silence and Dialectics," 140.

99. James, "How I Would Rewrite *The Black Jacobins*," 67.

100. Colás, "Silence and Dialectics," 136.

101. Sylvia Wynter, "Beyond the Categories of the Master Conception: The Counterdoctrine of Jamesian Poiesis," in *C.L.R. James's Caribbean*, ed. Paget Henry (Durham, NC: Duke University Press, 1992), 63–91.

102. Ibid., 64.

103. Ibid., 68.

104. Ibid., 69.

105. Ibid., 64–65.

106. Ibid., 84.

107. Ibid., 64.

108. Ibid., 65.

109. Ibid., 69.

110. Ibid., 82.

111. Kelly, foreword to *Black Marxism*, xvi.

112. I am also not prepared to reject the problematic instantiated by Cedric Robinson's thrilling and provocative five volumes of thought (as though it is something that you could just simply reject). My next project is an attempt to think the political thought of Cedric Robinson as an "unfinished totality."

113. Robinson, *Black Marxism*, 168.

114. *The Black Jacobins-history*, 88.

115. Ibid.

116. Ibid., 88–89.

117. Lewis R. Gordon, "Tragic Revolutionary Violence and Philosophical Anthropology," in *Fanon and the Crisis of European Man: An Essay on Philosophy and the Human Sciences* (New York: Routledge, 1995), 67–83; Maurice Merleau-Ponty, *Humanism and Terror: An Essay on the Communist Problem* (1947), trans. John O'Neill (Boston: Beacon Press, 1969); Fredric Jameson, "Actually Existing Marxism," in *Marxism Beyond Marxism*, ed. Saree Makdisi, Cesare Casarino, and Rebecca E. Karl (New York: Routledge, 1996), 32–33.

118. Sophie Wahnich, *In Defense of the Terror: Liberty or Death in the French Revolution* (2003), trans. David Fernbach (London: Verso, 2012).

119. Vassilis Lambropoulos, *The Tragic Idea* (London: Gerald Duckworth & Co., 2006).

120. Bertolt Brecht, "On Violence," in *Bertolt Brecht: Poems, 1913–1956*, ed. John Willett and Ralph Manheim (New York: Methuen, 1976), 276.

121. *The Black Jacobins-history*, 391.

122. San Juan, *Beyond Postcolonial Reason*, 314.

123. *The Black Jacobins-history*, 392.

124. Ibid., 407.

125. Ibid., 394.

126. Ibid., 197.

127. San Juan, *Beyond Postcolonial Reason*, 237.

128. *The Black Jacobins-history*, 275.

129. Ibid., 281.

130. Peter Sloterdijk, *You Must Change Your Life: On Anthropotechnics*, trans. Wieland Hoban (Cambridge: Polity Press, 2013), 19.

131. Ibid., 21.

132. Ibid.

133. Ibid.

134. Carby, *Race Men*, 68.

135. Bertolt Brecht, "AND I ALWAYS THOUGHT," in *Bertolt Brecht: Poems*, 452.

NOTES TO CHAPTER 4

For a useful critical overview of Lorraine Hansberry's life work, consult the following: Steven Carter, *Hansberry's Drama: Commitment amid Complexity* (Urbana: University of Illinois Press, 1991); Ben Keppel, *The Work of Democracy: Ralph Bunche, Kenneth B. Clark, Lorraine Hansberry, and the Cultural Politics of Race* (Cambridge, MA: Harvard University Press, 1995); Lorraine Hansberry, *A Raisin in the Sun/The Sign in Sidney Brustein's Window* (New York: Vintage, 1994); Lorraine Hansberry, *The Movement: Documentary of a Struggle for Equality* (New York: Simon and Schuster, 1964); Samuel S. Hay, *African-American Theatre: A Historical and Critical Analysis* (Cambridge: Cambridge University Press, 1994); Lorraine Hansberry, *Lorraine Hansberry Speaks Out: Art and the Black Revolution*

(Caedmon Records, 1972); Lorraine Hansberry, "The Negro Writer and His Roots: Toward a New Romanticism," *Black Scholar* 12.2 (1981): 2–12; and Brian Norman, "Jim Crow Jr.: Lorraine Hansberry's Late Segregation Revisions and Toni Morrison's Early Post–Civil Rights Ambivalence," in *Non-Segregation Narratives: Jim Crow in Post–Civil Rights American Literature* (Athens: University of Georgia Press, 2010), 21–51. The epigraphs to this chapter come from the following: Lorraine Hansberry, *To Be Young, Gifted, and Black: An Informal Autobiography of Lorraine Hansberry*, ed. Robert Nemiroff (New York: New American Library, 1970), 222, and Gang Starr, *Moment of Truth* (Virgin Records, 1998).

1. Considering how Hansberry's life ended tragically at such a young age, it is important to note that my sense of lateness evoked here is not chronological but (borrowing from Edward Said by way of Adorno's theorization of "Late Style") conceptual: "What of artistic lateness not as harmony and resolution but as intransigence, difficulty, and unresolved contradiction?" Said, *On Late Style*, 7.

2. Aijaz Ahmad, "Jameson's Rhetoric of Otherness and the 'National Allegory,'" in *Marxist Literary Theory*, ed. Terry Eagleton and Drew Milne (Oxford: Blackwell, 1996), 392.

3. Lorraine Hansberry, *Les Blancs: The Collected Last Plays*, ed. Robert Nemiroff (New York: Vintage, 1994).

4. Note Hansberry's utilization of "haunt" in her mention of *The Emperor Jones*: "We have grown accustomed to the dynamics of 'Negro' personality as expressed by white authors. Thus de Emperor [Jones] de Lawd, and, of course, Porgy still haunt our frame of reference when a new character emerges." Lorraine Hansberry, "Willy Loman, Walter Younger, and He Who Must Live," *The Village Voice*, 12 August 1959, 8.

5. Philip Eko Effiong, "History, Myth, and Revolt in Lorraine Hansberry's *Les Blancs*," *African American Review* 32.2 (1998): 283.

6. Hansberry, *Les Blancs*, 32–33.

7. Jean Genet, "Four Hours in Shatila," *Journal of Palestine Studies* 12.3 (Spring 1983): 3–22; Hisham Sharabi, "Review: From Ajlun to Shatila," *Journal of Palestine Studies* 16.4 (Summer 1987): 129–32.

8. Robert Sandarg, "Jean Genet and the Black Panther Party," *Journal of Black Studies* 16.3 (March 1986): 269–82.

9. M. Feinstein, "Genet Calls Black Panthers Camarades," *CCNY Observation Post Newspaper*, 10 April 1970, 3.

10. Ibid., 1.

11. Alain Badiou, *Pocket Pantheon* (London: Verso, 2009), 113. See also Hadrien Laroche, *The Last Genet: A Writer in Revolt*, trans. David Hormel (Vancouver: Arsenal Pup Press, 2010), originally published in France as *Le dernier Genet* (Paris: Éditions du Seuil, 1987). The epigraph source is Jean Genet, "After the Assassination" (August 1971), in *The Declared Enemy: Texts and Interviews*, ed. Albert Dichy, trans. Jeff Fort (Stanford, CA: Stanford University Press, 2004), 17.

12. Jean Genet, introduction to George Jackson, *Soledad Brother: The Prison Letters of George Jackson* (New York: Coward-McCann, 1970), i.

13. Jean Genet, *Prisoner of Love*, trans. Barbara Bray (Hanover, NH: Wesleyan University Press, 1992), 204–5, originally published by Editions Gallimard in 1986 as *Un captif amoreux*.

14. Slavoj Žižek, "The Family Myth of Ideology," in *In Defense of Lost Causes* (London: Verso, 2008), 81.

15. Jackson, *Soledad Brother*, 180–81.

16. Ibid., 126.

17. Ibid., 58.

18. George Jackson, *Blood in My Eye* (London: Jonathan Capte, 1972), 130.

19. Ibid., 61.

20. Jackson, *Soledad Brother*, 14.

21. Ibid., 26.

22. Hansberry, *Les Blancs*, 61. The epigraph source is Dhoruba Bin Wahad, Mumia Abu-Jamal, and Assata Shakur, *Still Black, Still Strong: Survivors of the U.S. War Against Black Revolutionaries*, ed. Jim Fletcher, Tanaquil Jones, and Sylvère Lotringer (New York: Semiotext[e], 1993), 114.

23. Adrienne Rich, "The Problem of Lorraine Hansberry," *Blood, Bread and Poetry Selected Prose, 1979–1985* (London: Virago Press, 1987). This essay originally appeared in a *Freedomways* special issue on Hansberry entitled "Lorraine Hansberry, Art of Thunder, Vision of Light," *Freedomways: A Quarterly Review of the Freedom Movement* 19.4 (1979).

24. Hansberry, *Les Blancs*, 20.

25. Amiri Baraka, "A Critical Reevaluation: *A Raisin in the Sun*'s Enduring Passion," introduction to Lorraine Hansberry and Robert Nemiroff, *A Raisin in the Sun (Expanded Twenty-Fifth Anniversary Edition and The Sign in Sidney Brustein's Window* (New York: New American Library, 1987).

26. Hansberry, *Les Blancs*, 125–26.

27. Ibid., 80.

28. Ibid., 78.

29. Effiong, "History, Myth, and Revolt," 277.

30. James R. Hooker, *Black Revolutionary: George Padmore's Path from Communism to Pan-Africanism* (1967; reprint, New York: Praeger, 1970), 16.

31. Grace Lee Boggs, *Living for Change: An Autobiography* (Minneapolis: University of Minnesota Press, 1998), 47; Frederic Warburg, *An Occupation for Gentlemen* (London: Hutchinson, 1959), 182.

32. I'd like to thank my brilliant colleague Ramesh Mallipeddi for his insistence on the advanced utility of the straight razor.

33. The epigraph source is James, *Toussaint Louverture*, 177.

34. Steven R. Carter, "Lorraine Hansberry's Toussaint," *Black American Literature Forum* 23.1 (1989): 143–44.

35. The work of both Brecht and Sean O'Casey was a key influence on Hansberry's choices as it relates to her dramatic aesthetic.

36. This spelling is Williams's.

37. Williams, *Modern Tragedy*, 234–36.

38. I realize that these two forms—social and economic structures—are not the same. A model that thinks the economic structure as primary contrasted with the more general formulation "social organization" reaches different conclusions in terms of what forces they prioritize as revolutionary and worthy of attention as well as what needs to be done in terms of transformation. It is the difference between a classical Marxist analysis offered by Marx and Engels versus the type of analysis offered by Omi and Winant in both privileging key actors and processes. It is my contention that Hansberry's thinks both analyses together in her plays. Michael Omi and Howard Winant, *Racial Formation in the United States: From the 1960s to the 1990s* (1985; reprint, New York: Routledge, 1994).

39. This is Adrienne Rich's point in her essay on Hansberry.

40. Harold Cruse's engagement with Hansberry and her milieu wavers from infuriating to fascinating to utterly bizarre. At one point he refers to her as "the Joan of Arc of People's Integration." His standard of comparison, his example of the authentic radical writer, is George Orwell (solely it seems for Cruse because Orwell washed dishes when he lived in Paris). Harold Cruse, *The Crisis of the Negro Intellectual: A Historical Analysis of the Failure of Black Leadership* (1967; reprint, New York: William and Morrow, 1984), 410.

41. Margaret B. Wilkerson, "The Sighted Eyes and Feeling Heart of Lorraine Hansberry," *Black American Literature Forum* 17.1 (1983): 8.

42. Lucien Goldmann, *The Human Sciences & Philosophy* (1966), trans. Hayden V. White and Robert Anchor (London: Jonathan Cape, 1969), 129.

43. Ibid., 153–54.

44. Cruse, *The Crisis of the Negro Intellectual*, 284.

45. Ibid., 276.

46. The epigraph source is Joy James, "Black Suffering in Search of the 'Beloved Community': Political Imprisonment and Self-Defense," *Trans-scripts: An Interdisciplinary Online Journal in the Humanities and Social Sciences at UC Irvine* 1 (2011), http://sites.uci.edu/transscripts/files/2014/10/2011_01_14.pdf (accessed 13 June 2015).

47. Hansberry, *To Be Young, Gifted, and Black*, 137.

48. Lorraine Hansberry, *Toussaint* (1969), in *9 Plays by Black Women*, ed. Margaret B. Wilkerson (New York: New American Library, 1986), 47–67.

49. Hansberry, *To Be Young, Gifted, and Black*, 67.

50. Carter, "Lorraine Hansberry's Toussaint," 140.

51. Ibid., 140–41.

52. Hansberry, *Toussaint*, 52–53.

53. Ibid., 55.

54. Hansberry, *Les Blancs*, 6; Sean O'Casey, *Three Plays* (1957; reprint, London: Macmillan, 1966).

55. Hansberry, *Toussaint*, 56.

56. Ibid., 60.

57. Ibid., 58.

58. Ibid., 56.

59. Ibid., 57.

60. Ibid., 59.

61. Ibid., 61.

62. Ibid., 57–58.

63. Ibid., 58.

64. Ibid., 61.

65. Ibid., 62.

66. Saidiya V. Hartman, *Scenes of Subjection: Terror, Slavery, and Self-Making in Nineteenth-Century America* (New York: Oxford University Press, 1997), 3.

67. Hansberry, *Toussaint*, 62–63.

68. Ibid., 63–64.

69. Ibid., 67.

70. Ibid., 65.

71. Ibid., 66.

72. Ibid., 58.

73. Hansberry, *Les Blancs*, 34.

NOTES TO THE CONCLUSION

1. The source of the title of the heading is Jan Carew, *Ghosts in Our Blood [With Malcolm X in Africa, England, and the Caribbean]* (Chicago: Lawrence Hill Books, 1994), 68.

2. Ibid., 61.

3. Two germane, phenomenal essays on Malcolm X's time in England are Marika Sherwood, "Malcolm X in Manchester and Sheffield," *North West Labour History Journal* 27 (December 2002): 29–34; and Saladin M. Ambar, "Malcolm X at the Oxford Union," *Race & Class* 53.4 (2012): 24–38. See also Saladin Ambar, *Malcolm X at Oxford Union: Racial Politics in a Global Era* (Oxford: Oxford University Press, 2014).

4. Tariq Ali, *Street Fighting Years: An Autobiography of the Sixties* (1987; reprint, London: Verso, 2005), 103–7.

5. Hugh MacDiarmid, *The Company I've Kept* (Berkeley: University of California Press, 1967), 27.

6. Lebert Bethune, "Malcolm X in Europe," in *Malcolm X: The Man and His Times*, ed. John Henrik Clarke (1969; reprint, Trenton: Africa World Press, 1990), 232.

7. Carew, *Ghosts in Our Blood*, 74.

8. Bethune, "Malcolm X in Europe," 233.

9. Carew, *Ghosts in Our Blood*, 74–77.

10. Antonio Gramsci, *Selections from Prison Notebooks*, ed. and trans. Quinton Hare and Geoffrey Nowell Smith (New York: International Publishers, 1995), 5, 10.

11. Malcolm X, *Malcolm X Talks to Young People: Speeches in the U.S., Britain, and Africa*, ed. Steve Clark (New York: Pathfinder, 1991), 25–26. This transcription is edited and greatly truncated.

12. Ibid., 68–69.

13. For more on this concept and articulation, see Stuart Hall, "Race, Articulation, and Societies Structured in Dominance," in *Black British Cultural Studies: A Reader*, ed. Houston A. Baker, Manthia Diawara, and Ruth H. Lindeborg (Chicago: University of Chicago Press, 1996), 16–60; David Kazanjian, *The Colonizing Trick: National Culture and Imperial Citizenship in Early America* (Minneapolis: University of Minnesota Press, 2003); Ernest Laclau, *Hegemony and Socialist Strategy: Towards a Radical Democratic Politics*, 2nd ed. (London: Verso, 2001); and Brent Hayes Edwards, "The Uses of Diaspora," *Social Text* 19.1 66 (2001): 45–73.

14. *The Black Jacobins-history*, xi.

15. This stammer is not captured in the *Pathfinder* edition transcription.

16. Vladimir Ilyich Lenin, "Our Revolution: Apropos of N. Sukhanov's Notes," 16 January 1923, *Pravda* 117 (30 May 1923) http://www.marxists.org/archive/lenin/works/1923/jan/16.htm (accessed 4 February 2013).

17. Lukács, *Lenin*, 80–81.

18. Ibid., 81.

19. Arnold Rampersad, "The Color of His Eyes: Bruce Perry's *Malcolm* and Malcolm's Malcolm," in *Malcolm X: In Our Own Image*, ed. Joe Wood (New York: St. Martin's Press, 1992), 118.

20. Kamau Franklin, "An Ivory-Tower Assassination of Malcolm X," in *A Lie of Reinvention: Correcting Manning Marable's Malcolm X*, ed. Jared A. Ball and Todd Steven Burroughs (Baltimore: Black Classic Press, 2012), 59.

21. I want to express gratitude to my friend Michael Pelias for reintroducing me to this part of *The Autobiography of Malcolm X* and this line of inquiry.

22. The epigraphs to this section come from W.E.B. DuBois, "Of the Passing of the First-Born," in *The Souls of Black Folk* (1903), ed. Brent Hayes Edwards (New York: Oxford University Press, 2007), 142, and Sir Frederick Pollock, *Spinoza: His Life and Philosophy*, 2nd ed. (New York: Macmillan, 1899), 17–18.

Malcolm X, *The Autobiography of Malcolm X*, as told to Alex Haley (New York: Ballantine Books, 1990), 180.

23. Said, *Freud and the Non-European*; Sigmund Freud, *Moses and Monotheism* (1939; reprint, New York: Vintage, 1955); Herbert I. Bloom, "A Study of Brazilian Jewish History 1623–1654, Based Chiefly upon the Findings of the Late Samuel Oppenheim," *Publications of the American Jewish Historical Society* 33 (1934).

24. Etienne Balibar, *Spinoza and Politics* (1985), trans. Peter Snowdon (London: Verso, 2008), 125–26.

25. Lewis S. Feuer, "The Dream of Benedict de Spinoza," *American Imago* 14 (1957): 226–27.

26. Ibid., 230–31.

27. Ibid., 232.

28. *The Black Jacobins-history*, 283.

29. Bertolt Brecht, *The Messingkauf Dialogues*, 91.

30. Benedictus de Spinoza, *The Letters*, trans. Samuel Shirley (Indianapolis: Hackett, 1995), 125–27.

31. For further explication, consult the entry "Mind and Body (Parallelism)," in Gilles Deleuze, *Spinoza: Practical Philosophy* (1981), trans. Robert Hurley (San Francisco: City Lights Books, 1988), 86–91.

32. Feuer, "The Dream of Benedict de Spinoza," 228.

33. Antonio Negri, *The Savage Anomaly: The Power of Spinoza's Metaphysics and Politics*, trans. Michael Hardt (Minneapolis: University of Minnesota Press, 1999), 57.

34. Lukács, *Lenin*, 95.

35. Ruth Wilson Gilmore, "Race and Globalization," in *Geographies of Global Change*, 2nd ed., ed. P. J. Taylor, R. L. Johnstone, and M. J. Watts (Oxford: Blackwell, 2002), 261.

36. *The Black Jacobins-history*, 406.

NOTES TO THE CODA

1. The second epigraph to this section comes from G.W.F. Hegel, *The Encyclopaedia Logic* (1830), trans. T. F. Geraets, W. A. Suchting, and H. S. Harris (Indianapolis: Hackett), 214.

Simone de Beauvoir, *Force of Circumstance* (1963), trans. Richard Howard (New York: G. P. Putnam's Sons, 1965), 592.

2. Brandon Stosuy, "Interview: Swans," 8 May 2014, http://pitchfork.com/features/interviews/9400-swans/ (accessed 8 January 2015).

3. Ibid.

4. "C.L.R. James-E. Ethelbert Miller-The Aldon Nielsen Project 05," 1 February 2015, http://heatstrings.blogspot.com/ (accessed 2 February 2015).

5. Michael McKeon, *introduction to The Secret History of Domesticity: Public, Private, and the Division of Knowledge* (Baltimore: Johns Hopkins University Press, 2005), xxv.

6. G.W.F. Hegel, "Who Thinks Abstractly?" https://www.marxists.org/reference/archive/hegel/works/se/abstract.htm (accessed 19 June 2015).

7. I view the tension between thinking and acting, authenticity and the problem of speculative thought as linchpin of the spirited exchange between David Kazanjian and Susan Buck-Morss on Hegel, Haiti, and Liberia. David Kazanjian, "Hegel, Liberia," review of Susan Buck-Morss, *Hegel, Haiti, and Universal History*, exchange with Susan Buck-Morss, *Diacritics* 40.1 (2012): 6–41.

8. Raoul Peck, "Lumumba: Death of a Prophet (1991)," in *Stolen Images*, trans. Catherine Termerson (New York: Seven Stories Press, 2013), 138.

9. Frantz Fanon, "Lumumba's Death: Could We Do Otherwise?" in *Toward the African Revolution* (1964), trans. Haakon Chevalier (New York: Grove Press, 1988), 196.

10. Eugene Genovese, *From Rebellion to Revolution: Afro-American Slave Revolts in the Making of the Modern World* (Baton Rouge: Louisiana State University Press, 1979), 89.

11. Fischer, *Modernity Disavowed*, 260–61.

12. Derek Walcott, "What the Twilight Says: An Ouverture," in *Dream on Monkey Mountain and Other Plays* (New York: Farrar, Straus, and Giroux, 1970), 14.

13. Georg Lukács, "Narrate or Describe?" (1936), in *Writer and Critic: And Other Essays*, trans. Arthur Kahn (London: Merlin Press, 1970), 130.

14. C.L.R. James, "The Black Jacobins and Black Reconstruction: A Comparative Analysis (15 June 1971)," *Small Axe: A Journal of Criticism*, no. 8 (September 2000): 91.

15. Joseph Stalin, *Dialectical and Historical Materialism* (1938; reprint, New York: International Publishers, 1940), 13–14.

16. W.E.B. DuBois, *Black Reconstruction in America: 1860–1880* (1935; reprint, New York: Touchstone, Simon and Schuster, 1995), 57.

17. Sadly, I cannot recall if I heard this formulation during a talk given by Slavoj Žižek or if I indeed thought it up. In light of this, I happily give credit to him for this phrasing and the ideas that drive it. Streaming Žižek speeches and the music of Hank Shocklee's et al. Bomb Squad propelled the writing of this book and constitute its sonic backdrop.

18. Ibid., 10.

19. Victor Bulmer-Thomas, *The Economic History of the Caribbean Since the Napoleonic Wars* (New York: Cambridge University Press, 2012), 46–76.

20. *The Black Jacobins-history*, 291.

21. Trouillot, *Silencing the Past*, 70–107.

Index

About the Author

Jeremy Matthew Glick is Associate Professor of African Diaspora Literature and Modern Drama in the English Department of Hunter College, CUNY.